The Nigerian Army 1956-1966

STUDIES IN AFRICAN HISTORY
General Editor: A. H. M. Kirk-Greene
St Antony's College
Oxford

KINGDOMS OF THE YORUBA
Robert S. Smith

THE MILITARY IN AFRICAN POLITICS
W. F. Gutteridge

SENEGAL: A STUDY IN FRENCH ASSIMILATION
Michael Crowder

SWAHILI: THE RISE OF A NATIONAL LANGUAGE
Wilfred Whitely

THE NIGERIAN ARMY 1956–1966
N. J. Miners

N. J. MINERS

THE NIGERIAN ARMY 1956-1966

METHUEN & CO LTD
11 New Fetter Lane · London EC4

First published in 1971 by Methuen & Co Ltd
© *1971 N. J. Miners*
Printed in Great Britain by
Richard Clay (The Chaucer Press) Ltd
Bungay, Suffolk

SBN 416 08270 X   hardback
SBN 416 65860 I   paperback

Distributed in the USA by Barnes & Noble, Inc.

IN MEMORIAM

REGIS COLLEGII ALUMNORUM

QUI IN BELLO CIVILI PRO PATRIA MORTUI SUNT

PRO NIGERIA PROQUE BIAFRA

QUISQUE PRO SUA

Contents

Preface	*page*	ix
Abbreviations		xi
I	Introductory Survey	1
II	The Nigerian Military Forces in 1956	12
III	Nigerianizing the Officer Corps, 1949–1960	33
IV	Handing over the Army, 1956–1960	59
V	Cameroons, Congo, Tanganyika, Tiv	71
VI	Changes in the Army, 1960–1965	93
VII	Nigerianizing the Officer Corps, 1960–1965	108
VIII	Politics and Violence, 1960–1965	130
IX	The Military Coups of 15 and 16 January	155
X	The First Four Months of the Ironsi Regime	180
XI	The May Decrees, the Riots and the July Counter-coup	194
Postscript		227
Appendix: Officer Statistics 1959–1965		235
Notes		238
Sources and Select Bibliography		274
Index		284

Maps 1	Regions and Main Towns, 1956	16
2	Main Tribal Groups	16
3	The Congo	76

Preface

Until the military archives in London and Lagos are opened for study, any such history as this can only be a provisional account, influenced by the author's experiences and the sources open to him. From 1957 to August 1966 I was teaching at a government secondary school in Lagos, King's College. While there, I helped to run the Army Cadet Unit, which gave me frequent contact with the army units in Lagos and Abeokuta, and I also knew a number of ex-students who became army officers. The idea of writing this book was only conceived at the end of my stay in Nigeria, and my memories and impressions have since been amplified and corrected by studying Nigerian newspapers, parliamentary debates and official reports of the period.

As far as is possible for an expatriate I have tried to look at the changes in the Army from a Nigerian point of view, and particularly how it appeared to secondary school students who were contemplating a military career. From 1958 onwards, when the War Office relinquished control of the Nigerian Armed Forces, developments were inevitably largely determined by the prevailing political situation. Consequently I have not attempted to evaluate the individual contributions made by the British commanders and officers during this difficult period of transition. In dealing with the events of 1966 it has been particularly difficult to give an impartial account, since propagandists on both sides during the civil war have done their best to confuse the issues. I have tried to hold the balance as fairly as I can in the light of my own knowledge, but I can hardly hope that the conclusions given here will command universal assent.

The research involved in writing this book was only made possible by the grant of a fellowship for two years by the Social Science Research Council, for which I am most grateful. This award was obtained on the recommendation of the late Professor H. V. Wiseman of Exeter University, who originally encouraged me to take up this project and watched over its early stages. It is a great regret that my thanks to him can only be rendered posthumously. Earlier drafts of this book were read by Dr R. E. Dowse and Mr N. S. Butterfield who made valuable suggestions, and I must also mention the stimulating discussions that I had with Mr Martin Dent. In addition many Nigerian officers and expatriates who served in Nigeria have been most helpful in answering my questions. I am greatly indebted to them and I am sorry that it is not possible to acknowledge their help individually. Sources of information have only been revealed where the officer referred to is now dead.

I am glad to thank the following for permission to quote from copyright material: Dr S. A. Aluko for his article in *The Sunday Express* (Lagos) 4 April 1965; *The Times* newspaper for a passage from the issue dated 18 January 1961; Cambridge University Press, for passages from *My Life* by Sir Ahmadu Bello; and Major-General K. G. Exham for a passage from *The History of the Royal West African Frontier Force*, published by Gale and Polden of Aldershot. Overseas Newspapers Ltd. kindly allowed me to see their files of the Lagos *Daily Times* for the years where the British Museum collection of Nigerian newspapers was incomplete.

In conclusion I must express my gratitude to my mother who worked tirelessly to type the first draft; and also to Miss Anita Ng who typed the final version. My wife gave me constant encouragement and helped in innumerable ways.

N. J. MINERS

The University of Hong Kong 1970

Abbreviations

A   The branch at a military headquarters which dealt with personnel, promotions and transfers.

AG   Action Group – a political party founded by Chief Awolowo, mainly Yoruba.

ANC   Armée Nationale Congolaise – the Force Publique renamed after Congolese Independence.

CPP   Convention People's Party, Ghana.

COR   Calabar–Ogoja–Rivers. Three provinces in the Eastern Region where the non-Ibo minority tribes are mainly to be found. Agitation for a separate C–O–R State was supported by the AG.

CSM   Company Sergeant Major – a warrant officer, class II.

DAQMG   Deputy Adjutant and Quartermaster-General – a major on the staff of a brigade who deals largely with administrative matters.

G   The branch at a military headquarters which deals with training and the planning of operations.

HR Deb   Debates in the Nigerian Federal House of Representatives.

NA   Nigerian Army
           1 NA – the first battalion of the Nigerian Army. This designation was used from October 1963 onwards.

NAM   Nigerian Army Magazine.

NCNC   National Council of Nigeria and the Cameroons – a political party founded by Dr Azikiwe, mainly Ibo. After 1960 the name was changed to the National Convention of Nigerian Citizens.

NCO   Non-Commissioned Officer – a lance-corporal, cor-
           poral, sergeant or staff sergeant.

NEPU   Northern Elements Progressive Union – a political
           party opposed to the NPC in the North, mainly
           Hausa, an ally of the NCNC. Mallam Aminu Kano
           was its leader.

NMF   Nigerian Military Forces – the name of the Nigerian
           Army until Independence.

NNDP   Nigerian National Democratic Party – a political
           party founded in 1964 by former members of the
           Action Group who supported Chief Akintola,
           together with most of the former members of the
           NCNC in the Western Region.

NPC   Northern People's Congress – the governing party
           in the Northern Region.

NR   The Nigeria Regiment – the title of the five Nigerian
           battalions of the Royal West African Frontier
           Force before 1956.
           1 NR – the first battalion of the Nigeria Regi-
           ment.

OR   Other Ranks – all soldiers who are not commissioned
           officers.

Q   The branch at a military headquarters which deals
           with stores and equipment.

QONR   Queen's Own Nigeria Regiment – the title of the
           five Nigerian battalions after the Queen's visit
           to Nigeria in January 1956. The name ceased to
           be used after Nigeria became a republic in
           October 1963.
           1 QONR – the first battalion of the Queen's Own
           Nigeria Regiment.

RDA   Rassemblement Démocratique African, French
           West Africa.

RMA   Royal Military Academy, Sandhurst.

RNA   Royal Nigerian Army – the title of the Army

between Independence and the date when Nigeria became a republic.

RSM   Regimental Sergeant Major; a warrant officer, class I.

RWAFF   Royal West African Frontier Force – the collective title of the infantry regiments of Nigeria, Gold Coast and Sierra Leone until these countries became independent.

UMBC   United Middle Belt Congress – a political party in the southern half of the Northern Region which advocated the setting up of a separate Middle Belt State. It was mainly supported by the Tiv and was allied to the Action Group. Its leader was Joseph Tarka.

UPGA   United Progressive Grand Alliance – formed by the NCNC, AG and a few smaller parties to contest the 1964 Federal election against the NPC and the NNDP.

WO   Warrant Officer – RSMs and CSMs.

Army Units

Platoon – about 36 men, commanded by a subaltern (a lieutenant or second lieutenant).

Company – about 150 men, commanded by a major. (A captain is second-in-command of a company.)

Battalion – about 750–800 men, commanded by a lieutenant-colonel.

Brigade – two or three battalions, plus other supporting units, commanded by a brigadier.

Division – two (usually three) brigades, commanded by a major-general.

I · Introductory Survey

In January 1956 Queen Elizabeth made the first and only visit ever made by a reigning sovereign to Nigeria, which was then Britain's largest remaining colony. Among those who met her at Lagos airport was her equerry for the royal tour, Captain (acting Major) Aguiyi-Ironsi. Almost exactly ten years later in January 1966, Major-General Aguiyi-Ironsi made himself the head of a military regime in Nigeria, after the civilian government had been overthrown in a *coup d'état*. Just over six months later he was murdered in another military coup, along with more than two hundred other officers and men, and the Nigerian Army split into two. A year later former comrades-in-arms were engaged on different sides in a bitter civil war.

This dismal sequence of events was not foreseen at Nigerian Independence in October 1960. Hardly any observer then predicted that in a few years' time politics in West Africa would go the way of South America.[1] The Congo had already dissolved into chaos within a few weeks of the Belgian withdrawal, but this was blamed on the precipitate haste with which Belgium had handed over power within months of the first outbreak of nationalist violence. In contrast to this, the independence of the British West African territories had been foreseen and actively prepared for since at least 1948, and Africans had held ministerial office for nearly ten years.

With the benefit of hindsight it is easy to mock at this facile optimism about the prospects of these newly emancipated territories. But in fact at that time a very plausible case could be made out for complacency, based on certain common characteristics of the military establishments which Nigeria and the other West African colonies inherited from their former

British and French overlords. It seemed highly unlikely that the new African presidents and prime ministers, supported by the vast machine of a successful political party whose branches were to be found in practically every sizeable town, would be challenged by the minuscule armed forces that had been left behind by the colonial regime – small in numbers, defective in equipment, with few experienced African officers and generally despised among the politically conscious citizens of the new states.

Take first the question of size. The smallest of the West African armies was that of Togo, a mere 250 men out of a population of about 1,500,000. The Nigerian Military Forces numbered 7,500 at Independence, but for a country with at least 45,000,000 inhabitants this was proportionately no larger than that of Togo. (For comparison, Argentina, with half Nigeria's population, has an army of 120,000.) All the West African armies were equipped with the weapons used in the 1939–1945 war. They had no tanks or heavy artillery; Nigeria had a few armoured cars but no other sophisticated military equipment. Nigeria and Ghana had taken the first steps towards building a navy, but no country had yet begun an air force.

Soldiers also had little public prestige. The military forces in these territories had been created not to defend the inhabitants against foreign attack but to assist foreigners to conquer the country. They had British officers, but, at least as far as the rank and file were concerned, they were mercenary armies. The soldiers were generally enlisted in the more backward parts of the country and were quite ready to suppress rebellions against colonial rule that might arise elsewhere. They were excellent soldiers, loyal to their comrades, their regiment and (perhaps) to the British Empire or the French Republic. But they were certainly not national armies and they had played no part in the struggle for Independence. In the case of the French armies, they had recently been used to suppress the nationalists in French Indo-China and in Algeria, and this was a standing reproach against them. The African soldiers of the British Army had not been recently employed in this way, but their poor pay and the memory of their origins gave them a low status in the eyes of the local population generally.

A third factor was the lack of African officers. There had been no sense of urgency in pressing on with the Africanization of the officer corps by either the French or the British military authorities until the very last years before Independence. Only one West African was given the King's Commission during the Second World War, though native officers had commanded battalions in the Indian and Sudanese armies. In 1951 there were only thirteen African officers in the four territories of British West Africa; at Independence in Nigeria and Ghana there was no African officer higher than a major, and three-quarters of the officers were still expatriate. The organization of a coup thus seemed to present formidable difficulties.

All these might have seemed to be good reasons why military interventions were not to be expected in West Africa in the first years after Independence. In fact, none of them precluded a military coup. This was shown in 1963 when the first success-ful one was staged by the smallest army, that of Togo. The coup was apparently led by two former sergeants of the French Army. The conspirators succeeded in assassinating President Olympio and then installed a new government which agreed to their demand that the Army should be expanded five-fold.

The military coups in Nigeria and Ghana did not take place for another three years, but the factors listed above which made a coup seem unlikely at the time of Independence did not remain unchanged as the years went by. Armies were enlarged, either for reasons of prestige or because a larger army was needed to ensure internal security; new African officers were rapidly trained and promoted as the expatriates left and the prestige of the Army rose at the same time as that of the politicians declined. The corruption of the politicians was

B

blatant; the Army seemed remote and unsullied; its faults would only be revealed after it had seized power.

However, all these changes were still in the future. In the case of Nigeria in 1960, the new state's future stability seemed assured not only by the apparent weakness of the armed forces (which was common to all the West African territories) but also because of its peculiarly peaceful advance to Independence. The 'struggle for freedom' had been remarkably free of violence, even by comparison with Ghana. None of Nigeria's leading nationalists went to prison, as Dr Nkrumah and most of his cabinet did.[2] There were no riots on the scale of the 1948 Gold Coast riots, which were so dangerous that army reinforcements had to be flown in from abroad. When certain militant Nigerian nationalists issued a 'Call to Revolution' in 1948 they were promptly disowned by Dr Azikiwe and quickly rounded up by the police. With the exception of the Kano riot of 1953 Nigeria progressed peacefully through the same stages as Ghana, and all constitutional conferences were concluded with agreements accepted by all the major parties. Unlike Ghana, where the National Liberation Movement opposition to the CPP boycotted the final attempts to achieve an agreed constitution for Independence, the 1960 Nigerian constitution was accepted by all the main parties. No country, it might have seemed, could be set for a more harmonious passage after Independence. This was the normal impression of Nigeria as seen by superficial foreign observers.

In fact, the main reason for this impression of tranquil progress was that the British were quite willing to accede to nationalist demands. Once constitutional progress on the road to Independence had been conceded to the Gold Coast Nigerian leaders found that they were pushing at an open door when they asked for the same treatment for Nigeria. Conferences to revise the constitution during the 1950s were harmoniously concluded, whatever the bitter disagreements at the conference table, because each of the three main political parties had a secure power-base in its own region which could not be coerced; conciliation was thus inevitable. But above all there was the knowledge that the British Army was ready to intervene with overwhelming force in support of the Nigerian Military Forces to resist any attempt to overthrow the constitution by violence. The existence of this powerful external guarantor of the successive constitutional settlements of the 1950s gave every incentive to the delegations to compromise their differences. However much bluster might be made with threats of revolution or secession, such as those made by the NPC leaders in 1953 or the Action Group in 1954, all political groups realized that, however badly they might do at the conference table, they would be far worse off if they resorted to the arbitrament of violence.

Once Independence was achieved, this external policeman was removed from the scene. The Under-Secretary of State for the Colonies assured the House of Commons in 1958:

> There is no question of washing our hands of ultimate responsibility for the law and order of . . . Nigeria. There are plans for the reinforcement of each of these territories in the event of trouble arising which it is beyond the capacity of the local security forces to control. . . .
>
> It would be neither appropriate nor usual to offer assistance of this kind once a territory has achieved independence.
>
> (*Hansard*, 25 June 1958, col. 576)

So, after 1960 internal security was to be the responsibility of the local forces alone. Provided the British Government adhered to this policy of non-interference in internal affairs, it was no longer necessarily the case that attempts to alter the constitution by force would be disastrous for the perpetrators. Now, they might even offer more prospect of success than redress of grievances by the proper constitutional channels.

Quite apart from this change in the balance of military forces supporting the established constitution, there was a more fundamental reason why a political upheaval of some sort might have been foreseen in Nigeria. In most of the territories of West Africa the departing colonial powers had handed over power at Independence to the representatives of one of the new 'mass parties' which had built up an impressive grass-roots organization in the territory to demand the end of foreign rule. Such parties were the various branches of the RDA in French West Africa, like that of Sekou Touré in Guinea and Houphouet Boigny in the Ivory Coast, and Dr Nkrumah's CPP in Ghana. In the main, the leaders of these nationalist parties were teachers, lawyers, successful businessmen and labour leaders, and they owed little to the traditional élites of Africa, the chiefs and similar elements favoured by the colonial regime. Because of the practice of 'indirect rule' in British territories chiefs were frequently regarded by nationalists as subservient instruments of British policy, 'colonial stooges', 'Uncle Toms', who were mere ventriloquists' dummies, mouthing the words taught them by the imperialists who pulled the strings behind the curtain.[3] In self-defence the chiefs had tried to organize political parties of their own, sometimes with the covert support of the colonial administrators, but in most cases these had failed to gain popular support in the pre-Independence elections. The only territories where such traditionalist-oriented parties were the residuary legatees of the departing imperialists were Niger, Sierra Leone – and Nigeria.

The Northern People's Congress in Nigeria was originally founded to defend the traditional social order in the Northern Region, that is, the rule of the Fulani Emirs. It made no attempt to become a nationwide political party and was challenged in its home region both by the Northern Elements Progressive Union, which attempted to mobilize the Hausa subjects of the emirs, and also by the United Middle Belt Congress, which was largely supported by the tribes in the southern parts of the region which had not been conquered in the Fulani *jihad* in the previous century. In spite of these handicaps, the NPC emerged as the largest single party at the Federal elections of 1959 which were to decide the government that would lead Nigeria into Independence. (NPC and allies – 148, NCNC and NEPU – 89, AG and UMBC – 75.) The main reason for its commanding lead was the rivalry between the two main nationalist parties in the South, the NCNC and the AG, which also involved their respective allies in the Northern Region. As a result of this split in the radical vote, the NPC formed a coalition government with the NCNC, and was able to insist that the position of prime minister should go to its nominee, Sir Abubakar Tafawa Balewa; the key positions in the cabinet were also held by NPC ministers.

The outcome of the election was a bitter disappointment to all radicals in the south, but particularly to the NCNC. The NCNC had been the first mass nationalist movement after the war, and its members believed that the end of colonial rule had been achieved largely because of their agitation. Now the fruits of Independence were being enjoyed by the party which had taken no part in the 'struggle for freedom'. Moreover, they suspected that the commanding lead the NPC had gained in the 1959 election had been partly contrived by the expatriate officials who had carried out the 1952 census. This census was the basis on which the electoral constituencies had later been delimited, giving the Northern Region more than half the seats in the Federal House. Southern radicals were convinced that British officials who organized the count had deliberately inflated the population figures for the North in order to smooth the path to power of their protégés, the NPC. The resentment felt by the NCNC can be seen in this editorial in the *Eastern Outlook* written by Mr A. K. Disu, the secretary to Dr Azikiwe:

There is little to commend the new Federal Government to the Nationalists of Nigeria. . . . The late Federal government was notable for its supineness to expatriate British officials. Now that government are all back. There is no virile blood.

They would merit the O.B.E. since we are going to be the 'good boys' of the Empire even after independence. Is it not ominous that neither Dr Azikiwe nor the NEPU leader, Mallam Aminu Kano is in the Federal Cabinet?

(23 December 1959)

This view of the NPC as puppets of the British was a caricature of the truth. The emirs of the North had quite as much reason as the educated classes of the South to object to the restraints and humiliations of British rule. In his autobiography Sir Ahmadu Bello, the Premier of the Northern Region and President of the NPC, makes plain his strong feelings of disdain for many British officials and his determination to be under nobody's thumb.[4] But in the eyes of the NCNC, who were now compelled by their coalition with the NPC to acquiesce in policies that they disliked, such as the ratification of the Anglo-Nigerian Defence pact, Independence was only half achieved so long as the NPC held the reins of power. The Action Group, now the official opposition, had no inhibitions about claiming that the government was affected by 'colonial mentality', and referring to the prime minister as a 'Knight Commander of the British Empire and not a true nationalist'.[5]

This resentment felt by the more educated and politically mobilized Southerners against the dominance of the 'feudal' and 'reactionary' NPC was an underlying cause of instability in Nigeria, which belied the seeming calm of the political scene at Independence. However, radical nationalists were not too despondent about the future. Opposition parties in the North had won thirty-three seats and 35 per cent of the votes in the 1959 Federal elections, in spite of the patronage and pressures which the NPC regional government there could bring to bear on the voters, and it was hoped that with increasing education and political consciousness among the poorer classes the hold of the NPC over that region would be slowly eroded. Moreover, in 1962 there was to be a new census, this time under Nigerian control, and it was confidently expected that this would show that the two Southern Regions had a greater population than the North, and so tilt the balance of electoral advantage in their favour. Meantime, the NCNC leadership was mainly concerned to use its position in the government to weaken its old rival the AG, now in opposition in the Federal parliament, so that eventually the NCNC would be the sole beneficiary when the NPC lost power. This internecine struggle between the parties of the South could only be to the advantage of the NPC.

These hopes that the NPC could be easily brought down by constitutional means soon proved illusory. In May 1961 there was an election to the Northern Regional Assembly in which the opposition won only 9 seats, compared to 156 won by the NPC. After a recount the census of 1963 revealed that the Northern Region still contained a majority of the Nigerian population, though the results of the census were disputed and the NCNC leaders claimed that the figures had once again been falsified. In consequence, radicals in the South became convinced that the rule of the NPC could only be ended if the constitution were radically revised. The NPC were equally certain that the constitution as it stood guaranteed the dominance of the North over the rest of the Federation for ever, and refused to contemplate any but the most minor alterations.

A constitution is supposed to lay down the rules and conditions under which the political parties can carry out their contest for power and it should not itself be at issue. In practice, no constitution is absolutely impartial between all contestants for power. Every rule of the constitution, and in particular those which concern elections, constituencies, the electoral commission and the restrictions on parliament and the executive, favours one party as against another, or one region of the country, or one social class. When a constitution is drawn up these stipulations will represent the advantage that certain groups have over others in the balance of political power at that time, or, in the case of former colonies, the wishes of the departing imperial power. Perhaps the most blatant example of this in recent times is the constitution of Guyana (formerly British Guiana) which laid down that elections should be held on the basis of proportional representation, apparently with the main aim of preventing Dr Jagan from becoming prime minister.

In the case of Nigeria the interests of the Northern Region were particularly favoured by the stiff conditions laid down for creating new regions, and it was later found that the provisions about the conduct of censuses and elections gave the government in power unrivalled opportunities for influencing the results. If the NCNC or AG had come to power as a result of the 1959 election they would probably have been very happy to leave the constitution untouched. As it was, they demanded drastic alterations, but they had no hope of achieving them by the complex method of amendment sanctioned by the constitution, in the face of the objections of the NPC. So it became increasingly clear that southern radicals would have to acquiesce in the perpetual dominance of the NPC, or attempt to subvert the constitution by unauthorized means, that is to say, by violence.

Broadly speaking, there are three ways of subverting a constitution – by popular revolution, by executive action on the part of the government or by a military *coup d'état*.

The best-known example of a popular revolution is the overthrow of Batista's government in Cuba by the guerrilla fighters of Fidel Castro. Other 'freedom fighters' have attempted to follow this lead elsewhere in the world, but with little success so far. The only similar success in recent years was the deposition of the Sultan of Zanzibar in 1964. The crucial factor is the condition of the armed forces supporting the government. Nowadays it seems clear that a popular revolution cannot succeed against a well-equipped and disciplined army deploying its full strength, unless part of the army goes over to the rebels, or they receive massive assistance from a foreign power. In the case of Zanzibar, the Sultan had no army at all, but only a few lightly armed police. In Cuba, the army of Batista was demoralized by frequent purges to ensure its loyalty, and weakened by corruption and indiscipline.

Another way of subverting a constitution is when the executive head of government makes use of his power to command the Army and Police in order to ride roughshod over the restraints on his powers formally embodied in the constitution. This was the method used by Louis Napoleon in 1851, by the Nazis in 1933 after Hitler had been constitutionally installed as Chancellor of Germany, and by President Iskander Mirza of Pakistan in October 1958.

Thirdly, and most commonly, there is the *coup d'état* by a section of the Army. There is no need to give examples of this method. Every few months there is a successful coup somewhere in the developing world, or the report of an attempt that has failed.

In Nigeria between Independence in 1960 and the successful military coup of January 1966 all these methods of subverting the constitutional government were attempted by Southerners in the hope of removing the NPC from office. Certain members of the Action Group, possibly led by Chief Awolowo, tried to organize a popular revolution in 1962, with the help of Ghana. In the Federal election crisis of December 1964 to January 1965 Dr Azikiwe attempted to use his position as president to order the heads of the Armed Services and the Police to take over the government, but failed to carry them with him. And even before the military coups of Major Nzeogwu and General Ironsi there was at least one previous attempt by army officers at military intervention.

The reasons for these failures and the eventual success are examined in the second half of this book, but before that it will be necessary to trace the evolution of the Nigerian Army during the ten years before the military regime was installed, in order to see why it did not take over power earlier and the methods by which the government of the day secured its loyalty.

II · The Nigerian Military Forces in 1956

Early History

The Nigeria Regiment (renamed the Queen's Own Nigeria Regiment after the Royal Tour in 1956) traced its origin to several local forces raised in the second half of the nineteenth century to carry out the British conquest of what is now Nigeria. The earliest of these was 'Glover's Hausas', a constabulary force organized at Lagos in 1863 from runaway slaves who had attached themselves to Lt. Glover, RN, when he returned overland to Lagos after his ship had been wrecked at Jebba.[1] Another force was the 'Oil Rivers Irregulars' raised in the East after the proclamation of the Oil Rivers Protectorate in 1885. From 1891 these were known as the 'Niger Coast Constabulary' and were based at Calabar. In the North Sir George Goldie's Chartered Company had organized the 'Royal Niger Company Constabulary' in 1886. These soldiers were subsequently reorganized by Lord Lugard in 1900 as the Northern Nigerian Regiment and took part in the expedition against Sultan Attahiru Ahmadu of Sokoto in 1903 which led to the formal annexation of the whole of Northern Nigeria. All these military establishments were united to form the Nigeria Regiment of the West African Frontier Force in 1914, at the time of Lugard's amalgamation of Northern and Southern Nigeria.

During this period brief punitive expeditions were frequently mounted, as British control was made effective over the whole country. Between 1900 and 1914 there were forty-three such operations, for which campaign medals were awarded (Africa General Service Medal and clasp). The regiment only served once abroad, when a force was sent to take part in the Ashanti

War of 1900. On the outbreak of the Great War in 1914 the regiment was quickly expanded and took part in the conquest of German Kamerun. When this was completed in 1916, troops were then shipped around Africa to take part in the campaign against Von Lettow in German East Africa (Tanganyika). While these operations were taking place abroad, other soldiers were engaged in suppressing the last major uprising against British rule. The Egba around Abeokuta in Yorubaland had risen against the imposition of Lugard's version of 'indirect rule' on what had previously been the 'Independent United Egba Government'. The rebellion lasted less than two months. Ten companies of troops were engaged and about five hundred rebels were killed.[2]

The Egba rising was the last full-scale punitive expedition in Nigeria. After 1920 the regiment reverted to four battalions from its wartime expansion. Half companies were deployed over much of the North in the years between the wars, and there were still areas, particularly among the pagan tribes of the 'Middle Belt', where district officers had to travel with an escort of armed police and occasionally a company of troops might be sent to enforce payment of taxation.[3] But otherwise the rest of Nigeria was peaceful. The only serious incident was the so-called *yakin mata* in the Eastern Region – the 'Women's War' of 1929–1930, when the imposition of taxation provoked furious riots by women traders. On several occasions troops were ordered to open fire to protect government property from pillage.

In the Second World War Nigerian troops formed part of the force which liberated Ethiopia from the Italians and restored the Emperor Haile Selassie to his throne. Thereafter, when the war against Japan began, Nigerian troops were sent to India and fought in the Burma campaign as part of the 81st and 82nd (West Africa) Divisions. The most important battle in which both divisions were engaged was the capture of Myohaung on 24 January 1945, a date which has since been commemorated by¯an annual ceremony. In all, 28 battalions and supporting troops were raised in Nigeria during the war and 1 21,652 Nigerians served in the Army, of which approximately 30,000 served abroad, winning 86 decorations (8 D.C.M's, 58 M.M.'s, 20 B.E.M.'s) and 243 mentions in despatches.[4]

The government mounted a vigorous propaganda campaign to enlist recruits and these efforts were supported by Dr Azikiwe's *West African Pilot*. This encouragement was welcome since it was more difficult to persuade those with some education to volunteer than illiterates from the bush. Local rulers, chiefs and emirs were expected to support the government's efforts among their people and possibly 'moral pressure' was sometimes used to gain recruits.[5] Cases of compulsion were rare. There was one notorious case in 1944 when there was a schoolboy strike at the leading government secondary school in Lagos, King's College. Seventy-five of the mutinous boys were arrested by the police, but when they were brought before a magistrate's court the case against them was dismissed. The government promptly conscripted eight of the ringleaders into the Army. This high-handed action of the governor caused great offence and was long remembered by the old boys of the school.[6] But this was an isolated occurrence. The great majority of the soldiers were genuine volunteers, attracted by the pay, travel and the opportunities for trade-training that were stressed by government propaganda.[7]

When the war was over most of the troops were demobilized. Gratuities were paid ranging from about thirty pounds for an RSM, who had served through the war outside Nigeria, to about fourteen pounds for a private who had not.[8] A certain percentage of jobs were reserved for ex-servicemen in government and private employment and various veterans' associations were formed, often as adjuncts to the different political parties. Unlike the French African territories, where a number of leading nationalist politicians had served in the French Army (e.g. M. Senghor, President of Senegal, and M. Yace, President of the National Assembly of the Ivory Coast), none of the leading Nigerian nationalists was an ex-serviceman with the exception of Mr J. M. Johnson, Federal Minister of Labour 1960–1963. But there were a number of local leaders and back-benchers in the Federal and Regional legislatures who were eager to contribute to the debates on the Army estimates and to press the claims of ex-servicemen for higher benefits.

Control and Finance of the Nigerian Military Forces – January 1956

In 1956 the Nigerian Military Forces consisted of about 250 officers and 6,400 other ranks.[9] The main units were the five infantry battalions, each of about 750 men, stationed at Abeokuta, Enugu, Ibadan, and two at Kaduna. There was also an artillery battery and an engineer squadron at Kaduna and the regimental depot and recruit training centre at Zaria. In addition there were the usual supporting units, the workshops, transport, signals, pay and records office, military hospitals and supply depots. All these units were commanded by a major-general at his district headquarters in Lagos. The whole organization was completely self-sufficient and independent of the departments of the Nigerian Colonial Government.

Officially, the governor-general of Nigeria was commander-in-chief of the Nigerian Military Forces. But this was a titular command only. In January 1956 all units in Nigeria formed part of West Africa Command of the British Army, whose headquarters were at Accra in the Gold Coast. The major-general in Lagos was directly responsible to the G.O.C.-in-C. West Africa and thence to the War Office in London.

This had not always been the case. Between the two world wars the Nigerian Military Forces had been entirely paid for by the revenue raised in Nigeria and 'their composition, organization and strength were determined by the Government of Nigeria subject to the sanction of the Secretary of State

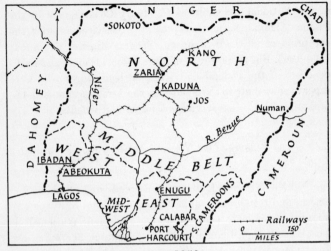

1. REGIONS AND MAIN TOWNS, 1956.

Garrison Towns underlined. The Mid-West Region was created in 1963.
Southern Cameroons left Nigeria in 1960.

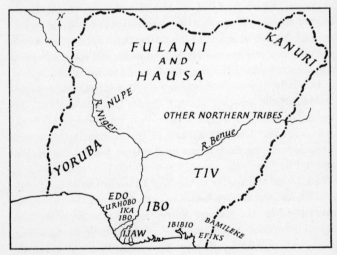

2. MAIN TRIBAL GROUPS

for the Colonies'.[10] The services needed by the military were
provided as economically as possible through the normal
channels of the Colonial Government. For example, the Nigerian Army in 1935 had only two lorries of its own, one at Lagos
and one at Kaduna.[11] But on the outbreak of war in 1939 the
Nigerian Government, along with all other colonial governments, had placed the Nigerian Armed Forces under the
authority of the Army Council in London, and this arrangement
continued after the war was over. Administrative control was
exercised in West Africa through the Command Secretary, the
local representative of the Permanent Under-Secretary of
State for War, who dealt with all matters of finance, accommodation, establishments and administration, audited all
accounts and referred doubtful cases to the War Office for
decision.

Financially this was an excellent arrangement for Nigeria.
The cost of the armed forces was borne by the budget of the
United Kingdom, and the Nigerian taxpayer was only required
to make a partial contribution. The size of this 'Contribution to
Her Majesty's Government on account of Military Expenditure
in Nigeria' (to quote the title of this item in the Estimates) was
periodically revised at conferences with the West African
governments. In 1952 the cost was £750,000. After the 1953
conference this was raised to £1,370,000. But the actual cost
of the military establishment in Nigeria was estimated at somewhere between £3,000,000 and £4,000,000, depending on what
value was placed on the services provided by the Command
Headquarters at Accra and the training establishments in
Britain.[12]

Since the Nigerian Government only paid directly for certain
small items such as cadet units in schools, the Boys' Company
and the training of African officers, the Nigerian legislature
could not lay claim to any influence on the way most of the
military budget was spent. One member stated the position
quite correctly:

I ask myself, is the Nigeria Regiment no more nor less than the British Army stationed in this country, subject to the Army Council of the British War Office? Is the Nigeria Regiment just Nigerian only in name?

(*HR Deb*, 21 March 1955, 415)

In the same debate Chief Akintola put the same point more rhetorically:

If it is only one million pounds that we can provide let that one million pounds be spent on a Nigerian Army over which we shall have control. . . . Let us have an army of two men, but let this appear in our Estimates that this is the nucleus of the Nigerian Army.

This did not mean that Nigerian ministers were not sometimes consulted on military matters. At the 1953 West African Forces Conference Nigeria was represented by two expatriate officials and two Nigerian ministers, Mallam Abubakar Tafawa Balewa[13] and Dr Eni Njoku. The former also attended the meetings of the West African Military Council set up by this conference, and in later years he told parliament: 'I would like to assure the House that, being connected with our military forces since 1952, I think I know quite a bit of what I am talking about.'[14] But Nigerian views obviously carried less weight in military matters than in questions about the Nigeria Police Force, which was entirely financed by the Nigerian taxpayer.

British Officers

In January 1956 only fifteen of the 250 officers were Nigerians. Rather less than half the officers were serving in the five battalions, which had between twenty and twenty-five officers each. The rest served in the various headquarters or in the supporting units and services. These included forty officers in the army medical organization (twenty-four army doctors and sixteen nurses) and also five army chaplains.[15]

Most of the British subalterns in the infantry battalions, the regimental depot and the artillery battery were newly commissioned officers doing their two years compulsory National Service. By the time they had completed their preliminary training and been to officer cadet school in England they usually had only fifteen months or less to serve in Nigeria and quite a number were in the country for less than a year. Most of the army doctors were also national servicemen, though these were usually in Nigeria for eighteen months as their initial army training was shorter. At any one time about sixty to seventy of the officers in Nigeria were British national servicemen, forming about 25 per cent of the total officer strength.

The rest of the expatriate officers were regulars, serving with West Africa Command on secondment from their British regiments and corps. This was the normal pattern for colonial forces, unlike the system in the pre-war Indian Army, where British officers were commissioned into Indian regiments and expected to spend their whole service career in India, building up an abiding affection for and commitment to that country. This was not the position in Nigeria. British regular officers normally served there for two tours of fifteen to eighteen months each, with a three-month leave in between. A few went on to a third tour and one officer who left in 1959 had been on the West Coast for eight years but this was quite exceptional. They had usually volunteered to serve with the RWAFF. West Africa was not a posting that was sought by ambitious young officers, and the War Office periodically publicized vacancies there. One such pamphlet, put out in 1955, emphasized the generous allowances, the opportunities for fishing, shooting (birds) and other sport, 'including at certain stations some of the cheapest polo to be found in the world'.[16]

This relatively short spell of duty in Nigeria for most army officers contrasted with the careers of officers in the colonial service. These expected to spend all their working life in the colonies and often all in the same territory. To a large extent

C

they identified themselves with the interests of Nigeria, as they conceived them, rather than with the interests of the British Government. For example, it is clear from the debate on 18 March 1953 that the expatriate Chief Secretary had vigorously opposed the attempt by the War Office to increase the contribution made by Nigeria towards the cost of the Army. On the whole, British officials accepted the idea of trusteeship, that colonies were being prepared for eventual self-government, even if the time-scale for achieving this was far lengthier than nationalists wished.

The same sort of identification could not be expected in the Army. For British officers in Nigeria their stay of three years or less was only an incident in a career in the British Army, organized by the War Office. As far as possible they expected the army units in Nigeria to follow the patterns and standards of the British Army elsewhere in the world, in Britain, Germany or Malaya, where they might be on their next posting. In the last resort, their frame of reference was, 'What is best for the British Army?' rather than, 'What is best for Nigeria?' Their job was to satisfy the War Office in London, not the Secretary of State for the Colonies or the Nigerian parliament in Lagos. Normally there need have been no conflict between these two criteria; both the War Office in London and the Nigerian Government in Lagos wanted an efficient army. But in the matter of Nigerianization of the armed forces the Army authorities placed far more emphasis on the need for maintaining standards accepted by the British Army all over the world than on the need to keep progress in the Nigerian Military Forces in line with progress in other government departments.

British NCOs

White officers were outnumbered by white non-commissioned officers and warrant officers. There were 336 of them in Nigeria in 1956.[17] Each battalion had an establishment of twelve of

them who were normally employed on the technical duties of
the unit, such as pay, vehicle repairs, signals, education and
specialist instruction. Five years before, the establishment for a
battalion had been twenty-two,[18] so there had been some
improvement. Many more were employed similarly at the
headquarters, the depot and the base and service units.

There was a vast difference in pay and privileges between
British NCOs and warrant officers and their Nigerian counterparts. For example, an African RSM drawing full allowances
received less than £20 a month, travelled second-class on the
railway and had to pay for his wife to travel with him. But a
British Army *sergeant* whose wife was with him in Nigeria was
paid more than £20 a *week*, travelled first-class and had leave
passages paid for his wife and children. The reason for this
disparity was that BNCOs received their British Army rate of
pay plus substantial overseas allowances, while the African
soldier was paid at the lowest rate that the War Office considered adequate to attract recruits. Elsewhere in the public
service white men were paid an expatriation allowance of
between £180 and £300 a year above their Nigerian colleagues.
But there was nothing like the differential which existed in the
Army. What made these discrepancies particularly galling was
the fact that BNCOs were often employed on duties, particularly
in matters of pay, stores and records, which were performed by
Nigerian executive officers in the rest of the government
service.

The presence and privileges of these BNCOs caused far more
comment and criticism than the lack of African officers. The
separate messes provided for British and African sergeants and
the Army schools maintained exclusively for the children of
white servicemen gave plenty of scope for accusations of racial
discrimination.[19] These anomalies were frequently raised in
the press and in the debates on the Army Estimates throughout
the 1950s. For instance, Mr Eneh, an ex-serviceman, complained
in parliament:

You have African warrant officers and British warrant officers. These people are not messing in the same place. They do not live together, they do not eat together. They are so separated that they are treated as people who are not working together, and in actual fact the payment which is given to these men is so different.

(*HR Deb*, 3 March 1958, col. 704)

Racial discrimination had long been a rallying cry for nationalist politicians. Almost all overt signs of this had been removed in Southern Nigeria by the middle 1950s. But the British Army in Nigeria remained a convenient butt for many complaints.

One reason for the continued presence of British NCOs was the shortage of skilled Nigerian tradesmen in the Army. The trouble was, as army spokesmen explained, that soldiers who had become proficient were eager to leave the Army as soon as their term of service was completed to sell their skills at a higher price on the civilian market.[20] In order to alleviate this shortage the 1953 Conference had recommended the setting up of Army Boys' Units where boys of fourteen could be enrolled for a four-year course of schooling and military training. One was set up in Nigeria at Zaria in 1954. Priority in selection was to be given to the sons of serving soldiers and it was hoped that these boy soldiers, having grown up in an army atmosphere, would remain loyal to the Army when they had been fully trained. The first boy soldiers to go on to Army Apprentices schools left for England in 1956. Later in the 1950s and 1960s the Boys' Company also produced a number of Nigerian officers.

Army Pay and Conditions of Service

Army pay was not very attractive in 1956. A recruit received 2s. 6d. a day, rising to 3s. 9d. when fully trained. At this time unskilled daily-paid government labourers were paid 4s. 8d. a day in Lagos, 3s. 6d. a day elsewhere in Southern Nigeria and it was only in the remotest parts of the North that the lowest government rate dropped to 2s. 4d. a day; but this is not a completely fair comparison since soldiers were provided with free food and accommodation in barracks. Rates of pay were no more attractive in the higher ranks; among the senior warrant officers a CSM (non-tradesman) was paid 8s. 6d. a day and an RSM 10s. The soldier felt particularly aggrieved when comparing his pay to that of the Police. A police recruit received 5s. a day, rising to 9s. a day as a first-class constable; a police lance-corporal received 10s. 4d. a day – more than an army RSM. When travelling on leave army NCOs were given travel warrants for a lower class than their equivalent ranks in the Police Force and, unlike other government employees, they had to pay for their wives and their baggage themselves.[21]

Another grievance of the Army was the condition of their barracks. When a Nigerian became Minister of Defence he claimed, 'Our inheritance consisted by and large in a lot of temporary buildings and mud huts.'[22] This was an exaggeration, but it was not entirely unfair. The Nigerian Government had taken over responsibility for buildings from the War Office after the 1953 Conference, and in 1954 a 'ten-year programme' had been drawn up. But implementation of the plans was slow; funds were not made available by government and progress was hindered by shortages of staff in the Public Works Department. As members of the House of Representatives pointed out, and ministers admitted, the accommodation provided for the Police was far superior to that of the Army.

The stations of the battalions were not permanent; each battalion changed places with another about every three years. This rotation was a postwar innovation. There were sound military reasons for it: it enabled the soldiers to know and train in different parts of the country; also some stations had more ceremonial duties and less amenities than others. Probably another reason, though not officially admitted, was that it prevented the garrisons from becoming too intimate with the local civilian population, which might have made them less reliable for internal security duties.[23]

The Pattern of Recruitment by Regions and Tribal Groups

Between the wars almost all the soldiers were recruited in the Northern Region. The Army consisted of little more than the infantry battalions and the artillery and it was believed that the 'fighting tribes of the North' produced excellent soldiers for these arms. But when the RWAFF was expanded during the Second World War large numbers of drivers, mechanics and other tradesmen were also needed, and there were no Europeans available to fill these posts. Accordingly the G.O.C.-in-C. West Africa laid down that every job that could be done by an African must be done by one. This policy led to the enlistment of many Southern Nigerians into the Army since the expanded Army needed men with education and the bulk of the educated were in the South. These recruits did far better than expected.

The services made greater advances than seemed possible at first, especially the West African Service Corps. . . . How they managed the technical words is a mystery, the answer to which is only known to themselves. The African of all types, even including those from the bush, showed amazing mechanical aptitude.[24]

After the war ended recruitment in the South was continued, but most of the infantrymen still came from the North. In the latter region recruits were only required to have a good physique and the ability to pass a simple non-verbal intelligence test. In the South the Army hoped that most of the potential recruits had completed their primary education, though some of these were also illiterate.[25]

This cleavage between tradesmen and clerks from the South and infantrymen from the North had its uses for the British. In May 1952 a hundred soldiers at the Command Ordnance

Depot, Yaba, staged a mutiny in protest against their living accommodation, burning army property and wounding two European officers. The mutineers were suppressed by the Military Police, assisted by soldiers from the infantry detachment in Lagos. These would be Northern riflemen suppressing a mutiny by Southern clerks.[26]

There was a marked discrepancy between the pattern of recruitment by regions, into the Police and into the Army.[27]

	% of population 1952 census	% of army recruits 1946–1958	% of police in 1955
North	54·5	62·5	17·5
East	23	25	45·5
West	20	11	33
S. Cameroons	2·5	1·5	4
	100	100	100

The reason for the predominance of the Southern Regions in the Police was that recruits were required to have a minimum standard of literacy, even in the North.

Within each region army recruits did not come equally from all areas. As one member explained to the House:

You must take into consideration the special aptitude of a certain section of the people. You will find extensions of the country where the people believe in the Army. In the East we know those who belong to the military section. But there are certain sections where immediately you say 'Ah' they run away.

(*HR Deb*, 12 August 1959, col. 1815)

There is, unfortunately, no publicly available evidence of the tribal composition of the Army. The Police published a detailed tribal breakdown of the Force each year in their annual report but the Army authorities refused to give this information. In general, the opinion of the Army was that the best recruits came from the areas farthest away from the recruiting centres at Zaria, Ibadan and Enugu.[28] These were the places where the minority tribes lived.

In the Northern Region most recruits came from the so-called 'Middle Belt', the lower half of the region, around the Niger and Benue rivers. Certain areas here had a particularly good record for providing recruits, such as Dakakori in Niger province, Tiv Division in Benue province and Numan in Adamawa province. Much of this territory had not been conquered by the Fulani *jihad* (holy war) at the beginning of the nineteenth century and had remained largely pagan until the arrival of the Christian missionaries in the last sixty years. Missionaries were largely excluded until recent times from the Fulani Emirates as a result of agreements made by Lugard when he annexed the whole of the region. Consequently, the so-called 'Holy North' remained almost entirely Muslim and untouched by European education. This difference in religion provides indirect evidence of the tribal origin of soldiers. In October 1966 a reporter of the London *Observer* was able to see the records of the fifth battalion at Kano.[29] At this time the battalion was entirely composed of Northerners since all the Ibo and Southern soldiers had fled or been killed. It was found that out of 681 other ranks, 328 were Protestant, 233 were Roman Catholic, 36 animists, and only 84 were Muslim (about 12 per cent). So most of these soldiers must have come from the small tribes of the Middle Belt. Army recruiting had only begun in this area during the 1914–1918 War, when replacements were needed for the East African campaign, but these tribes now far outnumbered the Hausa, who had originally provided the bulk of the Nigeria Regiment.[30] Another area of the North with a military tradition was Bornu province in the far North-East, where the Kanuri lived. A number of recruits also came from over the border in the French Colonies of Niger and Chad.

The senior warrant officer of the Nigerian Army in 1962, RSM Hama Kim, M.M. of the depot at Zaria, was one of these 'Frenchmen'.[31]

In the Eastern Region a clue to the main recruiting areas is provided by the constituencies which returned ex-servicemen as members of parliament. The provinces of Calabar, Ogoja and Rivers, where most of the non-Ibo tribes live, returned twelve ex-servicemen to the Regional and Federal legislatures, though they had less than half the seats; but the central Ibo heartland, with a majority of the seats, was represented by only two ex-servicemen.[32] Several of the first Nigerian officers came from or were educated in Calabar (Bassey, Ironsi, Ogundipe). This town had been a military station from 1891 right up to the end of the 1939–1945 War.

In the Western Region, the main tribe, the Yoruba, were most unwilling soldiers. In 1966, even though a regional recruitment quota had been in force for eight years, there were only 700 Yoruba soldiers out of an army of 10,500. Most soldiers came from the Mid-West area near the Niger river, or from Ondo province, which was next to it. Within the Mid-West itself, perhaps half the soldiers came from the Ibo minority there, the Ika-Ibo.[33]

The pattern in all three regions was the same: the best recruiting areas were those farthest from the regional capitals, in economically depressed parts with few natural resources. Few recruits came from the cocoa-producing areas of the West, or the main groundnut- and cotton-producing areas of the North. Similarly in the Eastern Region there were more alternative opportunities for employment in the Ibo heartland and along the lines of the railway than in the more sparsely populated minority areas where the roads were bad and few.

The Tasks of the Army

The functions of the Military Forces were defined as the immediate defence of Nigeria from outside attack, and aid to the civil power in the maintenance of internal security. In practice, the question of frontier defence did not arise in 1956, as long as the French still controlled their colonies which surrounded Nigeria. This did become a problem later, however, when the French were faced with a rebellion in the Cameroons in 1959–1960 and it was feared that trouble would spill over the border.

Troops were never required to take action in support of the Police in Nigeria during the 1950s, though they were ordered to stand by to assist if needed, notably during the Kano riots of April 1953, the riots in Eastern Nigeria over taxation in February 1958 and the riot in Ibadan in March 1958 after the death of Alhaji Adelabu. During the 1948 riots in the Gold Coast (now Ghana), two Nigerian battalions were sent there by air and remained for about two months. They were used for patrolling troubled areas and providing town piquets.

Apart from this incident, no Nigerian troops were sent on active service abroad between the end of the Second World War and the Congo operation of 1960. In the early 1950s there was some talk in Britain of increasing the number of West African battalions to form an Imperial Reserve, but any such plans were put aside after the decision of the 1953 Conference that no military formation should be moved out of any territory without the prior approval of the government of that territory.[34] It was rumoured in Lagos that Nigerian soldiers would be sent to the Middle East at the time of the Suez crisis in 1956, but this was promptly denied by the government.[35] British policy in this respect was a complete contrast to that of the French who made extensive use of African troops in their colonial wars in French Indo-China up to 1954, and later in Algeria.

Occasionally there were other calls for army assistance: to hunt marauding lions or elephants in remote areas; or the engineers might build a bridge in the bush which was helpful to the local people as well as being used for army manoeuvres. But for the most part the Military Forces were only seen on ceremonial parades such as that for the Queen's Birthday. The rest of the time they carried on with their normal round of training, treks through bush, range practices and sport, hardly noticed by most of the population.

The Reputation of the Army

Soldiers had never been very popular in Nigeria. Because of its brutality to friend and foe alike, the Niger Coast Constabulary was known in the nineteenth century as the 'Forty Thieves'. The origins of the military in Northern Nigeria were described by the Sardauna of Sokoto, Sir Ahmadu Bello, as follows: 'When the British came to the North, they started recruiting their army of soldiers by getting slaves who ran away from their masters, labourers from the markets and so on, and had them enlisted in the force. They had a bad start then.'[36]

To some extent their low reputation may have resulted from the part they played in establishing British rule. The Sardauna recalled his feelings when he was at school in 1926.

Within sight of the school we could see the square fort and the sentries behind the parapets. . . . We did not like the soldiers; they were our own people and had conquered us for strangers and had defeated our people on the plain just before us. This feeling was very common all over the North.

(My Life, 23)

Until 1960 the officers' mess of the first battalion displayed among its trophies the flag picked up beside the body of Sultan Attahiru after the Battle of Burmi. I remember the slight embarrassment shown by a Nigerian officer when explaining the history of this particular regimental trophy to a visiting party of schoolboy cadets in 1958. Occasional references to the suppression of the Egba rebellion were also made by Yoruba members of the House of Representatives.

During the Second World War the large expansion of the Army meant that temporary training camps were set up in areas where soldiers had not previously been known, and the soldiers' behaviour did not commend them to the local population. Major Eze recalled the view of the Army held by many people in the East at that time:

> The Army was a place for the illiterates and criminals whose duties were to kill and be generally brutal. The activities of some soldiers in the villages and markets during the last war only confirmed their opinions.
>
> (*NAM*, 1963, 12)

Similarly in the Western Region soldiers apparently caused havoc. Chief Longe told the Senate, 'I remember during the last war some soldiers were brought to my area at Ede. . . . Most of them committed atrocities; some of them were arrested and tried.'[37]

The soldiers' low rate of pay also did not help the Army's prestige. Mr Eneh, an ex-serviceman from the East, told parliament: 'People are jeered at when they want to join the Army, the reason being that soldiers are treated no better than labourers. . . . There is a psychology in this country that when someone is badly paid that man is inferior.'[38] In towns, and particularly among the Yoruba in Lagos, soldiers were more frequently a butt for ribald wit than an object of national admiration. At the time of the Queen's visit in 1956 an expatriate wrote a letter of complaint to the *West African Pilot*:

> I have visited many countries in my life, but in none have I seen soldiers being treated with such discourtesy as I have in Nigeria, and especially here in Lagos. . . . What I see in Lagos is abuse, insult and derision, amounting to causing some minor degree of dissatisfaction among the rank and file. . . . Scarcely a year passes without some irresponsible

citizen inventing some abusive epithet or another for the soldiers.

(8 February 1956)

The leader writer of the *Pilot* agreed:

If the present state of affairs exists simply because our soldiers are drawn mainly from the illiterate class and do not compare favourably with their counterparts in the outside world, then a case has been made for government to answer, but certainly on no account should soldiers be molested or abused. Such epithets as *afamaco* and *abobaku*, whatever they may mean, must be stopped.[39]

Nor did the military fare much better in debates in the House of Representatives. Complaints about British control of the Army have already been mentioned, but the soldiers themselves were also unpopular. Chief Akintola, the future Premier of the West, asked the Chief Secretary to move army units out of Lagos: 'The proximity of some of these army headquarters to the areas where civilians live is most embarrassing to us. So many barbed wires.'[40] He renewed his request in the debate on the Army Estimates in the following year, when he was supported by a prominent Ibo businessman, Mr Louis Ojukwu, who declared amid general laughter:

During the war we collected some military stores in a cluster of buildings in Clifford Street, which is now an eyesore. . . . I agree that during the war years we liked to accommodate them, but nobody likes to live with soldiers. We like them; they are our brothers; but at the same time we would like them to be far from us.

(*HR Deb*, 17 March 1956, col. 1174)

Mr Louis Ojukwu was knighted in 1960 as Sir Odumegwu Ojukwu, K.B.E. He was the father of the future Lt.-Col. Ojukwu, who at this time was still a district officer in the administrative service.

The soldiers thus had a low prestige among most sectors of the population, except in the poorest parts of the country where military service was a traditional form of employment. It was a pity. It was true that the Army was in origin, and in 1956 still remained, a mercenary and not a national force, engaged to serve the ends of its 'imperialist masters'. But it had helped to free Ethiopia from its Italian conquerors and restore the Emperor to his throne in Addis Ababa. Also, and more important, the Army was one of the few institutions in the country where Northerners and Southerners worked together. As 'Peter Pan' (the brother of Chief Anthony Enahoro) put it in his column in the *Daily Times*:

> We may have been ruled by expatriate tax collectors as one for upwards of fifty years, but in fact the national feeling in this country began in the war years when Southerner met Northerner in the British Army.
>
> (1 March 1966)

The same impression of the national comprehensiveness of the Army is given by a perusal of the list of medals and 'Mentions in Despatches' won in the Second World War. Most of the names are Northern, or even come from places in French territory, such as CSM Issa Sokoto, Pte. Mailafia Shangev (from Tiv Division) and Sgt. Moma Fortlamy (from French Chad); but the list also includes obviously Eastern names such as Cpl. Bassey Okon and Cpl. Emeka Ogoja, and Western names like Sgt. Akanbi Salami.[41]

But this was not a common point of view in Nigeria in 1956. Most of the Nigerian public regarded the Army as a thing apart, an alien institution to be ignored or despised.

III · Nigerianizing the Officer Corps, 1949-1960

Energetic efforts to promote Nigerians to senior posts in the public service did not begin until the arrival of a new governor, Sir John Macpherson, in 1948. He immediately appointed a committee to consider the subject headed by the chief secretary, Hugh Foot, and including Dr Azikiwe and Muhammadu Ribadu. This committee laid down the principles on Nigerianization which officially remained the basis of government policy for the next ten years: no non-Nigerian was to be recruited when a qualified and suitable Nigerian was available; no discrimination in favour of Nigerians for promotion; and no lowering of standards.

Rigid adherence to these last two principles would have put off complete Nigerianization of the top posts in the civil service to 1970 or later. Since there were very few Nigerian graduates available at this time, sufficient Nigerian entrants to the administrative grade of the public service, the 'senior service' posts, could only come from a lowering of standards. And if new Nigerian entrants were not given accelerated promotion over the heads of expatriates already in the service, they would not reach the top by normal processes for twenty years. In practice, both these impediments to Nigerianization were gradually abandoned during the 1950s, though lip service to these principles continued to be paid up to 1960.

First Plans to Produce Nigerian Officers

A few Africans were commissioned in the early years of the West African Frontier Force; its official history lists the casualties suffered by African officers as well as European officers in the Ashanti War of 1900. But after 1914 the officer corps, like the administrative service, was reserved for white men. During the Second World War only one West African was given the King's Commission – Lt. Seth Anthony of the Gold Coast, who retired from the Army after the war with the rank of major.

Nigerianization in the Army did not come within the terms of reference of the Foot Committee since the military forces in Nigeria did not form part of the Nigerian public service, but the army authorities could not remain entirely uninfluenced by political events in Nigeria and the Gold Coast. The first proposal made by the G.O.C.-in-C. West Africa, General Nicholson, in 1949 was that a West African Military Academy should be set up to train African officer cadets for commissions. But there were two objections to this proposal: the cost seemed excessive for the small number of officers who would be trained; and, when these officers passed out, they would not be considered the equivalent of an officer in the British Army holding the King's Commission. This last point completely damned the proposal. Nationalist leaders had always insisted that certificates and qualifications awarded in West Africa must be internationally recognized, even if the content of the examination was unsuitable to local conditions. (For example, in 1929 strong local opposition had killed a proposal to establish a Nigerian School Certificate in place of the Cambridge examination.) So the proposal for a West African Military Academy was turned down by the Nigerian Government.[1]

Instead, a number of places were reserved for West African officer cadets at Sandhurst, who would be given regular commissions in the British Army when they passed out after the eighteen-month course there. In addition to this, serving NCOs and warrant officers were to be eligible for short-service commissions if they successfully completed a sixteen-week course at Mons or Eaton Hall Officer Cadet Schools in England.

These were normally converted to regular commissions after three years service as an officer.

However, the requirements laid down for admission to these courses were quite stiff. Before a candidate for a short-service commission could appear before a selection board, he had to have passes at 'O' level in the General Certificate of Education in English Language and three other subjects (or its equivalent), be of high medical category, between the ages of twenty-five and thirty, and a British subject.[2] Considering that most army recruits were illiterate when they joined, this hardly opened the door very wide. It is not surprising that most of the early officers came from the technical branches of the Army. Six out of the first seven Gold Coast officers to be commissioned came from senior NCOs and WOs in the Army Educational Service. Of the first Nigerian officers, CSM Ironsi had begun his army service as a clerk in the Ordnance Stores and RSM Ademulegun came from the Signals.

The same educational qualifications were required for a student leaving secondary school who was a candidate for a regular commission, and he also faced a long series of hurdles. He had to pass the following tests:[3]

1. General Written Examination
2. Medical Test
3. Interview at District Headquarters
4. Interview at Army Headquarters
5. Recruit Course at Teshie, Gold Coast (six months)
6. Final Selection Board at Teshie
7. Officer Cadet Course at Eaton Hall, England (four months)
8. Regular Commissions Selection Board
9. Course at Royal Military Academy, Sandhurst (eighteen months).

None of these stages was a mere formality. On one course at Teshie in 1956 only two of the nine Nigerians passed the final selection board. In 1955 another cadet was sent out of the

D

Army after failing the Regular Commissions Board in England
at two attempts.[4]

The Army was clearly 'determined not to be satisfied with
anything but the highest standards', as the Foot commission
had recommended. In fact, the tests were much more severe
than those set for a British candidate for a regular commission.
A British officer cadet did not have to pass two selection boards,
nor did he have to go through the Eaton Hall course (intended
for British National Service officers) before going on to Sandhurst. It seems to have been assumed that there was all the
time in the world to produce Nigerian officers. When a new
G.O.C.-in-C., General Whistler, came out to West Africa in
1951 and talked of having Nigerian captains within five to ten
years and majors in ten to fifteen years, he was considered to be
a dangerous radical and he was warned by the Governor of
Nigeria that he would 'bump into a lot of trouble from his
battalion commanders' who would resist the speed of his
proposals very strongly.[5] In fact, even General Whistler's
modest timetable was soon outstripped by events.

The first short-service officer was commissioned in 1948,
Lt. Ugboma. The following year four more were commissioned,
Lts. Bassey, Sey, Aguiyi-Ironsi and Ademulegun. Thereafter
progress was slower, one in 1950, Lt. Shodeinde, and one in
1952, Lt. Wellington. It was February 1953 before the first
regular officers passed out from Sandhurst, 2/Lts. Maimalari
and Umar Lawan.

Not all these officers remained in the Army. Sey resigned his
commission in 1952. Both Ugboma and Wellington disappear
from the Army List by 1954; and one of the first two officers
from Sandhurst, Umar Lawan, resigned in 1956 after only
three years commissioned service.[6] However, by January
1956 there were fifteen Nigerian officers, as listed in the table
on pages 38–39.

Most of these officers came from traditional army recruiting
areas – Bornu and the Middle Belt in the North, the minority

areas of the East, and the Mid-West. It is surprising that five of the fifteen were Yoruba, but three of these came from Ondo province, which borders on the Mid-West. In view of the later predominance of Ibos in the officer corps it is also odd that there were only three Ibos in the first eighteen officers commissioned, and of these three only one, Lt. Imo, came from the 'Ibo heartland', which is now the East Central State; Lt. Nwawo was a Mid-Westerner, and Major Ironsi was only half Ibo (his mother was Ibo but his father came from Sierra Leone).[7]

None of the Northern NCOs and WOs in the infantry regiments was sufficiently educated to qualify for a short-service commission, but the senior warrant officer of the Nigeria Regiment, RSM Chari Maigumeri, was given the honorary rank of captain on his retirement in 1953. This remarkable soldier began his military career in the German Army in Kamerun and won the Iron Cross for gallantry against the British. After the conquest of German Kamerun in 1917 he enlisted in the WAFF, and then fought against the Germans in the last year of the East African campaign. He was still in service in the Second World War when he fought in the Ethiopia and Burma campaigns, winning the Military Medal.

In view of the backwardness of the Northern Region in education it is very surprising that the first five regular officers to graduate from Sandhurst were all Northerners. In 1954 only 85 boys from the North passed the School Certificate Examination, compared with 1,334 boys in the South. All five Northerners had been at the same school, Government College, Zaria. This was the most prestigious school in the North and was for a long time the only government school there. It had been founded in 1922 as Katsina College, had moved to Kaduna in 1937 and finally to Zaria in 1949. The Sardauna, Sir Abubakar Tafawa Balewa, and most of the Northern Federal and Regional ministers were educated there. In 1956 another

NIGERIAN OFFICERS AT JANUARY 1956

Name	Joined Army	First Commissioned	Rank and Seniority January 1956
A. *Officers Commissioned from the Ranks (former NCOs and WOs)*			
Bassey	1936	April 1949	Capt. Oct. 1948
Aguiyi-Ironsi	1942	June 1949	Capt. Oct. 1951 (acting Major)
Ademulegun	1942	June 1949	Capt. Dec. 1951
Shodeinde	1943	April 1950	Capt. Sept. 1952
Ogundipe	1942	Aug. 1953	Lt. Jan. 1951
Adebayo	1948	Dec. 1953	Lt. Dec. 1953
Nwawo	1950	May 1954	Lt. Aug. 1954
Fajuyi, B.E.M.*	1943	Nov. 1954	Lt. March 1952
Imo	1946	June 1955	Lt. Aug. 1953
B. *Officers given Regular Commissions from RMA, Sandhurst (former*			
Maimalari	1950	Feb. 1953	Lt. Jan. 1955
Umar Lawan	1950	Feb. 1953	Lt. Aug. 1955
Kur Muhammed	1951	Feb. 1954	Lt. Feb. 1956
Largema	1951	Feb. 1954	Lt. Feb. 1956
Pam	1953	Dec. 1955	2/Lt. Nov. 1954
Kurobo	1953	Dec. 1955	2/Lt. July 1955

Notes: All officers in Group A were originally given short service commissions; by 1956 Bassey, Ironsi and Ademulegun had been converted to regular commissions; all the rest were also converted before 1960.

Government College, Zaria was formerly known as Kaduna College. It moved in 1949 and became Zaria Secondary

GION, TRIBE AND TYPE OF COMMISSION

Tribe	Region	Home Town, District or Province	Other Information
Efik	East	Uyo, Calabar	
Sierra Leone/ Ibo	East	Umuahia-Ibeku, Bende	Father a railwayman. At school at Calabar and Kano.
Yoruba	West	Ondo	Father a tailor and farmer. A teacher before joining Army.
Yoruba	West	Abeokuta	Father a tax clerk.
Yoruba	West	Lagos	At school at Calabar.
Yoruba	West	Ado-Ekiti, Ondo	Father a railwayman.
Ika-Ibo	West	Mid-West	
Yoruba	West	Ado-Ekiti, Ondo	Father a carpenter and farmer. A clerk before joining Army.
Ibo	East	Amaekpu-Ohafia, Bende	
secondary school students)			
Kanuri	North	Bornu	Government College, Zaria.
Kanuri	North	Bornu	Government College, Zaria.
Kanuri	North	Bornu	Government College, Zaria.
Kanuri	North	Bornu	Government College, Zaria.
Birom	North	Jos, Plateau (born Kaduna)	Government College, Zaria.
Ijaw	East	Bonny, Rivers	Government College, Umuahia.

School till 1956. The present name is used throughout to avoid confusion.
* Fajuyi was awarded the B.E.M. in 1951 when he succeeded in maintaining calm in his squadron when trouble broke out among troops as a reaction against the rationing of food for soldiers (*West African Pilot*, 11 January 1962).

officer cadet from this school was in his last year at Sandhurst – the future General Gowon.

Why did the Army have such success here in persuading secondary school leavers to join, but not elsewhere? One reason was that a particular effort was made at this school, which was situated in the same town as the Regimental Training Depot. A close liaison was established and schoolboys were able to visit the Depot to see demonstrations. The school also had a rifle club which used the army range.[8]

Another reason was perhaps the traditional glorification of the warrior in Islam. The Emirates had been established as a result of the Fulani *jihad* at the beginning of the nineteenth century. One Northern member of the House of Representatives boasted: 'There was no region so much prepared for war as our own. Dan Fodio by chivalry and war art gave the North fifty per cent representation in this House.'[9]

There was also family tradition. At least three of the Northern officers commissioned before Independence had close relatives who had served in the war; Gowon (a brother), Hassan Katsina (an uncle) and Akahan (father).[10]

The Army did not show the same eagerness to attract secondary school leavers from Southern Nigeria. In 1952, after the liaison scheme at Zaria had been running for several years, the Army was still only 'considering' similar arrangements for the government colleges in the south at Ibadan and Umuahia. Southern members of parliament complained that no attempt was made to inform schools of the opportunities in the Army. The Army replied that schools had been circularized; but it is not surprising that it was accused of prejudice against Southern officers and deliberately attempting to go slow on commissioning Southerners until there were an equal number of Northern officers.[11]

It is certainly true that the Army was much slower to Nigerianize than the Police Force. In 1948 there were ten Africans holding gazetted rank in the Police, which is the grade corresponding to commissioned rank in the Army. By April 1956 this figure had risen to 56 out of an establishment of 238 officers.[12] Thus almost a quarter of the police officers were Nigerians, compared to a mere 6 per cent in the Army.

The Failure to Attract Southern Officer Cadets

Even though the Army made no special effort in Southern Nigeria to promote military service as a career, the army entrance examinations were still advertised and details were circulated to secondary schools. But the response was poor. Abubakar Tafawa Balewa, then Minister of Transport, told parliament in 1955, 'At present we are given a lot of vacancies in Sandhurst but which unfortunately we cannot fill.' The same complaint was made year after year by the chief secretary in the debates on the Army Estimates. Brigadier Browne told the press in 1957, 'Young people in Eastern and Western Nigeria with the required education do not appear to like the army as a career.'[13]

There were many reasons for this. First and foremost was the general mistrust of and contempt for the Army that existed over most of the South, which was coupled with considerable ignorance of what life in the Army was like. The rigid discipline of army life was quite foreign to the ebullient easy-going attitude of the average secondary school student. Major Eze recalled his experiences as an officer cadet in 1955:

The first few weeks of polishing, washing, starching and pressing, general cleaning, fatigues, 'square-bashing', physical training, military and educational studies, sports and general chasing around by non-commissioned officers shattered the potential officers' hopes. The feeling then was to 'pack it all up' and go back to civil life. This was when some fell by the wayside.

(*NAM*, 1963, 12)

Furthermore, the Army was an occupation of very low prestige. Only one army officer, Capt. Ademulegun, was named in a handbook of the Nigerian *élite* published in Lagos in 1956.[14] Fathers who had invested money on school fees wished their sons to become lawyers, doctors or engineers. As the *West Africa Pilot* put it:

> Until very recently Nigerians, particularly Southerners, had looked on an army career as a last resort. They saw service as a menial job, not good enough for people with good education, social status and good birth.

> (4 June 1957)

This disparaging attitude to the Army was not, in 1956, the result of poor pay. Nigerian officers had just received a substantial pay increase, and a newly commissioned subaltern now received £600 a year instead of £350, which had been his previous salary.[15] For comparison, a graduate just out of university was paid £624 a year on entering the 'senior service'. This would probably be at least five years after obtaining his School Certificate. But an officer cadet could complete his full course of training and pass out of Sandhurst in less than three years. The graduate would have had to find school fees and expenses of about £50 a year for his last two years at school while studying for his Higher School Certificate, and more than £100 for each of his three years at university, unless he was fortunate enough to get a scholarship. On the other hand, an officer cadet had no fees to find; he was paid by the Army while in training.

However, there were other factors besides basic pay to be considered. In the 1950s almost any graduate could find employment in the pullulating Federal and Regional public services and the new government corporations. Once appointed the graduate immediately qualified for a salary advance of up to £800 to buy a car. This advance had to be paid back over five years. But each month the graduate received a 'Car Basic

Allowance' of £13, free of tax, which was more than enough to cover the repayments. In addition he was entitled to a mileage allowance when he used the car on government business. Thus, in effect, a newly appointed senior service officer was given a free car. He also qualified for a government loan to build himself a house, if he did not live in government quarters.

None of this applied to the Nigerian army officer. He was serving in part of the British Army, and the War Office is not accustomed to give housing loans or free cars to all officers. This was not a trifling matter; a car, preferably as large and long as possible, was the status symbol above all others of the young man who had 'arrived'. It was next to impossible for the newly commissioned Nigerian officer to save up enough money to buy a second-hand car when he was beset by the urgent demands of needy relatives for money and when he was expected to pay the fees of his younger brothers and nephews still at school. This grievance was frequently aired in parliament and in the press. The *Daily Times* commented:

> Perhaps the Nigerian stands alone in his attitude to car ownership, which is largely psychological. Granting allowances for the purchase of cars may well turn out to be the tonic army officers need to end their general feeling of depression.
>
> (4 June 1957)

But the War Office could not grant such a privilege to Nigerian officers nor to British officers serving in Nigeria. That would be racial discrimination. British officers received substantial overseas allowances for which Nigerian officers were not eligible, but this was not considered relevant.

There were also other drawbacks to an army career in the eyes of a secondary school student. The training course at Sandhurst did not confer a degree and the army officer could not put any letters after his name. It was true that an officer could go on to take a degree in engineering at the Royal

Military College of Science at Shrivenham, but only one officer did this before 1960, Lt. Banjo. The prestige attached to being a graduate was immense. In part this was because of the rarity of the qualification. It also reflected the fact that a graduate could be assured of a senior service salary and its perquisites, since the salaries and conditions available in commercial firms corresponded fairly closely to those paid by the government. But pay was not the only consideration. Expatriate managers in commercial firms bemoaned the fact that Nigerian trainees left to go up to university as soon as they had acquired the necessary paper qualifications, even though their financial prospects would have been better if they had stayed on as trainee managers with the firm. The glory of wearing an academic hood was unbeatable.

Another discouragement to the potential officer was the high rejection rate during cadet training. Once a student had been accepted for a university he could be reasonably sure that he would eventually emerge with a degree. If he failed one examination he would probably be allowed to repeat it the following year. Not so in the Army. A cadet who was discharged after failing the Teshie course normally did not have a second opportunity, and if he then tried to qualify for university entrance he would find himself a year or more behind his former classmates. This could make a profound difference to a man's promotion prospects at a time of rapid advancement. So it is not surprising that any student who believed himself capable of getting to university considered an army career a poor gamble.

Promotion prospects were also poor in the Army in the 1950s compared to the civil service. As can be seen from a perusal of the Regional and Federal Staff Lists a number of Nigerian administrative officers who first entered the senior service grade in the early 1950s were promoted to 'superscale' posts earning £2,000 and more within six or eight years.[16] These were the fortunate and talented few, but their success stimulated the hopes of others. Not one similar example can be found in the Army. Nigerian officers moved gradually up the normal ladder of promotion in the British Army: two years from second-lieutenant to lieutenant, four years from lieutenant to captain, seven years from captain to major. Even acting rank was rarely given. Captain Ironsi was made an acting major three years before this was due when he served as equerry to the Queen in 1956, but Bassey and Ademulegun had to serve their full seven years as captains before promotion. Lt. Kur Muhammed was promoted acting captain in 1959 only three months before this was due to him on a time basis.

All these considerations were important to the Nigerian school-leaver considering a career in the Army, but the most important point was the question of the financial reward. Fees for a child at secondary school placed an immense burden on most families. Often a number of relatives would club together to find the money required, and the schoolboy would be expected to support them or their children in return, once he started earning. He was under great pressure to succeed, and every boy in the lowest form in the school knew exactly what the government scale of salaries was for a School Certificate holder (about £150 per annum) and a graduate (£624 per annum). He knew his opportunities – and his obligations. The army authorities apparently did not realize the importance of this. Until August 1957 advertisements for the army examination for potential officers did not include information about the officer's rate of pay on commissioning. It is hardly surprising that the first advertisement to do so produced a number of surprised letters to the newspapers and three times the number of applications that previous advertisements had achieved.[17]

Senior British officers showed the same lack of comprehension when addressing an audience of schoolboys to persuade them to join the Army. One speech by a British colonel in 1960 to King's College cadets stressed the more intangible benefits of army life – the joys of leading men, the camaraderie of the officers' mess, the open air life, travel, the opportunities for sport – and ended with the emphatic statement that the speaker had been in the Army for twenty years and enjoyed every minute of it. The following year a Nigerian, Lt.-Col. Ademulegun, addressed the same audience. He hardly mentioned any of the matters the British colonel had spoken of; but he gave full details of the rates of pay, contrasting them with the civil service, and also dwelt on the economies of living in the mess with soldier servant provided, and the likelihood of future expansion of the Army with opportunities for swift promotion.

Reasons for the Army's Failure to Nigerianize

So far a formidable list of difficulties has been given which stood in the way of attracting sufficient potential officers into the Army. It is now necessary to ask why the army authorities failed to act energetically to counteract them before 1958. Only two of these disadvantages were quite irremediable: nothing could make life in the Army as comfortable as a clerical post in the civil service, nor could Sandhurst turn itself into a university in order to satisfy Nigerian ambitions. The rest could have been dealt with if the necessary money and will had been present, as was shown by what happened once the Army was completely under Nigerian control.

The chief obstacle was the fact that, until 1958, the ultimate authority for changes in the Army was the War Office in London. This body was far enough away from Nigeria to be effectively insulated from the pressures to Nigerianize that were exercised on the Colonial Government in Nigeria by Nigerian ministers, members of parliament and the press. Nigeria only paid half the cost of the Nigerian Military Forces, so critical comment had far less effect than similar complaints about Nigerianization in the Police Force, where the Nigerian taxpayer footed the whole bill.

The Army was also unaffected by another potent argument for Nigerianization, the shortage of expatriate staff. In 1953 the senior grade of the public service had an establishment of 5,124 posts. Over 1,000 of these posts were vacant. This was before regionalization. In 1954 the unified public service was split up into one Federal and three Regional services. All these four services continued to expand, so that by 1961 the Federal service *alone* had an establishment of 5,133 senior service posts, and again over 1,000 vacancies.[18] Suitable expatriates were just not available to fill these vacancies, so there could be little argument against employing every Nigerian who was available, even if a man's qualifications were rather below the optimum requirement.

There were no similar pressures on the Army. Between 1956 and 1960 the number of army officers expanded slightly from 250 to 286. But the War Office never had any difficulty in filling these posts when officers ended their period of secondment. For the vacancies in the junior ranks of the battalions and for army doctors there were always the National Service subalterns available from England. For the higher ranks there were a number of officers who would otherwise become redundant now that the British Army was being slimmed down in the reorganization initiated by Duncan Sandys in 1957.[19] There was thus not the same incentive to search for suitable Nigerian officers at all costs as was felt by the Federal and Regional public service commissions.

It was particularly unfortunate that the Army did not feel itself compelled to Nigerianize swiftly since it was in one respect *better* placed to do so than the public service. The main obstacle to the accelerated promotion of Nigerians in government posts was the impossibility of displacing the incumbent expatriates, who often wished to remain in Nigeria until they qualified for compensation on retirement at Independence. The Nigerian Government was normally unable to offer them posts elsewhere in order to persuade them to retire earlier and so had to create special supernumerary posts for Nigerians to give them adequate experience in the higher ranks. But the frequent turnover of British officers in West Africa was continually creating vacancies to which Nigerians could have been promoted as the departing expatriates continued their careers elsewhere in the British Army.

Within the limits set by the War Office, the army authorities did what they could before 1958. To make up for the lack of car advances, Nigerian officers were allowed to use army transport twice a week for their private engagements. In 1957 the starting salary of a Nigerian subaltern was raised from £600 to £660 a year, a higher salary than that of a newly appointed university graduate. But this made little impact when the salary of a graduate in the public service was effectively increased by the £156 tax-free Car Basic Allowance.

Another means of attracting young men into the Army was the setting up of Army Cadet Training Units in suitable educational institutions. The necessary legislation for this was passed in 1955 and the first units were started that year at the University College, Ibadan, and at three government colleges (that is, secondary schools) at Zaria in the North, Umuahia in the East and King's College, Lagos. By 1960 they had also been set up at the technical colleges at Lagos and Zaria, Government College, Ibadan (West), Government College, Keffi (North) and Katsina Secondary School (North). All the units were in institutions directly run by the government. The first officers who organized these units were expatriate members of staff who had served in the Army in wartime or during their National Service. Not all the units were successful. The one at University College, Ibadan, ceased to function after less than twelve months, following a disagreement between the Army and the university authorities. Other units fluctuated in efficiency, depending on the continuity provided by the members of staff who were the officers in charge of them.

Besides giving secondary schoolboys some familiarity with

military life, a more tangible inducement to cadets to enter the Army was the institution of 'Governor-General's Cadetships'. Those selected for these awards were given £50 a year for the two years before taking School Certificate, and were then required to enter the Army for the first stages of the potential officers' course. The first of these cadets were selected in 1958 and four of them were eventually commissioned after Independence. Two were from Government College, Zaria – Shuwa Muhammed and Muhammed Murtala (who later became divisional commanders in the Civil War). The other two were from Government College, Umuahia in the East – Emelifonwu and Okoye (who were both murdered in the counter-coup of July 1966).

No attempt was made to advertise for graduates to enter the Army before 1960, either for the fighting arms or the technical corps. There were quite a number of Nigerian doctors who had qualified abroad who might have been attracted into the Army earlier, but none was commissioned before 1961. There was one unexpected graduate recruit in 1957: Odumegwu Ojukwu, who had taken his B.A. in History at Oxford in 1955 and then served as assistant district officer in the administrative service for two years, was commissioned in March 1958.

Nigerianization 1958–1960

In April 1958 the Nigerian Military Forces ceased to be under the control of the War Office in Britain and Nigeria took over full responsibility for the cost of their upkeep. Since January 1956 there had been a net increase of seventeen in the number of Nigerian officers, from fifteen to thirty-two. The rate of commissioning had increased from approximately two per annum over the period 1948–1955 to seven per annum from 1956 to 1958. But even if this rate of progress was maintained, it would still be a quarter of a century before the Army was completely Nigerianized; and Nigerian Independence was now only two years away. Even this modest rate of progress was doubtful; only nine more cadets were in course of training who would pass out of Sandhurst by August 1960.

The Nigerian ministers were faced with mounting pressure from the House of Representatives. A select committee, representing all major parties, had been appointed in March 1958 to survey the whole field of Nigerianization. This committee issued an interim report in June 1958 which advocated swift and massive measures, including the immediate displacement of senior expatriates on the ground that their loyalties to Nigeria after Independence would be divided. The cabinet rejected these recommendations, on the ground that the proposal was unrealistic, but the report clearly showed the anxieties of the House.

Action to increase the supply of potential officers was taken quickly on a number of lines. There were greater efforts at publicity; officers were sent to speak in schools and the information service made a film about the training of an army officer, featuring a cadet who was just about to pass out of Sandhurst. More cadet units were established. The long-standing complaint about cars was finally settled by giving Nigerian officers (but not expatriates) the right to a car advance and Car Basic Allowance. Pensions for Nigerian officers were improved. There was no further improvement in officers' pay; but, as the prime minister told parliament, terms and conditions of service for officers were now more favourable, in some respects, than in the rest of the public service.[20]

There was only one decision taken in 1958 that had an immediate effect on the number of Nigerian officers commissioned before Independence. Before 1958 all officer cadets who had come into the Army straight from secondary school had been sent to Sandhurst for training, taking about two and a half years; the short course at Mons and Eaton Hall of sixteen weeks was only used by those long-serving regular soldiers who were eligible for short-service commissions. This meant that,

DISTRIBUTION OF OFFICERS BY TRIBAL/
REGIONAL ORIGIN, OCTOBER 1960

North	West (not Ika-Ibo)	East (plus Ika-Ibo)		South Cameroons

Serving Soldiers originally given Short Service Commissions

North	West (not Ika-Ibo)	East (plus Ika-Ibo)		South Cameroons
—	Ademulegun	Bassey*	Ironsi	Malonge
	Shodeinde	Nwawo†	Imo	
	Adebayo	Njoku	Ekanem*	
	Ogundipe	Ekpo*	Trimnell†	
	Fajuyi	Okonweze†	Effiong*	
		Akagha	Ogunewe	
		Okafor, D.O.	Adigio	
		Okafor, D.C.	Ivenso	
		Okoro	Ochei†	
		Brown*		
(nil)	(5)	(19)		(1)

Officers Commissioned after course at R.M.A. Sandhurst

North	West (not Ika-Ibo)	East (plus Ika-Ibo)		South Cameroons
Maimalari	Ejoor†	Kurobo*	Anwunah	—
Kur Muhammed	Banjo	Madiebo	Unegbe	
Largema		Okwechime†	Ogbonnia	
Pam		Nzefili†	Eze	
Gowon		Nwajei†	Ezeugbana	
Katsina		Keshi†	Ude	
Akahan		Nzeogwu†	Chude-Sokei	
(7)	(2)	(14)		(nil)

Graduates given a Regular Commission after a short course

North	West (not Ika-Ibo)	East (plus Ika-Ibo)		South Cameroons
—	Olutoye	Ojukwu		—
(nil)	(1)	(1)		(nil)

Short Service Commissioned Officers (not serving soldiers)

North	West (not Ika-Ibo)	East (plus Ika-Ibo)		South Cameroons
Kyari	Sotomi	Amadi	Aniebo	Kweti
	Obasanjo	Igboba†		
(1)	(2)	(3)		(1)

North	West (not Ika-Ibo)	East (plus Ika-Ibo)		South Cameroons
8	10	37		2
14%	17·5%	65%		3·5%

Notes : * denotes an officer whose place of origin is in the Calabar/Rivers/Ogoja area of the Eastern Region.

† denotes an officer whose place of origin is in the Mid-West. (All are Ika-Ibo, except Ejoor–Urhobo.)

In a few cases there is some doubt if an officer who served for a short time in the ranks should be classified in the first group or the last (e.g. Igboba). All those in the last group did not serve long enough in the ranks to be given immediate promotion to lieutenant on commissioning.

There was one other officer commissioned before 1960, Lt. Onuaguluchi (East, short-service commission, 1956); he died in a traffic accident in 1959.

E

since Nigeria was only allocated six vacancies a year at Sandhurst, only six former secondary school students could be
allowed to pass the final selection board at the end of their
preliminary training at Teshie. From September 1958 this was
changed and former secondary school students as well as
regular soldiers were sent to take the short course at Mons
OCS. By the use of this short cut an officer cadet could be
commissioned less than twelve months after leaving secondary
school. Seven officers were trained in this way before Independence.

As a result of all these measures there were sixty-one
Nigerian officers at the date of Independence. Three of these
were clergymen commissioned as army chaplains, and there was
also one warrant officer in charge of the Army Physical Training
School at the Depot who had been given an executive commission (Lt. Shadrack). So there were fifty-seven Nigerian officers
who held combatant commissions on 1 October 1960 (see table
on p. 51).

The main change over the four years from 1956 was the great
increase in the number of officers of 'Eastern' origin.[21] There
were now thirty-nine of them, compared to only five in January
1956, and they now made up 68 per cent of the officer corps,
compared to 33 per cent in 1956. Only about half of these
'Easterners' were Ibos from the central area of the Eastern
Region (now the East Central State). The rest came from the
outlying areas where the Army had always been more popular –
Ika-Ibos from the Mid-West, the minority tribes of the provinces of Calabar and Rivers, and the Southern Cameroons.
There were only eight Northern officers, making up 14 per cent
of the officer corps, compared to five, comprising 33 per cent,
in 1956. Four more Northern officers had been commissioned
since then (Gowon, Katsina, Kyari and Akahan) but one had
resigned (Umar Lawan).

There were two main reasons for this influx of 'Eastern'
officers. Serving soldiers who were candidates for short-service

commissions had to have high educational qualifications, and NCOs and WOs with these standards were mainly to be found in the technical arms, where Easterners predominated. Every one of the eighteen officers promoted from the ranks between 1956 and 1960 was an Easterner. Secondly, two Southern schools began to develop a military tradition like that of Government College, Zaria. These were Government College, Ughelli in the Mid-West, the school of Ejoor (an Urhobo), Okwechime, Nzefili and Nwajei; and Government College, Umuahia in the East, which produced Kurobo, Anwunah, Eze and Madiebo.

This predominance of Easterners naturally caused some anxiety, particularly in the North. One Northern member, Abdullahi Magajin Musawa, said:

> I am appealing to the hon. Prime Minister, that we in Nigeria should be united in diversity. I think it would be a good idea if we equalized our army officers . . . so that the officers in the Eastern Region, the Northern Region and the Western Region are equalized.
>
> (*HR Deb*, 14 April 1960, col. 1252)

But Sir Abubakar had already refused to do this:

> I do not like only one section of the Federation to be over-whelmingly dominating the other sections if it is possible, but at the same time we want to have Nigerian officers in the Army and certain educational qualifications are required of such officers. Still, if people who present themselves to the Army are from one section and they have the qualifications, what can government do other than accept them?
>
> (*HR Deb*, 12 August 1959, col. 1818)

The prime minister was in a dilemma. British officers were unacceptable to nationalists in the South and they were also extremely expensive. It was possible to calculate that the

government could employ three Nigerian majors for the price
of one British major, when the costs of all his allowances and
travel were included. But if British officers were to be replaced
the only alternative seemed to be more Eastern officers.

In the Northern Region the NPC government was following a
policy of preferring expatriates to Southern Nigerians, when
there was no Northerner available to fill a vacancy in the
Northern public service. But such a policy was politically
impossible in the Federal public service at this time. The NPC
was the largest party in the Federal parliament but it did not
have an overall majority and it was extremely important for
the NPC that the two main parties of the South should not join
together against it after the 1959 Federal election. The NPC
seems to have had some understanding with the NCNC to
oppose the AG, even before the 1959 election. Any attempt to
discriminate against Easterners in the Federal service would be
likely to stimulate the NCNC to seek an alliance with the AG
against the North. So no attempt was made to rectify the
regional imbalance in the officer corps until after Independence.

However, the picture was not entirely unfavourable to the
North. Northerners made up only 14 per cent of the Nigerian
Army officers but they were even more of a minority elsewhere.
Northerners formed 5 per cent of the Nigerian Police officers at
Independence (13 out of 236) and there were only 29 Northerners
out of 2,607 Nigerians in the Federal administrative and higher
executive posts, less than 2 per cent.[22]

Moreover there was scope in the Army to change the ratio of
Northerners to Southerners, which did not exist elsewhere.
Eighty per cent of the officer establishment were still expatriates, all of whom would leave in the next few years. But in
the Police Force 50 per cent of the officer establishment was
already Nigerian by the date of Independence, and Nigerians
filled 57 per cent of the senior service posts in the Federal
public service as a whole.[23] The Army's record in Nigerianization was very poor; but from the point of view of the NPC it

would have been even worse if half the entire officer establishment, instead of merely 13 per cent, had been Eastern.

Nigerian Officers in their Units

In the first years of Nigerianization there was a tendency to post
Nigerian officers to technical units rather than to the infantry
battalions. For example, in 1956 Capt. Ademulegun was serving
with the Army Signals in Lagos, where he was described to the
press as 'one of the top officers in the most Nigerianized unit
in the Army'.[24] There was nothing necessarily discriminatory in
this: many of them had been NCOs and WOs in these services.
Similarly, when more Nigerian officers began to be posted to
the battalions in the later 1950s they were often to be found in
charge of the battalion signals or transport. Often the reason
for this was that the Nigerian officer, whether he had done the
long course at Sandhurst or been commissioned from the ranks,
was more competent for these technical posts than a British
National Service subaltern who had had a very brief period of
training and was more suitable for the relatively unspecialized
post of infantry platoon commander.

There were fears that Northern infantrymen would not accept
Southern officers, as is shown by this question asked by the
Select Committee on Nigerianization: 'What has been the
relationship between the senior Nigerian army officers who are
mostly Southerners and the rank and file who are mostly
Northerners?' The answer given to the committee by the army
representative was 'Excellent'.[25] What else could he say? This
was not the opinion of the British officers. Many British subalterns had been told by their platoon sergeants that the soldiers
preferred the white men to the Southern Nigerians and that they
would never be happy to serve under them. This knowledge
flattered the white men's pride. It was intended to. Nigerians
are very polite and will often prefer to give the answer that will
give most pleasure. There are some contrary indications. For

example, one Northern CSM referred to Major Shodeinde (a Yoruba) as the best platoon commander he had had, and spoke very warmly of him to me. It is impossible to settle the question now. But it is worth emphasizing that the Nigerian officers at this time were the product of a stringent process of selection; that the average soldier anywhere respects competent leadership; and it is likely that a Nigerian from another part of the country would have more understanding of a Nigerian soldier's point of view than an officer of a different race from overseas. An Englishman has never experienced alien rule and finds it difficult to appreciate what an insult this is to a man's or a nation's self-respect.

Social relationships between white and black officers in the mess were superficially friendly. The customs of the mess were the same as those to be found in British stations all over the world; British food was normally served and the mess subscribed to various British newspapers as well as Nigerian ones. Until after Independence Nigerian officers formed a small minority in all units. Some who had spent a long period of training in England found this entirely to their liking, and were practically 'black Englishmen'. Others have recalled how everything about the mess stuck in their throats as 'foreign'; but they kept their feelings to themselves.

Between the Nigerian officers themselves there seems to have been little tribal feeling. They were too small a group for that. General Gowon has recalled how he quarrelled violently with an Ibo officer, Arthur Unegbe, when they first met, but later he became one of his best friends and was best man at his wedding. Similarly, when Lt. Pam (a Birom from the North) married in Kaduna in 1957, his best man was Lt. Ejoor (an Urhobo from the Mid-West), and the wedding reception was held at the house of Lt. Adebayo (a Yoruba from the West).[26]

Where there was tension between Nigerian officers it was more likely to arise between those who had achieved a commission the hard way, through the ranks, and the bright young men from Sandhurst, with superior education whose opportunities seemed to be so much better.[27] All Nigerian officers were well aware that once Nigerianization was really pushed forward they could expect rapid promotion to the top posts in the Army. So questions of seniority were of great importance, and sometimes caused hard feelings.

Conclusion: the failure to Nigerianize

The main burden of this chapter has been the ineffectiveness of the Nigerianization policy in the Army before 1960. Yet all the time British generals and colonels were proclaiming their eagerness to welcome Nigerian officers. It is easy to accuse them of cynical hypocrisy and racial prejudice, as was done at the time. The reality was more complex. Their efforts suffered from two handicaps.

In the first place, they were not allowed, until too late, to offer the financial inducements that were necessary to offset the poor 'image' of the Army that was common in the South, which was the only place where sufficient numbers of educated potential officers could be found. Financial control was exercised from London, and this handicap was only removed when Nigeria had complete control.

The second difficulty was more deep-seated. British army officers found it difficult to believe that 'the right sort of chap' to be an officer was likely to be persuaded to join the Army by increased offers of pay. The whole ethos of army life, the belief in the virtues of service and self-sacrifice, was against it. The task of the army officer was to set the standard, to let the demands of army life be made known, and to trust that sufficient numbers would come forward to fill the vacancies. To ask for less was like asking a clergyman to seek converts by adulterating the gospel. The economic burdens placed on the young school-leaver by the extended family system did not come into this purview at all.

The same attitude influenced consideration of accelerated promotion for Nigerians. It seemed morally wrong that a young officer should by-pass the hard grind at the bottom by escalating quickly to field rank. The swift promotions of wartime were now long passed; why should the Nigerian officer expect to have it easier than the British officer had had? The British Army was rightly proud of its achievement in leaving behind successor armies in India and Pakistan as good as their original mentors. To connive at a lower standard for Nigeria, as the politicians seemed to be demanding, would be a gross betrayal of the trusteeship of empire.

Their attitude was never explicitly verbalized in such terms as these, nor can it be shown that this was the sort of thinking which in fact influenced the actions of senior British officers in Nigeria.[28] It is merely suggested that this gives a persuasive account of the rationale behind the actions – and omissions – of the decade of the 1950s.

IV · Handing over the Army, 1956-1960

When the French Government granted independence to the West African territories of the French Union in 1960, there was no question of handing over the control of the military units stationed there to these new states. The French Army was one and indivisible, unaffected by the transfer of sovereignty. Treaties were concluded with all the new states (except Guinea and Mali) formalizing the arrangements for the continued presence of the French Army and specifying the conditions under which these units might intervene directly to assist in internal security. The new armies of these states had to be built up from nothing; a nucleus of African officers and NCOs was transferred from the French Army in each state and demobilized veterans were enrolled to fill the ranks.

Action on these lines was never considered by the British Government. It was clear that the precedent of India would be followed, where the military establishment was handed over in its entirety to the successor governments. However, the British Government was anxious that the framework of military co-operation between the four West African territories should continue after they became independent. With this end in view, the 1953 Conference recommended the establishment of an Army Advisory Council for West Africa of government representatives to ensure 'uniformity in organization, equipment and methods of training'.[1]

The first stage of the British withdrawal was the break-up of West Africa Command. This took place in July 1956, nine months before the Gold Coast was to become the sovereign state of Ghana. The military forces of the four British West African territories now became independent of one another, each with its own commander and staff, but still part of the British Army and subject to the Army Council in London until such time as control passed to the local governments. The Advisory Council did not have a very long life. Three months after Ghanaian Independence Dr Nkrumah gave a year's notice of withdrawal from this body, and the perambulating military adviser to the council, having nothing to do, left in February 1958. The only relic of the former system of defence co-ordination between the West African territories was the training school for officer cadets at Teshie in Ghana, which continued to operate under a joint board, until Nigeria set up her own school at Kaduna in 1960.

The next stage in the decolonization of the Nigerian Military Forces was the transfer of control from the Army Council to the government in Lagos. This was agreed at the 1957 Constitutional Conference, and took place on 1 April 1958. As a consequence of this transfer of control, the Nigerian taxpayer had to take over the full cost of the Army, though the British Government made a grant of £500,000 in 1958–1959 and the same amount the following year to ease the increased financial burden. Control did not pass to the Nigerian prime minister but to the British governor-general, who was to be assisted by a Defence Council, composed of representatives of the Federal and Regional Governments. But once the 1959 Federal elections were over and the Nigerian Government that would take the country into Independence was installed in office there was no reason for further delay, and Sir Abubakar took over full ministerial responsibility for Police and Defence in February 1960.

This completed the hand-over of the Army, but it did not end the importance of Nigeria to Britain's global defence policy. The War Office wanted to use Nigeria as a staging post for aircraft on the way to the Middle East, and considered that the best way to secure this was to have the use of a British base at Kano. A draft agreement was drawn up and initialled by the

Nigerian political leaders at the 1958 Constitutional Conference. These conversations were referred to briefly in the Conference report, but the details were not made public.[2] Then in May 1960, Chief Awolowo, who was now Leader of the Opposition following the 1959 Federal elections, caused considerable embarrassment to the government by revealing the details of the draft agreement and leading a campaign against any British base on Nigerian soil. Because of this outcry the proposal for a British base at Kano was dropped, and Sir Abubakar undertook that the draft Defence Agreement would not be ratified by parliament until after Nigerian Independence.

The Agreement presented to the House of Representatives for ratification in November 1960 was a fairly innocuous document about the provision of instructors, equipment and training facilities, and arrangements for air-staging rights. But the Action Group and other radical nationalists organized demonstrations against this pact, and undergraduates came down to Lagos from Ibadan to try to force their way into parliament to protest. In spite of this opposition the government forced the measure through the House. But it remained a standing reproach against Sir Abubakar's government in nationalist eyes, and fifteen months later in January 1962 it was abrogated, by agreement with Britain.[3]

Consequences of the Hand-over in Nigeria

The first meeting of the new Federal Defence Council took place in November 1957. Since it was not expected that the Army would be required for more than internal security duties and minor frontier incidents, there was no justification for keeping the artillery battery. In April 1958 this unit was converted into a reconnaissance squadron of armoured cars, thereby giving the Army much greater mobility to patrol the open frontiers of the North. Approval was also given for plans to set up an officer cadet school at Kaduna and to raise an additional infantry battalion, the sixth. This last decision was not in fact implemented for seven years.[4]

All these decisions increased the cost of the military establishment. The Nigerian Government had acquired all the barracks, equipment and chattels of the Army as a free gift from Britain, but it now had to pay the full recurrent cost. This sum was now swollen by the increased secondment allowances to be paid to British officers and NCOs. The Army Estimates went up from £1,698,000 in March 1957 to £3,306,000 in March 1958 as a result. Later decisions, that the pay and privileges of other ranks should be brought up to the level of members of the Police Force and that Nigerian officers should be given car advances and Car Basic Allowance, also added to the costs of the Military Forces over the next two years.

But there were some savings to be set against these increases. Exclusive schools run for the children of white servicemen could no longer be maintained by Nigeria and were handed over to committees of local expatriates. Instead of food being supplied to soldiers in barracks, all troops except boy soldiers and recruits were given a cash allowance for rations, enabling two supply depots to be closed down.[5] Other similar economies were possible by using established government agencies rather than a separate army organization.

But the principal source where economies were sought was in the replacement of expatriates by Nigerians. Nigerian clergymen were appointed as chaplains, the first in April 1959. The rundown of British NCOs and WOs was accelerated. From April 1956 to April 1960 their number decreased from 336 to 80.[6] Another economy was the employment on contract terms of officers who had retired from the British Army. These officers only received the Nigerian officer's rate of pay plus the normal government expatriation allowance and did not qualify for the generous allowances paid to officers seconded from the British Army.[7]

Arguments on the Size of the Armed Services

Up to 1958 there had usually been a few members in the Federal
House of Representatives who, in the annual debates on the
Army Estimates, protested at the money being spent on the
military, and emphasized the prior claims of education, hospitals, agriculture or industry. The vast increase in the Estimates in March 1958 brought a renewal of these complaints,
and fears were expressed that the burden of defence expenditure
would lead to an increase in taxes.[8] The most weighty expression
of this point of view was given by Chief Awolowo at the Calabar
Conference of the Action Group in April 1958. He asserted that
after Independence Nigeria must choose between 'power
politics' and 'welfare politics'. It was quite sufficient to maintain the Nigeria Regiment at its current strength; 'We require
the regiment mainly for ceremonial purposes. I hope and pray
that the Federal Government will never have to call upon them
to put down disturbances in any part of the Federation.'
Internal security was a job for the police, and the Army would
only be called in for an unusually violent and large-scale disorder. Nigeria's neighbours were friendly; they had no territorial claims against her, nor Nigeria against them. 'We have
neither the money nor the need to embark on such crazy
ventures as building a Nigerian Navy and Nigerian Air
Force.'[9]

But such pacific advice was very much in the minority. Chief
Awolowo's views were attacked by other speakers at the conference, including the deputy leader of the party, Chief Akintola, and the leading member of the Nigerian Bar, Chief
Rotimi Williams. The latter claimed that Nigeria needed an
army sufficient to give her national dignity and not for ceremonial purposes only. He recalled the recent incident at Sakiet,
where French aircraft bombed a town in independent Tunisia,
and asked, 'What would Nigeria do if Nkrumah said we did
something to Ghana and planned to bomb us?'. Awolowo's

views were also attacked in the Action Group paper, the *Daily Service*, and he formally recanted them at the next party conference in September. But he seems to have kept to the same opinion, since passages from his Calabar speech are repeated verbatim in his autobiography, written in June 1960.

Before 1958 demands for a vast increase in military expenditure had been made by only a few nationalists of little political weight. Dr Chike Obi, the founder of the small Dynamic Party, in his book *Our Struggle* published in 1955, advocated the total mobilization of the nation's resources at Independence under a 'Kemalist' regime, in fear of an imminent invasion by South Africa. Mr R. A. Fani-Kayode, then an Action Group backbencher, called on the government in March 1955 to initiate a vast military expansion programme: 'We can only reach the God-ordained hegemony destined for Nigeria – supremacy south of the Sahara – sword in hand.'[10]

In 1955 such views were a subject for gentle mockery, but now that Nigeria had taken over the Army the tide was running the other way. In August 1959, when Alhaji Abubakar's government proposed a supplementary estimate for the Army, the news was greeted in parliament with applause and Chief Mariere, a leading member of the NCNC, asked for a further million-pound increase the following year, saying that no additional sum was too high. When the Estimates for 1960–1961 showed an increase of only £600,000 the opposition spokesman (Chief Rosiji, AG) attacked them as insufficient: 'Nigeria should be prepared to give Africa not only political leadership but also military leadership.'[11]

Quite apart from considerations of prestige, there were good reasons for some increase in spending on the Armed Forces. When Nigeria took over control of the Military Forces in 1958 the surrounding countries were all relatively peaceful. But in June 1959 terrorism broke out in the western areas of the French Cameroons bordering on Nigeria and continued through the following months. In October 1959 an infantry battalion was sent into the Southern Cameroons (a part of the former German Cameroons which was then included in Nigeria) in case trouble might spill over the border. There was also unrest in French Niger to the north of Nigeria from the banned Sawaba party. It was with this situation in mind that the prime minister addressed the House of Representatives in January 1960 on the motion asking Britain to grant Nigeria Independence:

> You may say that Nigeria is a peaceful country which has no territorial ambitions and has no intention of attacking her neighbours. I agree. You may also say that there is no evidence that we are going to be attacked. Superficially I should say that view is correct but I must tell the House that in my opinion we are confronted by a very serious situation. Over the past year or so there has been a good deal of trouble going on in some of the countries which border on Nigeria and as I see it, the danger is that disaffected elements in these countries will come over the Nigerian border and hide and will then carry out sporadic raids on their own country. This could very easily lead to border incidents and to serious misunderstandings between Nigeria and her neighbours. . . . We must have adequate military forces to safeguard our long land frontier; for guaranteeing the inviolability of that frontier we shall in future be dependent on our own resources.
>
> (*HR Deb*, 14 January 1960, col. 33)

Another external stimulus to increased military spending was the example of Ghana. During the first three years of Independence there had been no expansion in the modest military establishment which Ghana had inherited from the British. But in July 1959 the Estimates for Defence increased by £700,000 and in November a plan was announced to increase the Ghana Army by 50 per cent, re-equip it with new weapons and create a Navy and an Air Force.[12] With this example before

them, many Nigerians felt that their country, the most populous
state in Africa and six times as large as Ghana, should follow
suit. Mr Eneh asked: 'If a small country like Ghana has already
established an Air Force, why should not this government think
in terms of establishing an Air Force immediately?'[13]

An example of this competition with Ghana was the decision
to equip the infantry with the new FN self-loading rifle. The
Lee-Enfield rifle had been the standard weapon in the Second
World War, but the British Army had changed to the self-
loading rifle in 1956-1957. In February 1959 the Nigerian prime
minister refused to do the same: the Lee-Enfield cost only £5
while the new FN rifle cost nearly £50 each. In May 1959 Ghana
announced that it was making this change; so in 1960 parliament was told that the Nigerian Army would have the new
rifles before Independence.[14]

While external pressures and popular demands encouraged
the government to enlarge the Army, this course also had its
dangers. 1958 was a most successful year for military conspirators. Generals took over power by *coups d'état* in Pakistan,
Burma, Iraq, Thailand and the Sudan, and in France General
de Gaulle became president as a direct result of the danger of a
coup d'état by a section of the French Army. There was also the
discovery of an alleged plot in Ghana, and the Granville Sharp
Commission of Enquiry found unanimously that two members
of the opposition party had purchased military accoutrements
and 'were engaged in a conspiracy to carry out at some future
date in Ghana an act for an unlawful purpose, revolutionary in
character'. The Ghana Government feared that the opposition
party was plotting to assassinate Dr Nkrumah and his cabinet
in the same way that this had been done in Burma in 1946, by
party members disguised as soldiers, but this was not proved
before the commission.[15]

During 1959 there were occasional references in the press to
the dangers of a *coup d'état* in Nigeria, but there was never any
discussion of this in parliament.[16] Sir Abubakar referred to the

possibility of the Army entering politics only on one occasion, and then by implication only, in reply to Mr Eneh of Calabar:

My hon. friend said he would like to see us making some of our Nigerian officers either major-generals or something like that. As an ex-serviceman he knows how long it takes to become a general and I think it will be very, very dangerous simply because we want to Nigerianize to promote a colonel to major-general. That will be very, very dangerous.

(*HR Deb*, 16 February 1959, col. 536)

Questions were also asked in parliament about the regional (i.e. tribal) origins of army officers. One reason for such questions was the desire to be sure that the North was getting its 'fair' share of Federal posts; but fears of a possible future military intervention may also have prompted them.[17]

The Army and the 1959 Federal Election

All the parties referred to the question of defence in their election manifestos. The NPC referred to the danger of trouble spilling over from neighbouring countries and the need for an army 'large enough and adequately equipped to safeguard the long land frontiers'; Nigeria also needed forces that were impressive in size and equipment to exercise her influence and act as a stabilizing factor in Africa; expansion of the Armed Forces would be necessary so that they could fulfil their commitments. Finally, 'It will be our policy to maintain a high standard of discipline so that the Nigerians may be proud of their Army and all visitors may be properly impressed.' This was the only manifesto which specifically proposed an increase in the Armed Forces.[18]

The NCNC was much more modest. It merely promised to improve the conditions of service in the Armed Forces and to develop them 'on the basis of neutrality and considerations of national interest' after Independence. It intended to 'maintain

F

efficient and disciplined Armed Forces for the purpose of protecting Nigeria internally and externally.'

The manifesto of the Action Group was the most interesting. Reversing the party's previous attitude of indifference to ex-servicemen, it promised to set aside £500,000 as a first instalment to spend on schemes for veterans' welfare, as soon as Chief Awolowo formed his government. This was the only reference to the Army in all the many AG policy documents issued. However, the paper on internal security proposed to set up a new type of police formation 'to deal with any large-scale unrest or revolutionary situation'. These new police units would not be required to perform normal police duties, but could provide ceremonial guards of honour if required. The AG also proposed to establish a Frontier Protection Force, whose sphere of action would be restricted to the country's borders. Detailed methods of control for these new forces were proposed, and the policy paper concluded that such a Police Force would not be tempted to seize power. Since these two new police formations appear to engross all the normal functions of an army, it would seem that some Action Group policy-makers proposed to set up a new Police Force as a rival to the Army, or perhaps even to take the place of it altogether, if the AG came to power, though it did not say so in so many words. This would be a rational policy for the AG, since there were very few Yorubas in the Army, either in the rank and file or in the officer corps.[19]

Security over the election period was still the responsibility of the British governor-general. To discourage potential disturbers of the peace military units were sent on marches round the country to 'show the flag' in the period before the election. In addition fifteen companies were posted at strategic centres to be ready if needed. The stationing of soldiers in Northern towns caused some embarrassment to the NPC, since the opposition leader in Kano had already asked the governor-general to do this, because thugs had been attacking his sup-

porters. So the Northern Regional Government issued a statement that the army move was part of a long-standing training
programme and not the result of NEPU protests. The sending of
the troops was naturally welcomed by the AG who believed
that the Army would be more impartial in law enforcement
than the native authorities. In fact, polling was unexpectedly
peaceful and the troops did not have to take any action.[20]

The Changing Reputation of the Army

Belief in the impartiality of the Army was part of a change in
the popular view of the military over the past four years. There
had been a number of reasons for this, such as better Army
public relations (Press days had been instituted), the reduced
scope for charges of racial discrimination, and particularly the
increased rates of pay and allowances that had resulted from
local control. But most of all, the Army was now seen as a
symbol of the new national consciousness. The celebrations for
regional self-government in the North in 1959 included a military tattoo which culminated in a display of 'modern battle'
enacted by an infantry company and armoured cars from the
Recce Squadron. In 1960 a detachment from the Army went to
Britain to take part in the annual Royal Tournament. A
fortnight before Independence it was announced that a battalion of infantry was to be sent to join the United Nations operation in the Congo. And on the eve of Independence itself the
final act of the tattoo on Lagos Racecourse, before the Union
Jack was lowered for the last time at midnight, was an improved
version of the display already given in the North. After the
traditional horsemen and dancers had performed, the Army
seemed to symbolize the modern and technically efficient
Nigeria that was hoped for in the future.

The final token of the changed status of the Queen's Own
Nigeria Regiment was a ceremony that took place on the
durbar ground at Sokoto in November 1960. The flag of Sultan

Attahiru Ahmadu, kept since 1903 by the first battalion as a trophy of their victory, was paraded and solemnly handed over to the reigning Sultan of Sokoto in the presence of the premier of the Northern Region. In the words of the official history of the Royal West African Frontier Force:

> In the many speeches made at this parade there were repeated references to this 'symbolic gesture'. To many of those present, and particularly the Army officers, the real significance of the event was that it marked, more than anything in the Independence Celebrations, the changed nature of the Nigerian Army. The ceremony was symbolic of the fact that the Army was no longer the agent of the United Kingdom and the Colonial Government. Henceforth it was Nigeria's own Army.

(Haywood and Clarke, 518)

V · Cameroons, Congo, Tanganyika, Tiv

The main focus of this book is the question why the Nigerian Army took over the government in 1966. But the question could equally well be put in a different way: why did the Army not take over before then? Part of the reason was that in the five years from 1960 to 1964 the Army was engaged almost continually in a series of operations which allowed little time or opportunity for conspiracy until all the battalions were back in Nigeria at the end of 1964.

Southern Cameroons, 1959–1960

After the conquest of the German colony of Kamerun in the 1914–1918 war, the country was divided between the British and French, first as a Mandated Territory under the League of Nations and then as a Trust Territory under the United Nations. The French, who had much the larger part of the country, administered their part of Kamerun as a separate entity, the French Cameroons, while the British, in effect, annexed their mandate to Nigeria and administered it as part of the Northern and Eastern Regions. This arrangement continued until 1954 when the southern part of the Trust Territory was split off from the Eastern Region to become the quasi-federal territory of the Southern Cameroons, with its own government.

Like most boundaries in Africa, the division between the British and French mandates took little account of tribal areas, and the Bamileke tribe was split between the British and French sectors. In 1955 the French governor banned the Union des Populations Camerounaises, a political party which had wide support in the south-west of the French Cameroons but particularly among the Bamileke. The UPC continued to exist as an underground organization, directed from abroad by its Marxist leader, Felix Moumié, and resorted to terrorism. At first the French Army seemed to have this incipient rebellion under control; but when the premier of the French Cameroons negotiated its Independence from French rule for 1 January 1960, Moumié denounced this Independence as a sham, and terrorism was renewed in June 1959. This led the French authorities to proclaim a state of emergency in the western areas of the country which bordered on the Southern Cameroons.

The problem for the Nigerian Government was that guerrilla bands of the Bamileke were accustomed to cross over to their fellow-tribesmen on the British side of the frontier for rest and training. In October 1959 1 QONR from Enugu was sent to do military training in the Southern Cameroons, both to protect the local inhabitants and to encourage them to give information on terrorist camps to the police. The trouble then seemed to die down and the troops returned to Enugu before Christmas. But this lull was only temporary; there was a renewed outbreak of violence in the Cameroon Republic to coincide with the proclamation of Independence on 1 January 1960, and shortly after this the whole of 1 QONR returned to the area and were concentrated in the northern part of the Southern Cameroons (Bamenda) where the Bamileke live. The guerrillas then began to make more use of the area farther south towards the coast, between Douala in the Cameroon Republic and Kumba in the Southern Cameroons. To deal with this, 4 QONR was moved by sea from Ibadan to Kumba in February 1960. 1 QONR was relieved by 5 QONR at Bamenda in March, and 4 QONR by 3 QONR at Kumba in May. Then 2 QONR took over duties from both battalions as troops were thinned out, and remained in the Southern Cameroons until the end of September. When Nigeria became independent on 1 October, the British Cameroons Trust Territory remained under British sovereignty, pending the outcome of a plebiscite to determine whether it could

achieve its own independence by joining the Cameroon
Republic or Nigeria. The premier of the Southern Cameroons
refused to allow Nigerian troops to remain after 1 October, so
2 QONR was replaced by a British battalion.

Thus by the end of this period all five infantry battalions
had spent about four months each in the Southern Cameroons.
The pattern of operations was that companies set up camps
along the border and then sent out patrols of about ten men
and an officer along the bush paths for up to five days, looking
for signs of the terrorists or laying an ambush. One such patrol
came on a guerrilla camp by surprise, capturing thirty of them
and a strong-box containing £10,000. Battalion reports speak
feelingly of the 'perpendicular rain' in the later months of their
stay (the area round Mount Cameroon has one of the heaviest
rainfalls in Africa), but agree that 'the experience of self-help
and maintenance in the field was inestimable and the best
training that the battalion has had since Burma'.[1] It was un-
doubtedly a good preparation for service in the Congo the
following year.

In February 1961 a plebiscite was held under the supervision
of the United Nations, and the Southern Cameroons voted to
join the Cameroon Republic. It was formally incorporated in
the Federal Republic of the Cameroons on 1 October 1961. The
Southern Cameroons had already begun to form its own army
from a nucleus of Cameroonian soldiers who had volunteered to
be transferred from the Nigerian Army, and this force, assisted
by the Cameroons gendarmerie, took over internal security
duties when the British battalion left.

The internal security of the Southern Cameroons had ceased
to be a concern of the Federal Nigerian Government after 1
October 1960. But there was still anxiety about the border
between the Eastern Region and the Cameroons. Units of 1
QONR and scout cars of the Recce Squadron were deployed
along the frontier at the time of the 1961 plebiscite. The old
British/German border was resurveyed by foot patrols and

new police posts were built along it. But there was in fact no further trouble here. However, the possibility of some disturbance on this border was probably one reason why 1 QONR was the last Nigerian battalion to be sent for service in the Congo.

The Congo, 1960-1964

The former Belgian Congo achieved Independence on 30 June 1960. The Force Publique mutinied five days later and on 11 July, in conditions of escalating confusion, the Prime Minister, Patrice Lumumba, asked for help from the United Nations. The first troops arrived from Ghana on 15 July and by the beginning of September the UN force had reached about 16,000.

Nigeria was asked to help even before her own Independence, and the first announcement in the press in mid-September said that a battalion of infantry with elements from the signals, engineers and medical services would be sent under the command of Aguiyi-Ironsi, who was then second-in-command of the battalion at Enugu. Ironsi was promoted acting lieutenant-colonel a few days before Independence and took over command of 5 QONR at Kaduna. It had been promised that at least half the officers sent to the Congo would be Nigerians; but since there were only fifty-two Nigerian officers in the country at the time this promise caused some difficulty and officers were posted into the fifth battalion from training establishments and the Recce Squadron to make up the numbers.[2] 5 QONR left in mid-November – 26 officers, 640 soldiers and 4 British NCOs. By this time the Secretary-General of the United Nations had asked for more troops, and so shortly afterwards 4 QONR was sent to the Congo from Ibadan. This event was less noted in the press since the battalion was commanded by an expatriate, Lt.-Col. Price. Finally Brigadier Ward (also an expatriate) left to set up a brigade headquarters to command the two battalions. This meant that Lt.-Col. Ironsi was not the senior officer with the Nigerian troops and there were protests in the press at the failure to live up to earlier government promises. By the end of November there were 1,350 Nigerian soldiers in the Congo.

The Nigerian force was sent to Kivu province and the northern part of Katanga province. Chaos was fairly general in the Congo by November 1960 but this area was in a particularly unstable situation. Katanga, under its Premier, Moise Tshombe, had proclaimed its secession from the rest of the Congo on 11 July, but the Baluba tribe in the north of the province had refused to accept the authority of the Tshombe regime and were in rebellion against it. These tribesmen were unable to distinguish between the Katangese gendarmerie and the UN troops sent to protect them and had just murdered nine men of an Irish patrol near Albertville. In Kivu province the Congolese administration was nominally loyal to the government in Leopoldville headed by Col. (later General) Mobutu who had ousted Lumumba from the premiership. But the Kivu provincial authorities were threatened by the regime set up farther north in Stanleyville, Orientale province, by Antoine Gizenga, who supported the deposed Lumumba.

On arrival, 5 QONR under Lt.-Col. Ironsi was sent to Bukavu, capital of Kivu province, and three companies of the battalion were detached to Goma, Kasongo and Kindu. 4 QONR was ordered to take up position at Manono in North Katanga. In order to reach this position it had to make a difficult road journey of two hundred miles from the Kamina air-base, being impeded and ambushed all the way by Baluba tribesmen. Brigade headquarters was set up between the two battalions at Albertville.[3]

In early December an Austrian ambulance unit arrived at Bukavu. The local Congolese authorities became suspicious of this non-combatant unit, arrested them and imprisoned them in the local jail, claiming that they were Belgian parachutists. Negotiations for their release between Ironsi and the Congolese

ORIENTALE
STANLEYVILLE

EQUATOR

GOMA
KIVU
BUKAVU

KINDU
KASONGO

LEOPOLDVILLE

PORT FRANCQUI

KASAI

KWILU

LULUABOURG

ALBERTVILLE

MANONO

KATANGA

KAMINA

ELISABETHVILLE

0   100   200   300   400   500
MILES

3. THE CONGO

provincial president were fruitless and the Nigerians were finally authorized by UN headquarters to issue an ultimatum for their release and to effect it by force if necessary. The operation was mounted by three platoons of the Bukavu force, one of which was hastily formed from the cooks, mess staff and storemen of battalion headquarters. The Congolese numbered about three hundred. The action lasted three hours, after which the Congolese requested a ceasefire and released their Austrian prisoners. The Nigerian casualties were one dead and five wounded, the Congolese far more. Later, the Austrian Government awarded their medal for gallantry to Lt.-Col. Ironsi, Major Njoku, two expatriate officers and twelve Nigerian soldiers. Lt. Matthews (an expatriate), was awarded the Military Cross.

At the end of December Kivu province was invaded by soldiers from Stanleyville who ejected the provincial government and set up a new, pro-Lumumbist administration. This column then went on to invade North Katanga and reached Manono where 4 QONR was stationed. Here a four-hour battle was fought for control of the airport, which the Congolese eventually conceded. Previous to this the battalion had been in action when providing escorts for trains that were subject to attack by the Baluba. As a result of these actions Lt.-Col. Price was awarded the D.S.O., Major Fajuyi and Major Edge the M.C. and CSM Jibrin Gulani the M.M. The citation for Major Fajuyi was as follows:

He led C Company of 4 QONR against a large band of hostile tribesmen in North Katanga. Knowing that the majority of his men had never been under fire before, he personally led the advance. The successful outcome was largely a result of his gallantry and determination. During the next two days Major Fajuyi again set a splendid example of courage and leadership during the advance of his company through hostile tribal country. Again on 3 Jan. 1961 Major

Fajuyi was commanding a train escort on a journey through North Katanga. The train was derailed and attacked by tribesmen. In beating off the attack and extricating his company he displayed a high degree of leadership and military ability.

The next incident was at Kindu in Kivu province where a company of 5 QONR was detached. On 2 February 1961 a skirmish at a road block manned by troops from Stanleyville led to an attack on a Nigerian position which then expanded until all the Nigerian company was engaged against a far larger force of Congolese. A platoon was sent to secure control of the airstrip at Kindu in case it was necessary to call in reinforcements, but this unit was ambushed on the way there and the officer in command, Lt. Ezeugbana, was killed. Eventually a ceasefire was agreed, and after a conference between Lt.-Col. Ironsi and General Lundula of the Stanleyville regime, the Nigerian troops were withdrawn to Bukavu and later replaced by a much larger force from the Malay regiment.

Meanwhile, what little civil administration that there had been in Kivu province began to disintegrate after the Lumumbist troops had taken over. Mr Dayal, the representative of the UN Secretary-General in the Congo, reported on the situation in Kivu province as follows:

> Several rival claimants to office have arrested one another or sought sanctuary with the United Nations Force; there is therefore no effective government in the province. . . . The population has been exposed to the violence and lust for loot and revenge of undisciplined armed bands.
>
> (*The Times*, 24 February 1961)

These chaotic conditions had their effect on the Nigerian troops. A special correspondent of *The Times* visited the battalion at Bukavu and sent back a long report on deteriorating discipline among the soldiers, which he blamed particularly on the 'equivocation and indecision' of the United Nations High Command:

The effect of this ambiguous position has been worse on the whole among the African troops, because they are under stronger pressure to take sides, and are more often the recipients of thoughtless complaints and sneers from Belgian civilians and tend naturally to fraternize when they can with Congolese soldiers from whom they may pick up undisciplined habits. Among the Nigerians there has developed a particularly demoralizing split between some of the African officers and their British colleagues, causing an infectious indiscipline in the ranks. So far, at least ten Nigerians have been sent home with detention sentences for insubordination and one man has been dismissed the service with ignominy. . . .

The trouble with the Nigerians seems to have begun after the incident in December when they forcibly released an Austrian ambulance team. . . . Afterwards some of the Nigerian officers and men appear to have developed a sort of guilt complex about the affair.

Since then, and especially following the coup in Bukavu on Christmas Day by forces loyal to Lumumba and the resulting disorders in the province, there have been frequent differences of opinion in the Nigerian force about the extent of the protection they should give to Europeans or Africans molested by the Congolese soldiers.

Some Nigerian soldiers who have fraternized with the Congolese have been openly insubordinate, and on one occasion, according to reliable informants, soldiers who had been put on a charge by a British officer were dismissed unpunished by an African superior officer.

Observers in Bukavu and Goma, where the Nigerians were also stationed until 10 days ago, suggested that there were faults on both sides between the British and African officers, and happily there are now signs that both groups are sufficiently alarmed at the deterioration of general discipline to be ready for drastic counter-measures.

(*The Times*, 18 January 1961)

The information in this report obviously derives largely from expatriate officers, and some allowances must be made for this. For example, there may have been good reasons why the charges brought against a soldier by a British officer were dismissed by the African superior officer – presumably Lt.-Col. Ironsi is referred to. The stiff sentences noted in the first paragraph of the extract do not suggest that Ironsi's discipline was usually weak. But the main details of the story were later confirmed by the Nigerian Minister of Defence:

Shortly after the Bukavu incident . . . the very great strain under which the fifth battalion were living revealed certain weaknesses in administration and morale. From these stemmed a slight loss of confidence between a minority of the Nigerian and seconded officers and a slight weakening of discipline among the men.

The subsequent concentration of the whole battalion at Bukavu and the greater sense of security resulting from it, coupled with the cross-posting of three officers have rectified what was never more than an isolated and domestic difficulty. . . . There have been no courts martial resulting from this or any other incident in the Congo. A total of seven men have been dismissed from the service and ten NCOs have been reduced to the ranks by the commanding officer, for disciplinary reasons.[4]

The Nigerian troops were not the only ones in the Congo to suffer from disciplinary troubles. Also in January 1961, the third battalion of the Ghana Army staged a full-scale mutiny in Kasai province. The whole battalion was immediately flown home, the ringleaders court-martialled and the battalion formally disbanded. General Alexander blames the mutiny on overwork, lack of clear orders from UN Headquarters, the atmosphere of hate, the language barrier, the infectious example of indiscipline in the Armée Nationale Congolaise and the ready availability of beer, Indian hemp and the local women.[5]

It is possible to suggest further reasons. Nigerian troops received copies of the main Nigerian newspapers twice weekly by air, and from December 1960 onwards these papers began to feature letters and articles demanding the withdrawal of Nigerian troops from the Congo, on the ground that they had failed to support Lumumba and prevent his arrest. There were also allegations about the role of the British officers; that they ordered Nigerian soldiers to fire on unarmed Baluba in defence of wealthy Belgians with whom the British fraternized, and similar accusations. All such hostile propaganda was vigorously refuted by the Ministry of Defence in Lagos, but it must have had some effect on the morale of the less sophisticated soldiers who would tend to give exaggerated credence to anything which appears in print. Some newspapers also printed alarmist reports of the dangers which the Nigerian garrisons were said to be facing.[6]

Lt.-Col. Ironsi's inexperience must also have added to the difficulties at Bukavu. When he was second-in-command of 1 QONR he had not gone to the Cameroons but had been left behind in Enugu to supervise the rear details. At Bukavu he found himself faced by unusual difficulties which would have taxed an experienced battalion commander. But he was evidently held partly to blame. When 1 QONR returned to Nigeria in May 1961 Ironsi was posted away to London to the obscure position of military adviser to the Nigerian High Commissioner, and he did not hold another command in the Nigerian Army until October 1964.[7] The next commander of 5 QONR was a British officer, Lt.-Col. Morgan.

The Nigerian authorities were sufficiently alarmed by the situation in Bukavu to ask the UN headquarters that the Nigerian troops should be given a period of rest elsewhere in the

Congo. This request was first made at the end of January 1961, but at that time the UN was in no position to grant it.[8] Because it was alleged that the UN had failed to protect Lumumba, Morocco, Indonesia, Guinea, Egypt and Ceylon had all withdrawn their forces from the Congo, reducing the size of the UN force from 19,000 to 14,000 soldiers. On 13 February the Katangese authorities announced that Lumumba had been killed, allegedly while escaping from imprisonment. This murder caused an outbreak of rioting in many Afro-Asian capitals, and there were threats of further withdrawals of troops. The Nigerian force was only 1,400 men but it now made up 10 per cent of the UN strength and if this had also been withdrawn the Secretary-General would have been hard put to it to maintain the UN position on the ground.

In Nigeria as much anger was felt at the murder of Lumumba as in other independent African states. There was a nasty little riot in the centre of Lagos in which some Europeans were attacked. Letters in all newspapers demanded the immediate recall of the Nigerian troops and this call was supported by the *West African Pilot* and some opposition leaders. Sir Abubakar remained admirably calm in face of these demands. He insisted in parliament that the Nigerian troops were in the Congo to preserve law and order and not in the interest of any particular Congolese faction; they had been in action against troops supporting Mobutu at Bukavu in December 1960, and against Lumumbist troops at Manono and Kindu in January and February 1961; the problem in the Congo was a political one and the Nigerian troops would support the UN in seeing that there was no outside interference in Congolese affairs.[9] This firm Nigerian support for the UN operation at this time must have been of crucial importance to the Secretary-General.

So the Nigerians remained in their positions and the only concession made to their difficulties was an increase in their allowances. 5 QONR did not leave Bukavu until May 1961, when they handed over to another Nigerian battalion, 2 QONR under Lt.-Col. Ademulegun, who remained there until July. 4 QONR remained at Manono until June 1961 when they handed over to an Indian force. Nigerian Brigade HQ then moved to Luluabourg in Kasai province. One battalion was stationed in Kasai and the other on guard duties in the Congolese capital, Leopoldville.

Kasai was hardly less chaotic than North Katanga. In the words of the *Nigerian Army Magazine*:

> Within a few days of the arrival of the Nigerians some 400 people were massacred not far from Luluabourg. Many of the tribes were in open conflict with each other. The Baluba expansionist movement in South Kasai under the self-styled King Albert Kalonji was a contributory factor to this unrest. However the two greatest factors were that the Central Government troops in occupation of various Kasai towns were completely ill-disciplined and looted at will and that several towns in this province were occupied by troops from the neighbouring province of Stanleyville. The police force in Kasai was hopeless, corrupt and very much afraid of the Army.
>
> (*Royal Nigerian Army Magazine*, May 1962, 47)

Kasai province was about half the size of France, and the Nigerian headquarters had to attempt to restore normal conditions of life and keep three mutually hostile Congolese armies apart with a total of five companies of troops, four Nigerian, one Liberian. It had been the scene of the mutiny of one Ghanaian battalion in January 1961 and the massacre of forty-two officers and men of the Ghana Army at Fort Francqui in April by troops nominally loyal to General Mobutu.

The plan adopted by Brigadier Goulson of the Nigerian headquarters was for intensive patrolling on the ground to keep the peace, coupled with visits by officers accompanied by officials of the UN Civil Affairs Administration, who went by air to all the main towns to try to persuade the people to co-operate with each other and to bring in medical supplies, food and other relief. This pattern of operations continued for the next two years until Kasai ceased to be a Nigerian responsibility in May 1963. 3 QONR was relieved in turn by 1 QONR, 4 QONR and finally by 3 QONR again. The battalion notes of 3 QONR on their second tour of duty in Kasai read very much like those of their first spell there: a patrol sent out to investigate reports of tribal clashes; a patrol sent to investigate the killing of a local administrator; a strong company group sent to stop tribal fighting and looting in the town of Tshikapa; a company patrol assisted by an armoured car squadron sent to capture a local bandit chief and several hundred thugs who were terrorizing the neighourhood and whom the local Armée Nationale Congolaise was unable to deal with; troops sent to take over the local broadcasting station to prevent inflammatory broadcasts by local politicians leading to street demonstrations, and so on. It is easy to believe the writer's summary: 'After arriving in Kasai we did not have a dull moment. Life has been busy and exciting.'[10]

The Nigerian troops in Kasai were only marginally involved in the attempts to force the reintegration of Katanga into the Congo. In October 1961 General Mobutu attempted to invade Katanga through Kasai. But the soldiers of the Congolese Army were soon forced to retire, and in their retreat ran riot through Luluabourg, causing considerable difficulties for the Nigerian garrison. A few months later Gizengist troops from Stanleyville attempted again to invade North Katanga and occupied some towns in Eastern Kasai. These troops from Stanleyville were not well-disciplined and two officers from Nigerian Brigade headquarters, Major Lawson and Major Nwawo, helped to evacuate a number of missionaries who were endangered by their advance. For this series of actions Major Lawson was awarded the D.S.O. and Major Nwawo the M.C.

At the time of the final reduction of Katangese resistance in

January 1963 the Nigerian battalion was reinforced by elements of the Recce Squadron with armoured cars. Brigade headquarters took temporary command of the Malayan battalion in Kivu and the combined force moved across the Lualaba river into North Katanga. But there was no fighting and the commander of the Katangese gendarmerie in this area surrendered his men without resistance. Their surrender was received by Brigadier Ogundipe, who was the first Nigerian to command the brigade in the Congo.

Apart from Kasai, the other half of the Nigerian commitment in the Congo was to provide one battalion for duties in Leopoldville. This began with 2 QONR, who moved from Bukavu in August 1961, followed successively by 5 QONR, 2 QONR (again) and 1 QONR. They were largely occupied with guard duties and patrols in the Congolese capital and with ceremonial parades for distinguished visitors, but the battalion also had time for some sport and military training at the Kitona army base near by. The only potentially serious incident was in April 1962 when Moise Tshombe wished to return to Elizabethville from peace talks in Leopoldville and the ANC surrounded the airport and blocked the runway to prevent his departure. The Nigerians were ordered by the UN to use force if necessary to ensure his departure, but the ANC drew back at the last moment and Tshombe was able to leave unmolested.

In January 1964, during the final months of the Congo operation, a new rebellion broke out in Kwilu, south of Leopoldville, under Pierre Mulele, a former Lumumbist. United Nations troops were not asked to help in suppressing this uprising, and in any case there were too few of them left in the Congo to be of much help. But rescue teams were formed by the battalion to help evacuate missionaries from the troubled area. Apart from these two incidents, life for the Nigerians in Leopoldville was comparatively uneventful.

Summary of the Congo Operation

The Nigerian Army was involved in the Congo for rather more
than three and a half years. Up to June 1963 the contingent
comprised two battalions with supporting troops totalling about
1,400 soldiers, with a high point of 1,703 in March 1962 when the
Nigerians were the third largest national force in the Congo,
after the contingents from India and Ethiopia. After June 1963,
when the commitment in Kasai was given up, only one battalion
remained for the final year. The normal tour of duty in the
Congo was six months, but in fact several battalions stayed
beyond this, notably at the end of the Congo operation when
2 QONR stayed for eight months and 1 QONR for twelve
months as the UN mandate for the Congo force was grudgingly
extended by the General Assembly, first from June 1963 to
December 1963, and finally up to June 1964. By the end, each
Nigerian battalion had completed two tours of duty in the
Congo.

The effect of all these moves was that at any time from the
end of 1960 to July 1963, Army headquarters in Lagos could
normally count on only two of the five battalions being available for internal security duties inside Nigeria. Usually two
would be in the Congo, and another either preparing to fly out,
in transit home or on block leave once it was back. During the
years of the Congo operation soldiers in certain static units in
Nigeria such as stores, workshops and record offices were given
special training and exercises for internal security duties, should
this become necessary. But this was a very makeshift arrangement.

The dangers of this situation were made clear in May 1962
when Chief Akintola was dismissed from the premiership of the
Western Region by the governor, but refused to vacate his
office. The Western House of Assembly was summoned to a
meeting in Ibadan to resolve the crisis. At that time the dispo-
sition of the five battalions was as follows:

	Normal Station	*Actual Position*
1 QONR	Enugu	In transit from Kasai
2 QONR	Abeokuta	Abeokuta
3 QONR	Kaduna	Kaduna
4 QONR	Ibadan	In transit to Kasai
5 QONR	Kaduna	Leopoldville

So 3 QONR was immediately ordered to move from Kaduna to take up position in the barracks at Ibadan that had just been vacated by 4 QONR. But this move meant that the only troops available to deal with any trouble in the whole of the Northern Region were half the Recce Squadron at Kaduna – a couple of hundred men at most, even if all the clerks and storemen at Brigade headquarters are added in with them.

Service in the Congo was popular in the Army, mainly because of the special allowances paid while serving there. In addition to his normal pay a soldier was entitled to a daily UN allowance, a Nigerian special overseas allowance, an additional allotment for his family and an allowance in lieu of leave that he was unable to take while in the Congo. Taken all together these meant that a private soldier whose normal month's pay was less than £10 might receive up to £26. 7s. 6d. a month in allowances. Higher ranks received considerably more.[11] Most soldiers were able to save substantial sums during their tours of service and this compensated in some measure for the hard soldiering in Kasai or the more boring duties in Leopoldville.

Whatever difficulties the Congo commitment may have caused for the Army, and whatever stringency may have been induced in the internal security situation at home, the Nigerian Government never withdrew their agreed contribution from the UN Congo Force and gave unswerving public support to the Secretary-General, even when many Nigerians had grave doubts about his policy. Without the support of the most populous state in Black Africa it would have been very difficult for Dag Hammarskjöld to carry on after the withdrawal of the troops of the Casablanca Bloc states in 1961. Nigerian troops were not involved in any of the hard fighting in Katanga, which was largely borne by the Indians, but they served in some of the most difficult areas of the Congo. They were not among the first UN troops to arrive in the Congo in July 1960, since Nigeria was not then independent, but they were the last to leave on 30 June 1964 when eighty-five Nigerian soldiers of the first battalion flew out of the Congo with Major-General (acting) Aguiyi-Ironsi who commanded all the remaining UN troops for the last six months of the operation.[12]

Tanganyika, April – September 1964

Even before the last soldiers had left the Congo, the Nigerian Army had accepted another task in Africa. In January 1964 the two battalions of the Tanganyikan Army had staged a mutiny, imprisoned their European officers and run riot through the streets of Dar-es-Salaam. The mutinous troops were only brought under control when the prime minister, Julius Nyerere, invited British troops to intervene. The causes of this mutiny are not yet certain. It took place soon after rebels had over-thrown the Sultan of the neighbouring island of Zanzibar, and communist influence was immediately suspected. But it seems more likely that discontent over pay and the slow progress in the 'Tanganyikanization' of the officer corps were mainly res-ponsible, though the example of the success of the Zanzibari revolutionaries no doubt served as a catalyst.[13]

Once Nyerere was restored to power by the British inter-vention he ordered the complete disbandment of the two Tanganyika battalions, except for the few African officers, who had been imprisoned by the mutineers along with their Euro-pean colleagues. He believed that under the British the Army had been an élite force, deliberately isolated from the people, and he told a reporter, 'Since you can't do without an army in these times, the task is to ensure that the officers and men are integrated into the government and party, so that they become no more of a risk than the civil service.'[14] Accordingly 1,500 young men were selected from the youth wing of the Tanganyika African National Union to form a completely new and truly national army.

These new recruits needed to be trained, and there was also the need for other African troops to take over internal security duties so that the British Army's necessary, but embarrassing, presence could be dispensed with as soon as possible. The ministerial committee of the Organization of African Unity met in February in Dar-es-Salaam and recommended that the British soldiers should be replaced by three African battalions; Algeria, Ethiopia and Nigeria were suggested as possible sources. But the Tanganyikan Government decided that one battalion would be sufficient, and Mr Kambona, the External Affairs minister, came to Lagos at the end of March to make arrangements.

The battalion chosen was the third, under Lt.-Col. Pam. 3 NA had returned from service in Kasai province in May 1963, and Lt.-Col. Pam had taken over the command shortly afterwards, on the departure of Lt.-Col. Etches, the last of the expatriate battalion commanders. There was still one British officer left in the battalion, but the Tanganyika Government did not object to his inclusion in the contingent, even though the Nigerians were going to replace the British troops.[15] The battalion flew out to Dar-es-Salaam in the first week of April 1964 – a total of 533 soldiers and 24 officers. The training mission was to be under the general supervision of Brigadier Ademulegun who had recently taken over command of 1 Brigade, Kaduna.

The immediate task of the battalion was to train the TANU youth wing recruits into competent soldiers. This was not quite as impossible as it might appear in the short time available, since a number of NCOs and warrant officers of the former Tanganyikan Army were unofficially allowed back into the force once the ring-leaders of the mutiny had been court-martialled. While the training was in progress the Nigerian troops were also available for internal security duties, if required, and they mounted the normal ceremonial guards in the capital.

The newly trained recruits officially passed out on 1 September 1964, less than five months after the Nigerians had arrived. On 21 September the battalion held a ceremonial parade and received a fulsome tribute from Julius Nyerere for their service. They then left by air, and were all back in Nigeria by the end of the month. The original plan had been that they would be replaced by Algerian or Ethiopian troops after six months, and a small contingent from the Ethiopian Air Force had arrived in May. But in the event the Nigerian soldiers were not replaced, and responsibility for internal security passed immediately to the reconstituted Tanganyika Army. This was taking a big risk, particularly as some officers and other ranks were arrested for 'doubtful loyalty and insubordination' even before the Nigerians left.[16] But up to the time of writing, the new Army seems to have remained loyal.

Tiv Division, 1964 – 1965

The million or so Tiv living in Tiv Division of Benue Province had long been the main centre of opposition to the NPC government of the Northern Region. In the 1959 Federal election 85 per cent of the voters there had supported candidates of the United Middle Belt Congress, an ally of the Action Group. Since then they had remained impervious to the normal methods of persuasion used by parties in power – that is, the manipulation of tax assessments, patronage and the local courts to the disadvantage of those who persisted in supporting the opposition. Among the proudly independent Tiv such methods were more likely to lead to riots than to compliance, as was shown by the wave of arson that occurred just before Independence.[17]

After this the government was naturally anxious not to take any risks on internal security, and army units were moved there for short periods to reinforce the police in April 1960, August 1961 and February 1964. On all these occasions the soldiers were able to leave within a few weeks.

But in July 1964 there were more serious disturbances than anything known before. By mid-August almost eight hundred people had been arrested, and though the official death roll was only eighty, an assistant police commissioner was quoted as saying that hundreds of bodies might still be lying undiscovered in the bush.[18] On 2 September the *Nigerian Citizen*, a newspaper supporting the NPC, admitted, 'The present Tiv riot is encircling Makurdi town (the provincial capital) as the environ villages have been invaded and looted by rioters.' In October rail services between Enugu and the North were interrupted when railway employees fled from their stations when attacked by rioters. The NPC claimed that the disturbances were instigated and the rioters subsidized by the NCNC government of the Eastern Region. UMBC supporters put the blame on arbitrary taxation and victimization by clan heads who were trying to force them to support the NPC.

In spite of this violence, the Federal Government refrained as long as possible from sending troops. But finally this step became unavoidable if sufficient public order was to be guaranteed to hold the 1964 Federal election there. On 18 November 1964 Sir Abubakar ordered the Army 'to take immediate steps to ensure a return to normal life in the area'. Almost the whole of 3 NA together with the Recce Squadron now moved into Tiv Division. The choice of 3 NA is rather surprising. When infantry were required in Tiv in February 1964, a company had been sent from 5 NA under the command of Capt. Onwuatue-gwu.[19] This battalion was still available, while 3 NA had only just returned from Tanganyika. A possible explanation is that Lt.-Col. Pam came from this area, being a Birom from Jos, and so would inspire more confidence in the local population. An

alternative explanation is that the government had some suspicion of Lt.-Col. Ojukwu who had recently taken over
command of 5 NA, since the official NPC view of the riots was
that they were Ibo-inspired. However, the Recce Squadron,
which was also sent there, was commanded by an Ibo, Major
Anuforo.

The soldiers were able to overawe the Tiv without any actual
fighting. Within a fortnight of their arrival they had arrested
122 rioters and confiscated a large store of home-made guns,
bows and arrows. By mid-December peace was returning to the
division and markets were beginning to function normally.
The correspondent of the London *Observer* reported that the
UMBC leaders, who might have been expected to protest
against the coming of the soldiers, had in fact welcomed them
as being far more impartial than the police.[20] Orderly polling was
now possible, and in the Federal general election at the end of
December the UMBC won four of the seven seats in the
Division, the only opposition victories in the whole of the
Northern Region. There was no official 'state of emergency' or
martial law in force at the time, but the Army was effectively
in control of the area, and the victory of the opposition party
was taken as proof of the Army's ability to act as an impartial
arbiter.

But the complete pacification of Tiv Division was a long
task. Soldiers were still there in February 1965 when the
governor of the North was able to report only that peace was
'in sight'. In June 1965 a company of troops under Major
Ademoyega still remained there. In August an NPC leader in
Tiv pleaded for the release of those arrested in the riots: 'It is
only by release of prisoners that peace and tranquillity can be
present in Tiv Division'. And when Maj.-Gen. Ironsi took over
power in January 1966 he gave as one justification of the
military take-over 'the current disorder in the Tiv area'.[21]

VI · Changes in the Army, 1960-1965

For the entire period from Independence to the 1966 coup ministerial responsibility for defence was kept firmly in Northern hands. Immediately after 1 October 1960 Sir Abubakar handed over the Defence Ministry to Alhaji Muhammadu Ribadu, who remained at this post until his sudden death in April 1965. The Ministry was then given to Alhaji Inuwa Wada, a Fulani from Kano. From February 1960 to August 1961 the post of minister of state for the Army was held by Dr Majeko-dunmi, a Yoruba and a personal friend of the prime minister. But during the remainder of the period this post too was held by a Northerner: first by Mr Jacob Obande, an Idoma business-man from the Middle Belt, and then from December 1962 by Alhaji Ibrahim Tako Galadima, a Nupe from Niger province who held that office until the military coup. The NCNC, though they were partners with the NPC in the coalition government, were only given the post of minister of state for the Navy, which was held by Mr Matthew Mbu (Ogoja, Eastern Region). Similarly, the post of permanent secretary to the Ministry was continuously held by Northern civil servants, first by Mr A. A. Atta, and then from 1964 by Alhaji Sule Kolo.

Muhammadu Ribadu was the man who made the Nigerian Army what it became in the first five years of Independence. Like the premier of the North, Ribadu was a Fulani and came from one of the leading families of Adamawa province. He had been a district head at the early age of twenty-six and was a member of the first Northern House of Assembly in 1946. In 1951, with Mallam Abubakar, he came to Lagos and became Federal Minister of Natural Resources. Thereafter he remained a minister until his death, holding a number of portfolios before he finally came to Defence in 1960. When the NPC was re-organized in 1954 Ahmadu Bello, the Sardauna of Sokoto, became president, Abubakar first vice-president and Ribadu second vice-president of the party. It was popularly believed that Ribadu was the strong man of the Federal cabinet, relaying the Sardauna's commands to Lagos. Certainly the prime minister was seen to lean heavily on him for advice and reposed 'unshakable confidence' in him. Hence the nickname 'power of powers' by which he was sometimes known in parliament. In spite of this he did not assume a proud demeanour in public. He had a reputation for sincerity and plain speaking, but in the House of Representatives he rarely sat on the government front bench, preferring to speak from farther back. He rose before daybreak every morning to pray and read the Koran, and made several pilgrimages to Mecca. He rarely listened to the radio or read a newspaper. It was possible to describe him as 'humble', 'unassuming and rather shy', and 'much more than a politician and a statesman; he towered above such nomenclature and he died a saint'. Okotie-Eboh and Inuwa Wada both broke down in tears while paying their last respects to him in the House.[1]

Whatever may have been his personal virtues, Ribadu was certainly an effective minister in securing a fair share of government revenue for his department. Immediately after taking over the Defence Ministry he had inserted an additional £1,000,000 for barracks development in the Supplementary Estimates of December 1960, and a further £750,000 was added to the Capital Estimates in April 1960 for military reorganization. These were both additions to the final stages of the 1955–1962 National Plan. When estimates were drawn up for the 1962–1968 six-year plan Ribadu secured an allocation of £30,000,000 for capital expenditure on defence. This compared with £5,500,000 actually spent in the previous seven years, the greater part on the Army and the rest on the initial stages of the Nigerian Navy. The new plans envisaged further expansion of the Navy, the creation of an Air Force, and a massive programme to rebuild and extend all the barracks and set up a new Military Academy and Ordnance Factory. In fact, in the first four years of the plan up to April 1966 about two-thirds of this sum was actually spent, as follows:[2]

Building and rebuilding barracks, depots, etc.	£10,850,000
New Ordnance Factory	2,700,000
Warships	3,750,000
Aircraft and Air Force equipment	900,000
Army equipment	1,400,000
	£19,500,000

This increased capital expenditure did not lead to any great increase in the size of the Army. The number of soldiers increased by about 3,000 in the seven years following Nigeria's assumption of responsibility, from 7,600 in 1958 to 10,500 in 1965.[3] Most of this increase was made up by the formation of a number of small units: the Nigerian Artillery, which had been disbanded in 1958, was reformed by the creation of two new batteries; there was an additional squadron of armoured cars; and a new Federal Guards company was formed, mainly to perform ceremonial duties on Lagos Island. In addition each of the original five battalions formed an extra company in 1963 and these were to be united to form the sixth battalion when a barracks had been built to house it, but this was not yet ready in 1966.

If Ribadu had had his way the Army would have been much larger. There was a large increase in recruits under training in 1961, but a freeze on funds available cut numbers back again in 1962–1963.[4] There was then some expansion in 1963–1964, but again in 1964 a review of the progress of the Development Plan showed that there was 'a gross imbalance between expenditure on the administrative sector and on productive projects'. This report led to a further reduction in building projects for the Army, and Ribadu was displaced from the chairmanship of the Economic Committee of the cabinet.[5]

Because of these economic pressures, defence took a very moderate proportion of government revenue up to 1966. The recurrent cost of the Army, Navy and Air Force varied just below 4·5 per cent of the total Federal and Regional budgets between 1959 and 1966, though it rose in money terms from about £4,000,000 in 1959–1960 to nearly £8,000,000 in 1965–1966. By contrast Ghanaian recurrent defence expenditure had already reached £9,000,000 by 1963, taking over 10 per cent of the budget.[6]

Criticism of Army Expansion

There was little sign of public protest at the increasing yearly total of the Defence Estimates. Quite the contrary. Demands for expansion were frequently made in the press and in parliament, along with suggestions that the government should introduce compulsory military service and that cadet units should be set up in all secondary schools. These demands came from both the government and the opposition sides of the House. Up to 1958 there had always been a few members who spoke out against expenditure on the Army. But between 1959 and the coup only one such speech was made in the House of Representatives; this was by Mr Akpan Brown (AG member for Uyo, Eastern Region):

To increase the Armed Forces of Nigeria means an increase in Nigerian troubles. At present there is nothing wrong in this country that should warrant wasting thousands of pounds on increases in the Police Force, the Army and the Navy. . . . What are we afraid of? . . . I remember in the colonial days one of the politicians accused one of the British Governors of giving us stones when we asked for bread and walking sticks when we asked for arms. This is exactly the position. When we asked the Federal Government for industries they gave us Federal Crown Counsel. Last year we asked the Federal Government for the extension of the railway; they gave us a naval base.

(*HR Deb*, 30 March 1963, col. 195)

But Mr Brown was not entirely disinterested. The rest of the speech showed that he was really concerned with the anti-smuggling activity of the Customs and Excise in his constituency, where they had recently been assisted by soldiers from 1 QONR.

One suggestion sometimes made was that the Army should engage in agricultural projects or carry out public works. This was done elsewhere, notably in the Ivory Coast, where short-service conscripts were given agricultural training during their service to make them better farmers afterwards. But this was not practicable in Nigeria where the Army was composed of long-service regulars. The military were ready to help in national emergencies, as in August 1963 when army engineers put up Bailey bridges after Lagos was almost cut off from the rest of the country by floods. They also helped occasionally with other engineering works in the bush, such as building a road to the formerly inaccessible Mambila Plateau in the remote North-East of the country. But any regular use of soldiers for such work would have laid the Army open to the charge of aggravating the problems of unemployment. In any case, the Army was fully stretched by the Congo commitment, which left little time for such non-military pursuits.

Tribal/Regional Composition of the Army

From 1958 onwards recruitment of ordinary soldiers was governed by regional quotas: 50 per cent from the North, 25 per cent West, 25 per cent East. It would take some years before the proportions in the Army as a whole approximated to these quotas, and no official statistics were ever made public. The only firm piece of information is that the Western Region continued to be under-represented and there were only seven hundred soldiers from there at the end of 1966, in spite of a special effort to bolster the proportion of Yorubas in the Army undertaken in 1965.[7] There was one other change since Independence, when 130 soldiers from the Southern Cameroons left in 1961 when a separate Cameroons Army was formed.[8] The figures for the regional composition of the Police in 1965 are available and the following table is a possible guess at the position in the Army then, for comparison with the figures for 1958 at page 25 above:[9]

Region of Origin	Police	Army
	%	%
North	27	?55
West and Lagos	12	6
Mid-West	19	?14
East	42	?25
	100	100

Since about half the soldiers from the Mid-West were probably Ika-Ibo,[10] it is possible that about one-third of the Army were 'Easterners' at this time, though the proportion in the battalions would be very much less.

The introduction of regional quotas for ordinary recruits was not uncontroversial. The measure tended to discriminate against the North where the majority of the infantry had previously been recruited, and this caused complaints there, just as introduction of regional quotas for officer recruitment in 1961 aroused complaints of discrimination against the East. Yerima Balla, an ex-serviceman from Adamawa in the North, raised the question in 1963:

It does not matter to this country if all the personnel of the Army come from one region, so long as they can defend the whole of the Federation. . . . During the colonial days we had in this country only one system of recruitment. But now we are independent some members of this House are trying to place recruitment on a regional basis. . . . During the war most of the soldiers who went to Burma and India came from the North.

(*HR Deb*, 17 April 1963, col. 1510)

There was no difficulty in filling the Eastern quota. In 1962 a crowd of 690 volunteers besieged the barracks at Enugu, eager to fill the fifteen vacancies for recruits available on one intake.[11]

Within the regional quota there was some effort in the North to spread recruitment evenly over the entire region, so that all the tribes were fairly represented. It had long been the practice that recruitment at the Depot, Zaria, was supplemented by teams which went to the outlying provinces. It now became customary for the authorities at the provincial capitals to pre-select a batch of recruits and send them down together to Zaria. This meant that the Middle Belt, formerly the main recruiting area in the North, felt that it was being treated unfairly. This resentment was most keenly felt and expressed by the Tiv.[12]

There was no similar concern with provincial balance in the other regions. This did not cause complaint in the Mid-West, since recruits from there could always take the places of the Yoruba whose reluctance to become soldiers was well known. But there were complaints in the minority areas of the East. Chief Enang, a former RSM and now NCNC member for Obubra, Ogoja province, asked the Minister of Defence for fairer treatment:

Most young school-leavers have tried to naturalize themselves by posing to be members of the major tribal groups or by other means to gain admission into the Armed Forces. Quite often when they leave their villages to go to the Regional Headquarters there is a lot of discrimination against

H

them, and so the only thing they have to do is to collect some money and settle down among the indigenes of the place possibly to study Hausa, Yoruba or Edo and then pretend to be natives of those places, so as to be given the opportunity of serving in the Army.

(*HR Deb*, 19 October 1965, col. 2628)

The normal ministerial justification of the regional quota system, both for ordinary recruits and officers, was the need to make the Army a fully representative body and 'to create an awareness in all sections of the community of their responsibilities for the defence of the borders of this country', as Ribadu once said. One reason not so often avowed was the question of ensuring the Army's loyalty. Alhaji Tako Galadima, Minister of State for the Army, told the Senate:

We introduced a quota system in the Army, thus preventing the possible fear that the Army would sometimes become unreliable. If any part of the country is not represented in the Army, we may harbour some fear that a particular section will begin to feel that it is being dominated. But now . . . this country's safety is assured.

(*Senate Debates*, 1 May 1965, col. 262)

Making the Army Safe from Subversion

In theory an army should be a passive instrument in the hands of the government, an efficient agent to carry out the ends decreed by its political masters without sentiment or complaint. Few armies achieve this ideal completely, but the Nigerian Military Forces before 1958 came very near to it. Their loyalty to the purposes of the British Government was dependent on a number of factors: that all the officers and many of the NCOs and WOs were British; that most of the troops were recruited from backward areas who found the low pay offered attractive and had not yet been touched by nationalist agitation; that the

battalions were rotated every few years so that they could not
form very close links with the local population; that the politically conscious Southerners needed for the technical services
were neutralized by being mixed with Northerners in the
battalions, or were separated in small specialized units where
they could do no harm.

After 1961 practically all these factors were no longer opera-
tive. The British NCOs and WOs had almost all left and the
British officers were leaving; even those that remained were
not entirely trusted to serve the purposes of a Nigerian Government.[13] Even the backward areas had by now been exposed
to politics and there was in any case a tendency to shift recruitment to the major tribes away from the minority areas.
Because of the Congo commitment it was impossible to continue to rotate battalions; the moves to and from the Congo
every six months caused quite sufficient disturbance, and the
last rotation was the move of 2 QONR to Abeokuta in 1961.

There was little the government could do about these
changes. The main anxieties centred on the officer corps. As
far as the rank and file were concerned, instructions were issued
in the year after Independence that every unit, however small,
must be tribally mixed. This mixing was to go down as far as
the sections in a platoon. This had always been the official
policy but it had often been unimplemented in practice because
Southerners preferred the technical units or were deliberately
posted to them because they were literate. Now officers were
instructed to see that this was fully enforced, as a means of
neutralizing any disaffected elements and enhancing the cor-
porate spirit of the Army.[14]

But the main means used to secure the loyalty of the Army
was higher pay. Between 1958 and 1960 the pay of most
soldiers was roughly doubled to bring them level to the equivalent ranks of the police. From 1960 onwards the soldiers received large bonuses on their pay for service in the Congo. In
October 1963, when the Congo operation was ending, the

Minister of Defence told the troops that a new salary review for
the Army was then about to be ratified by the Council of
Ministers. 'The Army,' he said, 'is like an engine and must be
regularly lubricated if it is not to lose its efficiency.'[15] This
review raised the pay of all soldiers, but not officers, by about
25 per cent. No other civil servants received a pay increase at
this time; but the government had just been forced to concede
a Salary Revision Commission under threat of a general strike,
and it expected that it would have to face another confrontation with the unions before long. The Armed Forces, who had
once been the Cinderella of the public service, now had rates
of pay which could be described in parliament as 'comfortable'
and 'very attractive'. Not to be outdone in generosity, an
opposition spokesman for the Action Group proposed to make
army pay tax free.[16]

Diversification of Training and Supplies

Until Nigerian Independence all advanced training of officer
cadets, senior officers and NCOs was naturally done in Britain
and all equipment was purchased there. This was bound to
change. In 1961 Major Maimalari was the first Nigerian officer
to go to the Pakistan Staff College, and officers were also sent
for staff training to the United States from 1962. For the first
two years after Independence all Nigerian officer cadets continued to complete their training in England, but thereafter,
when the numbers being trained rapidly increased, cadets were
sent to Canada, Australia, India, Pakistan, Ethiopia and the
United States. When Nigeria set up its own 'Sandhurst' to give
a full three years' training to officer cadets it was largely staffed
by an Indian training mission, with an Indian brigadier as
commandant.

There was a similar diversification in sources for weapons.
When the Lee-Enfield rifle and the sten machine carbine were
replaced in 1960, the Army bought the self-loading rifle and

Sterling MG from Britain. But when a replacement was sought for the bren light machine-gun a German gun was bought in preference to the new British GPMG. The newly reformed Artillery Battery was equipped with Italian field-guns, and in 1965 the Swedish Carl Gustav mortar was bought for the infantry. The contract for setting up the new ordnance factory to produce weapons and ammunition was given to the West German firm of Fritz-Werners. The new Nigerian Air Force was directed by a West German training team and its commanding officer was a German officer right up to the coup in January 1966.

The Reputation of the Army in 1965

The most obvious change from 1960 was in the Army's uniform and accoutrements. The old ceremonial dress of the RWAFF – red fez, zouave jacket, red cummerbund and khaki shorts – had long been a source of complaint. In 1961 the governor-general, Dr Azikiwe, had said: 'The fact that the uniform was designed originally for the colonial army of occupation makes it imperative for a complete departure from the past to take place.'[17] Some years before that one Nigerian officer described it to me as being fit only for performing monkeys. In 1963 it was replaced by a smarter green uniform of long-sleeved jacket, long trousers and peaked cap. At the same time the 'crowns' in the badges of rank of majors and above were replaced by 'eagles' and officers were issued with new swords bearing the Nigerian coat of arms rather than the monogram of Queen Elizabeth. The old RWAFF badge of the palm tree, which had been common to all four territories of West Africa, was now replaced by an eagle and star, though the former motto in Arabic script, 'Victory is for God alone', was retained. The title 'Queen's Own' was dropped from the names of the battalions and 'Royal' from the title of the Army at the same time.

The Army was now national not only in its nomenclature and

emblems but also in its personnel. The last expatriate battalion commander was replaced in June 1963 and all the battalion officers were Nigerian by the end of that year. In 1964 all the remaining staff appointments at Army and Brigade Head-quarters were Nigerianized, with the sole exception of the G.O.C., Major-General Welby-Everard, who left in February 1965. The last British seconded officer left in August 1965 (an engineer) and at the end of the year there was only one ex-patriate contract officer remaining, a Pakistani medical officer. In 1964 the only volunteer territorial army unit, the engineer squadron at Bukuru, was disbanded. This was originally formed by expatriate exployees of the tin mines of the Jos Plateau. In 1960 it had taken in Nigerian other ranks for the first time, but in 1964 it still had only one Nigerian officer, and so could not be allowed to continue.[18]

One welcome consequence of the complete Nigerianization of the Army was a new stability in command positions. Between 1960 and 1964 Nigerian officers were constantly moving on a merry-go-round from battalion to battalion on promotion and for further training. In June 1963 the fifth battalion noted that only ten officers remained of the twenty-seven who had been in the unit a year before.[19] This lack of continuity in the senior ranks meant that the mass of newly appointed subalterns were not given the necessary support and guidance in the enforce-ment of proper standards of discipline. The period of transition from British to Nigerian command also gave rise to tensions between senior Nigerian officers and British officers junior to them, just as there had been difficulties the other way round when the British held the senior ranks before Independence; and at a lower level some junior Nigerian officers were resentful that newly seconded British officers should be made company commanders rather than that they themselves should be promoted.[20] It would be surprising if some NCOs and privates did not take advantage of this situation; and the remaining British officers may also have felt unwilling to 'stick their

necks out' in matters of discipline, particularly if they were in
any doubt about the support they would receive from higher
authority. There were also occasional cases of political interference with military discipline.[21]

When all these factors were compounded by the difficulties
of the Congo operation with the constant moves which this
entailed, it is hardly to be wondered at that discipline came
under considerable strain in the early 1960s.[22] But once
Nigerianization was complete and all the battalions were once
more back in Nigeria at the end of 1964, it was possible for
those in charge to take a firmer grip on their commands. Four
of the five battalions had the same commanding officer for two
years before the coup: Lt.-Cols. Fajuyi, Njoku, Pam and
Largema were in command of the 1st, 2nd, 3rd and 4th battalions respectively, and there would probably have been
similar stability in the 5th battalion but for the court-martial
of Lt.-Col. Imo. Under their strong leadership former standards
of discipline were re-established and enforced.

Compared to the Police Force the Army had a much better
reputation for honesty and freedom from corruption. This was
partly because the soldiers had few opportunities and were not
often in contact with the public. The venality of the police,
particularly those on traffic-control duty, was a byword. In
1963 the Inspector-General of Police set up a special X Squad
whose sole function was to suppress bribery in the Force. The
Army was not without its blemishes. Recruits sometimes found
it necessary to offer bribes in order to be accepted. One subaltern, Lt. Okafor, was cashiered and sentenced to two years'
imprisonment for stealing £2,500 from the unit imprest account. Lt.-Col. Imo was court-martialled in February 1964 for
improperly acquiring property worth £96 from the Army
Ordnance Depot and for misusing army transport; he was
found guilty and sentenced to a severe reprimand. But the
remarkable thing is that such a senior officer was put on public
trial for a relatively trivial amount.[23] The Army never had any

scandals like that of the Nigerian Navy where three officers were court-martialled in 1964 for embezzling £60,000, almost 10 per cent of the annual naval estimates.[24]

The Army also had a better reputation than the Police when dealing with civil disturbances. Normally the military were only called to stand by, in case the trouble was too serious for the Police Mobile Force to deal with. These riot squads were composed of experienced police, specially trained and armed with automatic weapons if necessary. Each unit was fully mobile and contained men from all regions. They had a reputation, perhaps not entirely unjustified, for brutality and they were usually able to deal with any trouble. When the Army was required to intervene, as in Tiv Division in 1964, the change was welcomed by the local people.

The high point of the Army's reputation was reached at the time of the Federal election of 1964. Just as happened before the 1959 election, the Army was ordered to organize parades and demonstrations to 'show the flag' around the country, as a deterrent to trouble-makers. When the NCNC leaders found that sixty opposition candidates in the North had been unable to file their nomination papers because of obstruction by the native authorities, Dr Okpara, the premier of the East, demanded that the Army should supervise the election. 'The supervision of voting is necessary,' he declared, 'because the Army is the only public force that is independent today. . . . The police are doing nothing.' Later he said, 'In the West and the North the law enforcement agencies have been incorporated in the machinery of the political parties. One of my ministers was rescued by the Army from NPC thugs thirsting for his blood.'[25]

After the election crisis was over Dr Okpara continued to insist that the Army should conduct elections 'as the Army is generally recognized as the only really non-regional and non-tribal organization in the country.'[26] The same complimentary view of the Army was held in the North. The *Nigerian Citizen*, which at this time often voiced the views of the less conciliatory members of the NPC, commented:

> Thanks to our Armed Forces which kept the balance of power and saved the nation from shame, I can now rest assured that we have one of the most loyal and disciplined forces in the whole continent of Africa. The way in which all of them stood firm by the government of the day was very commendable.

(9 January 1965)

VII · Nigerianizing the Officer Corps, 1960-1965

When Muhammadu Ribadu took over as Minister of Defence in October 1960 only 22 per cent of the army officers were Nigerian (61 out of 283), a lower proportion of Nigerians than in any other branch of the public service. He found in the Ministry a plan for a controlled expansion which foresaw that all the subalterns and half the company commanders would be Nigerian in eighteen months' time, by April 1962, but which set no firm date for the complete Nigerianization of the Army.[1] The only forecast given to the public was that in the *Report of the Select Committee on Nigerianization*, which had been told by an army spokesman in April 1959 that the complete withdrawal of expatriate officers could not be completed efficiently in less than six years, that is by April 1965.

In spite of parliamentary pressure to accelerate this leisurely programme, Ribadu made it clear that he was not going to be hurried. In reply to a motion that the top posts in the Army should be Nigerianized as soon as possible he told the House:

> The motion underrates the difficulties, the qualifications and experience required for the efficient running of a modern army. . . . We do not want another Mobutu in Nigeria. . . . I appeal to both sides of the House not to bring politics into the Armed Forces. Because one has a brother in the Army he should not get up and say, 'Nigerianize the Armed Forces.'
>
> (*HR Deb*, 11 April 1961, col. 1257)

There was no increase in the numbers of army officer cadets accepted for each course at the new Officer Training School at

Kaduna. On each of the first four six-month courses from April 1960 to March 1962 there were twenty-five Nigerian Army officer cadets and only 60 per cent were allowed to pass the final tests (15, 17, 16 and 18 respectively on the four courses).[2] Of these cadets the best four or five went on to RMA Sandhurst and were commissioned about two years later; the rest did the short sixteen-week course at Mons OCS, Aldershot.

The British head of the Army, Major-General Foster, was due to complete his service in March 1962. After Dr Nkrumah had dismissed his British Chief of Staff, Major-General Alexander, in September 1961, it was expected that a Nigerian would now be appointed. But Ribadu was not moved by public pressure. He sent the Minister of State for the Army, Mr Obande, off to London to interview a number of British officers to find a successor. The newspaper of the Eastern Regional Government, the *Nigerian Outlook* grumbled:

> Are we to believe that if either Lt.-Col. Ironsi or Lt.-Col. Ademulegun was appointed to take over command of the Nigerian Forces that Northern Nigeria would one day be invaded by the South? Or could it be inferred that since one of the most important ministries – the Defence Ministry – is under the control of a Northerner and perhaps there is no Northerner yet qualified to command the Nigerian Forces, then the post of commander must continue to be occupied by expatriates?
>
> (23 February 1962)

However, as a concession to public opinion, Ironsi and Ademulegun were promoted brigadiers on the day the new British commander, Maj.-Gen. Welby-Everard, arrived, and also four majors to the rank of lieutenant-colonel – Shodeinde, Ogundipe, Adebayo and Maimalari.[3] It was also announced then that Nigerianization of the Army would be completed over the next three years, by March 1965.[4] This was exactly the date foreseen six years earlier.

At about the same time, in March 1962, the new six-year development plan was published. The plans for capital expenditure on the Defence Forces included the building of a new Defence Academy which would give officer cadets a full three-year course and make it unnecessary in future to seek training facilities for them abroad after they had completed their six-month course at Kaduna. This Nigerian 'Sandhurst' was scheduled to open in January 1964, and its first products would not be commissioned before the end of 1966. Consequently all the subalterns needed to Nigerianize the Army and to allow for any expansion foreseen in the next four years would have to begin their preliminary training in the next eighteen months; once the new Defence Academy began to function there would be a three-year gap before any of its new officers reached their units.

To fill this gap there was a marked acceleration in the number of officer-cadets selected for training. In April 1962 the number of cadets on the Kaduna course went up to forty-eight, and then to sixty-four on the course which followed. Instead of a failure rate of about a third, practically all these cadets were sent on for further training overseas. Since officer training schools in England could not accommodate this increase, cadets went on to military academies in Canada, India, Pakistan, Ethiopia, Australia and the United States. In addition some other regular soldiers from the ranks were sent overseas for officer training without passing through the Kaduna course first. Most of these cadets were commissioned in 1963 and 1964.[5]

The Supply of Potential Officers

The reason for the lack of potential officers in the 1950s had been that the British Army offered low pay and perquisites and demanded high standards to enter a profession which, in the eyes of most Nigerians, carried little prestige. Previous to

1960 an army career only appeared attractive to those secondary school students who came from areas of the country where military service was a traditional occupation, those from poor homes or where the father was dead and who had difficulty in finding the money for school fees, or those who could not hope to get to university.[6]

In order to find sufficient Nigerian officers the Army needed to be able to draw on a wider field of applicants. One means of doing this was to lower the minimum academic standards required. Up to 1959 potential officers had to have four credits, including English, in the School Certificate examination, the equivalent of four passes at 'O Level' in the G.C.E. In September 1959 this requirement was lowered to four School Certificate *passes*. The academic standard was further widened in May 1961: the advertisements specified that as an alternative qualification a Teachers Grade II certificate or the Royal Society of Arts examination, Stage II, would be accepted.[7] Applicants with these minimum academic requirements still had to sit an army entrance examination, but those with five School Certificate credits were excused this. Before 1959 such an academic standard was only sufficient to *qualify* a candidate to take the examination, from which only graduates were exempted. Apart from the academic requirements all candidates had to satisfy a selection board.

The maximum age for entry was also raised in 1959, from twenty-two to twenty-five for candidates who were not already serving in the Army. The reason for this change was that previously former secondary school students were sent only to RMA Sandhurst, and this institution would not accept those above the age of twenty-two. But from 1959 such cadets were also sent to Mons OCS for the short course, where there was no age limitation. The raising of the qualifying age meant that those who had already spent some years in other occupations could now try for the Army, if they wished.

There was no need to raise the financial inducements for

potential officers. The decisions taken between 1958 and 1960 now began to have their full effect. As a result of a general salary revision in 1960 a newly commissioned subaltern was now paid £768 a year, while a university graduate began at £720. It was now possible for a young man to take his School Certificate in November and enter Kaduna NMTC in the following April. If he passed the Kaduna course he could begin training at Mons OCS Aldershot in October and be back in Nigeria as a second lieutenant before the following Easter, less than sixteen months after leaving school. Meanwhile his more studious classmates who had stayed on at school to take their Higher School Certificate would still have to wait at least another four and a half years more before they could take a degree and enter the government service. Moreover, the young officer had reached his senior service salary without having had to pay university fees, and he could expect faster promotion in the Armed Forces where there was still room at the top, compared to the public services in the South where most of the expatriates had already left and most senior posts had been Nigerianized. I well remember the effect produced by one such newly commissioned officer returning to his old school. He arrived in uniform while the school cadet unit was on parade and received the salutes of his former classmates who were still in the sixth form. This sight produced an enthusiastic rush of potential officers for the next army entrance examination.

The attractive salary and the lowering of the academic standards required were not the only reasons why the number of applicants increased after 1960. The exploits of the Army in the Congo received wide publicity and gave a considerable boost to the Army's prestige. The cadet units that had been set up in schools over the previous few years now began to produce school-leavers who had acquired a taste for army life from what they had seen in their weekly training and annual camp. Another significant source of potential officers was the Boys' Company (now called the Nigerian Military School) at Zaria.

This had opened in 1954 and the first course of twenty-six boy soldiers passed out in 1958. Five of these then entered the cadet school at Teshie and were eventually commissioned (Usuman, Ally, Ukpong, Haruna, Ikwue). The number increased in later years. Fifteen of those who left the school in 1962 went on to become officers.[8]

Graduates, Direct Commissions, Executive Commissions

Two graduates were commissioned before Independence, Ojukwu in 1958, and Olutoye in 1960. The latter had a B.Sc. degree and was mostly employed in the Army Education Service, rising to be head of it in 1964. Three more graduates were given combatant commissions after 1960: Rotimi and Ifeajuna in 1961 and Ademoyega in 1962. Rotimi had been a cadet at school at King's College when the first unit was formed there; Ifeajuna was an outstanding athlete who had won the gold medal for the high jump at the Commonwealth Games; Ademoyega had been an administrative officer in the Federal public service for a short time between graduating and joining the Army. After these three no other graduates were given combatant commissions.

There were two reasons for this. The government was suspicious of undergraduates after the demonstrations against the Defence Pact and other government policies, and did not wish to encourage potential revolutionaries to join the Army. These same fears led the Ministry of Defence to close down the cadet units at the Ibadan and Zaria Colleges of Technology when these institutions were upgraded to be universities in 1962. Another reason was the opposition to the commissioning of graduates within the Army itself. Such graduates did the sixteen-week course at Mons OCS and were then given combatant commissions with their seniority backdated several years, to compensate for the time spent in studying for their degree. This was naturally resented by other officers who had been commissioned before them, but who now found themselves superseded.

Apart from these three, all other graduates who entered the Army after 1960 were given 'direct commissions' and were recruited specifically to practise their professional skills as doctors, engineers or teachers. (Direct commissions were also given to those with other specialist qualifications, such as nurses for the Army Medical Service, accountants for the Pay Corps and imams and clergymen for the Chaplains Department.) These officers had no more than the most perfunctory military training and generally served in the headquarters or technical units. As they would not normally be in command of any considerable body of troops, these graduates posed no threat to the government.

Up to 1960 serving soldiers had only been eligible for commissioning if they were under thirty and were able to pass the training course for infantry officers. Beginning in 1960 'executive' and 'quartermaster' commissions were instituted and were offered to senior NCOs and WOs, to take up officers' appointments in the workshops, pay, records, signals, education and stores branches of the Army. Most of those chosen by the new Executive Commissions Board had first joined the Army during the war or in the years immediately after it. Like officers with direct commissions, officers with executive commissions were normally to be found in headquarters units rather than in the infantry battalions, apart from the battalion quartermasters.

The great majority of the officers with direct and executive commissions were Southerners. It is difficult to be sure of their region of origin, but a very rough estimate can be made, relying mainly on the evidence of their names, of those commissioned up to the end of 1965.

There were very few Northern graduates, and most of these found much better opportunities in the Northern Region public service than in the Army. Most of the Northern officers

below were from the 'Middle Belt', apart from some imams
and an instructor in equitation for the Military Academy.

	North	West and Mid-West (not Ika-Ibo)	East and Ika-Ibo
Executive commissions	8 (12%)	18 (28%)	39 (60%)
Direct commissions (excluding nurses)	18 (20%)	43 (47%)	30 (33%)
	26 (17%)	61 (39%)	69 (44%)

Regional Quotas for Officers

At Independence only 14 per cent of the Nigerian officers were
from the North (eight out of fifty-seven). Anxiety had already
been expressed about this in 1959, but the prime minister had
refused to introduce a regional quota system for officers because
the Army needed all the officers it could get, from whatever
region. However, one possibility canvassed by Northern ministers was that there should be a discriminatory lowering of
standards for Northern officer cadets, and enquiries were made
whether there could be a lower level of entry to Sandhurst for
Northerners.[9] But nothing came of this. Officers commissioned
up to Independence still received British Army commissions
and they all did their preliminary training at Teshie in Ghana.
This was an inter-territorial cadet school not under Nigerian
control, so special double standards to accommodate Northerners could not be allowed.

There was more opportunity to influence the choice of
officers when the new Nigerian Military Training College was
opened at Kaduna in April 1960, to replace Teshie, but at first
no regional quotas were laid down. However, the selection
board was instructed that 'where there are potential cadets of

I

equal merit, consideration may be given by the board to the ethnic balance between regions'.[10]

This system seemed to work well on the first course which passed out in September 1960. Six of the fifteen cadets who went on to further training overseas were from the North and another was a Mid-Westerner who had been educated in the North.[11] But on the next course, which passed out in March 1961, the figures were much worse from the North's point of view. Only five of the seventeen successful cadets were Northerners and there were nine Ibos among the twelve Southerners who passed.[12]

It was at this point in 1961 that the Ministry of Defence gave instructions that a rigid regional quota system should be instituted. In future 50 per cent of all cadets must be from the North, and this was to apply both to the initial selection board and to the final pass list, *whatever the order of merit*. This instruction came too late to affect the composition of the third course at Kaduna, which had already been selected, but it did apply to their tests at the end. The original composition of this course was twelve Northerners and sixteen Southerners, but at the end, in September 1961, eight Northerners and eight Southerners were successful.[13] In future courses both the initial selection and the final success ratio were determined by the regional quotas.

At this time the NPC ministers also felt strong enough politically to enforce regional quotas for officers without worrying about the protests of their coalition partner, the NCNC. In the Federal parliament in May 1961 the NPC was only six short of an overall majority as a result of carpet-crossing by opposition members.[14] And in the recent May 1961 elections for the Northern Region Assembly the NPC had done far better than in 1959, reducing the opposition to ten seats compared to thirty-three in the previous election. So, if the NCNC had tried to object, it was more likely to end up on the opposition benches than to overthrow the NPC government.

Great efforts were made by the Northern leaders to find enough good Northern cadets to fill the new regional quota. Ministers and officials encouraged schoolboys to consider a career in the defence services and in one case known to me a student was directed to enter the Army by a relative, an emir, though he had no wish to do so. Six new school cadet units were opened in the North after 1960, compared to only two in the South.[15] But the North continued to be handicapped by its shortage of secondary school leavers, as the following figures of male candidates for the West African School Certificate make clear:[16]

	North		*Rest of Nigeria*	
Year	Sat	Passed	Sat	Passed
1958	407	293	3200	2268
1959	596	347	3750	2328
1960	572	345	3968	2538
1961	590	422	4134	2768
1962	723	420	5496	3200
1963	1003	493	8414	3960
1964	1437	850	9919	6455
1965	1709	930	11462	7389

Source: *West African Examinations Council Annual Reports 1958–1966*

The one advantage that the North had was the traditional prestige of the Army in certain areas of the region. One student from the Middle Belt, a Tiv, gained a good Higher School Certificate in 1961, but chose to enter the Army rather than a university. Another Northerner from Niger province passed out as the best cadet on the Kaduna course in March 1962. But in general the academic standards of potential officers from the North were somewhat lower than those of Southern candidates, where competition to enter the Army was now much keener.[17]

According to the *West African Pilot*, the effect of the institution of regional quotas for officers was 'to send subgrade people for training merely to satisfy Regional as opposed to

National interests'.[18] This depends on how we define the 'national interest'. If Nigeria had been in imminent danger of military invasion by a foreign power then obviously the need would have been for the most efficient army officers available. But this eventuality was highly improbable. The Army was most likely to be required for internal security duties in Nigeria; and in this case the 'national interest' might be better served by having an Army which was acceptable to all sections of the community because it corresponded in its composition with the make-up of the population as a whole.

The regional quota system took some time to have its full effect. Quite apart from the fifty-seven officers commissioned before Independence there were sixty-five officers who had begun their training before the system was introduced in 1961 and the last of these, those who went on to Sandhurst, did not receive their commissions until August 1963. A further 216 officers were given combatant commissions after the quota system was introduced. The tribal/regional breakdown of these officers is shown in the following table:

	North	West and Mid-West (not Ika-Ibo)	East and Ika-Ibo	South Cameroons
Pre-Independence	8 (14%)	10 (17%)	37 (65%)	2 (3½%)
Pre-Quotas	21 (32%)	12 (18%)	29 (45%)	3 (5%)
Post-Quotas	104 (48%)	46 (21%)	66 (31%)	—
	133 (39%)	68 (20%)	132 (39%)	5 (2%)

This shows how the number of Northerners was progressively increased, but the gain was not matched by a proportionate decrease in the number of Easterners commissioned. This was because the Mid-West and Lagos counted as part of the Western Region quota of 25 per cent, and Ibos living in these areas could be included in it. For example, eight of the sixteen successful cadets on the third course at Kaduna in August 1961 were from the South (this was the first pass-out after the quotas were introduced), but five of these were Ibo, including two from the Mid-West, and only one was a Yoruba.[19]

This table gives the figures for all officers given combatant commissions up to the end of 1965. Twelve of these left the Army for various reasons during this period.[20] The total of all male officers (combatant, direct and executive commissions) on the eve of the coup was 482, made up as follows:

North	West and Mid-West (not Ika-Ibo)	East and Ika-Ibo	South Cameroons
157 (32½%)	128 (26½%)	195 (40½%)	2 (½%)

There were also twenty-six female (nursing) officers in the Army Medical Services, making a grand total of 508 officers.

Thus the NPC government had had considerable success in altering the balance of the officer corps. About a third of all male officers, and two-fifths of all officers with combatant commissions, were Northerners on the eve of the January 1966 coup, compared to a mere 14 per cent of all Nigerian officers at Independence. But they were still outnumbered by Southern officers, whose loyalty the government could not entirely rely on. As with the other ranks, the main precaution taken was to see that Northern, Eastern and Western officers were mixed up as much as possible in the various units and headquarters. The position at the Federal Guards on Lagos island may serve as an example. When it was first formed in 1962 the commander was Lt.-Col. Bassey (an Efik from Calabar in the East), his second-in-command was Capt. Johnson (a Yoruba) and the senior subaltern was Lt. Wushishi (a Northerner). When Major Okafor (an Ibo) took over the unit in 1964 the second-in-command was Lt. Shande who was later replaced in 1965 by Capt. Garba (both Northerners).

Officer Promotions

The institution of regional quotas for officer cadets in 1961 only influenced the composition of the lowest ranks of the Nigerian officer corps. Only three officers who passed through their training course after the quota system was introduced were promoted to the substantive rank of captain before the first coup; all the rest were still subalterns. The highest ranks in the Army were held by officers who had been chosen while the Army was still under British control. Now that a Northerner was Minister of Defence after 1960 accusations were naturally made that Northerners were given accelerated and unjustified promotion over the heads of Eastern officers. It was also noted that when the last British colonel in charge of 'A' branch at Army headquarters left in June 1963 – (this is the branch which deals with all questions of promotions and postings) – he was replaced by a Northerner, Lt.-Col. Gowon, and then by another Northerner, Lt.-Col. Pam.

Such accusations were bound to be made, whether they were true or not. One member of the House of Representatives expressed an almost universal belief among Nigerians when he referred to promotion in the Nigerian Navy:

> In the Nigerian Navy nepotism and discrimination are the order of the day. . . . Promotion in the Navy is not based on merit. An Ibo officer will only promote his brother who may happen to be a very junior member of the staff. A Yoruba officer will also prefer promoting a Yoruba man to promoting an Ibo man or a Hausa man, and the same goes for a Hausa officer. As a result men who really deserve promotion are still at the bottom of the scale and those who are not qualified for promotion have been promoted.
>
> (Mr Ede, *HR Deb*, 22 August 1962, col. 2617)

'Tribalism' is an excellent excuse to explain away one's own failure to achieve advancement; few men are entirely impartial in assessing their own merits.[21]

The difficulty in deciding the truth of such allegations is that promotion in the most senior ranks is never purely on the basis of seniority but also on the opinion held of an officer's competence. But if there was a consistent pattern of preferring officers from the North it should be easy to detect, since it is highly unlikely that all the best officers would come from one region.

The most obvious change in the army seniority list between October 1960 and January 1966 was the promotion of officers who had been trained at RMA Sandhurst above officers who had been commissioned from the ranks and had done the short training course at Eaton Hall or Mons OCS.[22] These promotions were not confined to Northern officers; by 1966 all Sandhurst-trained officers had improved their relative positions. But since the first officers out of Sandhurst had been Northerners this could appear to be an instance of regional favouritism. For example, Kur Muhammed passed out of Sandhurst in 1954 and ranked fifteenth in the Army List at Independence. By January 1966 he had moved up to sixth position over the heads of seven Southern officers who had been commissioned from the ranks. Similarly, Nzeogwu, commissioned from Sandhurst in 1959, moved up from forty-eight to thirty-sixth place on the eve of his coup. Naturally there were some feelings of resentment at these changes and this was one cause of the tension between these two groups of officers that has already been noted.[23]

The best way to test the suggestion that Northerners were given unfair advantages is to trace the careers of officers from different regions who were originally commissioned from the same training institution on the same day.

As can be seen from this list, there are some examples at the top of the Army where Northerners do better than Easterners, but lower down the reverse also occurs.

Normally those who were commissioned at the same time moved up the Army in step with one another. There is no evidence of a consistent pattern of discrimination in favour of the North.

	Date and Place of Commission	Rank and Seniority on 1 January 1966	
Pam (Birom, North)	RMA 1955	Lt.-Col.	23.8.63	
Kurobo (Ijaw, East)	,,	Major	3.3.63	A/Lt.-Col.
Gowon (Angas, North)	RMA 1956	Lt.-Col.	1.4.64	
Unegbe (Ibo, East)	,,	Lt.-Col.	3.7.65	
Okwechime (Ibo, Mid-West)	,,	Major	11.3.63	
Anwunah (Ibo, East)	,,	Major	15.3.63	
Madiebo (Ibo, East)	,,	Major	16.3.63	
Aniebo (Ibo, East)	Mons OCS 1960	Major	30.3.65	
Ochei (Ibo, Mid-West)	,,	Capt.	29.7.62	A/Maj.
Kyari (North)	,,	Capt.	18.3.64	A/Maj.
Kweti (Cameroons)	,,	Capt.	18.3.64	A/Mai.
Anuforo (Ibo, East)	RMA 1961	Major	28.2.65	
Bissalla (North)	,,	Capt.	18.9.63	A/Maj.
Haruna (North)	,,	Capt.	18.9.61	A/Maj.
Onwuatuegwu (Ibo, East)	,,	Capt.	18.9.63	A/Maj.
Muhammed Murtala (North)	,,	Capt.	8.11.63	A/Maj.
Shuwa Muhammed (North)	,,	Capt.	1.9.64	A/Maj.

At the very top of the Army there were a number of changes of position, as was to be expected. Ironsi and Ademulegun moved above Bassey, and Ogundipe and Adebayo were promoted above both Bassey and Shodeinde. Maimalari, a Northerner, was another officer who improved his position, but so also did Njoku, an Ibo. There were no sweeping changes: in the ranks of major and above 60 per cent of the officers were Easterners or Ika-Ibo (32 out of 53) compared to 65 per cent of all Nigerian officers (37 out of 57) at the time of Independence. Major-General Ironsi was rather isolated at the very top of the Army,

SENIOR ARMY OFFICERS BY RANK AND TRIBAL/ REGIONAL ORIGIN, JANUARY 1966

	North	West and Mid-West (not Ika-Ibo)	East and Ika-Ibo	
Maj.-Gen.			Ironsi	
Brigadier	Maimalari	Ademulegun Ogundipe		
Col.	Kur Muhammed	Adebayo Shodeinde		
Lt.-Col.	Largema Pam Gowon	Fajuyi Ejoor Banjo	Bassey Njoku Imo Ojukwu Effiong	Nwawo Unegbe Kurobo (acting)
Sub-total	5	7	9	
Majors (substan- tive)	Katsina Akahan	Olutoye Adekunle Obasanjo Sotomi Adegoke Rotimi Ayo-Ariyo	Trimnell Ekpo Okwechime Anwunah Madiebo Nzefili Ogunewe Akagha Nwajei Eze Okonweze Okoro	Nzeogwu Ude Ivenso Kalu Keshi Ifeajuna Okafor, D.O. Anuforo Chude-Sokei Aniebo Obienu
Sub-total	2	7	23	
Grand Total	7 (13%)	14 (26%)	32 (60%)	

Notes: This table refers to officers holding combatant commissions only, and does not include such officers as Col. Peters in the Army Medical Service.

All information is taken from the notices of promotions in *Federal Gazettes*; it is possible that one or two officers may have been promoted substantive major before January 1966 whose notification has been omitted from the *Gazette*.

Major Adekunle has been placed in the Western column. He is the son of a Northern mother and a Yoruba father, educated in the North at Okene, so he might have been placed in the Northern column.

Officers are listed in order of seniority; all the left-hand column of Eastern majors are senior to those on the right.

since the three brigadiers and three full colonels below him were all from the West or North, but this was mainly because of the few Ibos among the first Nigerian officers to be commissioned (see table on p. 38).

Officers' Fears for the Future

The Eastern officers had no reasonable grounds for complaint about their treatment up to 1966. But they did have apprehensions about the future. All the highest positions had been Nigerianized and so it seemed that there could be no more promotions in future unless the Army were to be enlarged. In 1965 this must have seemed very unlikely. Plans for expansion had been cut back in 1962 and 1964 when it was found that funds were not available. It had taken six years to achieve an increase of one battalion. Nor was there any hope that more posts for senior officers could be created. The number of officers had almost doubled since 1959, from 283 to 508, though the total strength of the Army had only increased by about a third. So it seemed clear that any room for further promotions could only be found by prematurely retiring some of the more senior officers. (See Appendix, p. 236.)

There was another reason for believing that some officers would shortly need to be retired. The numbers of newly commissioned combatant officers had increased every year up to 1963, and had then declined. This was because the new Nigerian Military Academy had opened in 1964, and the officers commissioned in 1964 and 1965 were those who had done their preliminary training in 1962 and 1963 and had then gone on to complete their military studies overseas.

1959	12	1963	96
1960	21	1964	59
1961	42	1965	35
1962	37		

There would be hardly any new officers in 1966 until the first graduates of the new Nigerian 'Sandhurst' completed their three-year course at the end of that year. Places would then have to be found for these fifty or more new subalterns. Unless there was some expansion this meant that at least fifty of the present officers would have to be prematurely retired during 1966. Some Eastern officers were afraid that the Northern Minister of Defence would take the opportunity to adjust the tribal/regional balance in the higher ranks of the Army in favour of the North, just as the quota system of officer recruitment had already altered the balance in the lower ranks of the officer corps.

The Attitudes of Nigerian Officers in 1965

It is impossible to say how widespread such fears were and how much they affected the cohesion of the officer corps on the eve of the first military coup. Certainly there were a few officers who believed that they had been passed over for a temporary promotion or a desirable appointment because they were not of the correct tribe.[24] In the officers' mess, just as in any community where people have to live closely together, day-to-day contact may have occasionally given rise to personal enmities, particularly between officers from different parts of the country. Similar tensions had sometimes arisen between Nigerian and British officers in previous years.

On the other hand, at least equally common were the friendships which had arisen in spite of such differences, from common experiences and hardships shared in an officer cadet school overseas, by working together to solve a difficult situation in the Congo or by playing together in a battalion team. Every officers' mess contained as complete a cross-section of the tribes that make up modern Nigeria as could be found anywhere in the country; and experience of the few other Federal institutions where similar tribal mixing was to be found suggests that in such a community an individual is valued more for the contribution he can make to the common goal than for his place of origin. Several officers have contrasted the happy atmosphere in the mess before January 1966 with the unpleasant tension that followed the murders of the first coup.

The vast majority of the combatant officers in 1965 were young men under twenty-five who had been commissioned in the five years since Independence. Officers who had risen from the ranks with executive commissions would be rather older, up to thirty-five or forty. But in a normal battalion the only officers who were over thirty were the lieutenant-colonel, the quartermaster and perhaps one of the majors. Some writers on the military stress the puritan and ascetic elements in the military ideal and the hostility of army officers to what are believed to be 'self-indulgent urban values'.[25] This attitude certainly existed among certain officers, such as Major Nzeogwu, and has recently been exemplified by Lt.-Col. Ogbemudia's campaign of moral reform in Benin.[26] But it seems likely that these examples were not typical of the average Nigerian officer. Nigerian society does not rate the puritan virtues very highly. Abstemiousness is not normally much admired and an important man is expected to indulge in generous self-display. A certain measure of carefulness might be imposed on an officer by the financial demands of the extended family system. But, by and large, most officers preferred to follow another army tradition, perhaps less publicly acknowledged, of 'a short life and a gay one' – the idea that a man who may possibly die before his contemporaries in civilian life is entitled to enjoy his pleasures while they are available and where they do not interfere with military efficiency; and high spirits in the mess are indulgently viewed, even when there is no imminent likelihood of death in battle.

How far were most officers satisfied with their situation in 1965? In the years since Independence most of their grievances had been removed. Almost every barracks had been rebuilt in the past six years. The old-style 'colonial' uniforms had been done away with and almost all the obsolescent weapons and equipment had been replaced. Officers' pay had not been increased since 1960. But the same was true of all government senior service employees. The policy of the government was gradually to level up the inequalities of the colonial pay scales from the bottom, leaving the salaries of the highest civil servants to be eroded in value by inflation. So the officer could not feel that he was being treated worse than other similar sections of the community. Most officers who had recently entered the Army were very satisfied with their pay; for the more senior officers the effects of inflation were mitigated by rapid promotions as the expatriates left. It is probably fair to say that most officers were quite satisfied with their treatment at the hands of the government and had good reason to be.

There is insufficient evidence to say anything about the political opinions of the officers. There was certainly a fairly general contempt for politicians as was shown by General Ironsi and Major Nzeogwu during their tenure of power. But such disdain for politicians was quite common at all levels in Nigerian society. If there was one ideology which was distinctive and common to most officers it was a belief in the necessity for Nigerian unity; for the Army was almost the only truly national institution of importance left in the country. Since the regionalization of the public service in 1954 regional ministries and departments had been staffed almost exclusively by the indigenous inhabitants of each region. Even the Federal civil service tended to keep staff working in their own regions as far as possible. In 1965 Dr Aluko, Professor of Economics at Ife University in the West and later at Nsukka University in the East, wrote:

In the colonial period a civil servant could work anywhere in the country and through the opportunity he grew to know that the other people are not man eaters as the allegories about them depict.

Now, even in the Federal Public Service the Easterner is not welcome in the North and vice-versa. Such rigidity has been extended to secondary schools where formerly all Nigerians met and studied. Today no non-Westerners can be admitted to Government College Ibadan or Queen's School Ede. The Edo College and the Government College at Ughelli are exclusively for Mid-Westerners, King's College is predominantly biased in favour of Lagos and its environs.

Even in the universities there has been a subterranean attempt to favour the admission of some natives of the regions where the institutions are located or where the top administrators come from. . . .

(*Sunday Express* (Lagos), 4 April 1965)

The Police Force also tended to be regionalized since the laws and criminal code were different in each region and since policemen who knew the local language were more acceptable. It was only in Lagos at Police Headquarters and in the regionally mixed Police Mobile Force (riot squad) that men of all tribes could normally be found.

In contrast to this increasing exclusiveness an army officer might find himself posted to a barracks anywhere in the country. There he could command a unit which contained men from all over Nigeria. He probably picked up a smattering of all the main languages and older officers claimed to be able to speak them fluently. He had served in the Congo where he had been proud to be a member of the largest contingent from any African state in the UN Force. When on training courses abroad he had been assessed as a representative of Nigeria, not as an Ibo or a Hausa. He could contrast this working example of unity in the Army with the antics of politicians whose principal tactic for gathering votes was to play on tribal prejudices and chauvinism.

The dedication of Major Nzeogwu to the ideal of Nigerian unity is well known. Even after the massacres of Ibos in 1966 he could still tell a reporter just before the outbreak of the civil war: 'Secession will be ill-advised, indeed impossible. . . . If this country disintegrates I shall pack up my things and go.'[27] But exactly the same sentiments were expressed by Major Hassan Katsina in January 1966 before his first meeting with Ironsi on being made military governor of the North:

> It is our intention to build the nation on the foundation of honesty and hard work, and to bring about unity among all Nigerians living in whatever part of the country with respect, love and understanding towards one another. Everyone must realize that we are one nation irrespective of the tribe from which each originated. Our experience in the past has shown that political parties had not worked for the common good but for sectional interests. . . .
>
> (Daily Times, 20 January 1966)[28]

There is no reason to doubt that he was sincere in what he said, nor that most of the officers of the Nigerian Army would have echoed his sentiments, then and in the years before.

VIII · Politics and Violence, 1960-1965

The first attempt to overthrow the government coincided with Independence itself. Some kind of plot was hatched by a few junior officers of Eastern Region origin at 1 QONR, Enugu. They planned to seize control of the battalion, but what would have happened after that is obscure. Possibly they hoped that their action would be followed in the other battalions. In the event, the conspiracy was discovered and the officers arrested. They remained in prison for about six months and were then returned to duty. Nothing of this was ever made public and no officers disappeared from the Army List as a result.[1]

To all appearances the plot seems incredibly foolhardy. All the senior posts were held by British officers, and once there was a leakage of information these officers had no difficulty in taking action to forestall the conspiracy and arrest the plotters. If there had been an actual resort to violence in the battalion it seems highly unlikely that the Northern infantrymen, who had recently had a large increase in pay as a result of the transfer of the Army to Nigerian control and had no reasonable grounds for dissatisfaction, would have staged a mutiny on the orders of junior officers from the East.

On the other hand, the conspirators may have calculated that Ibo and Eastern officers now formed over two-thirds of the Nigerian officer corps, and this proportion could only decline in future under an NPC government. They may have also been encouraged in their gamble by the recent example of the Congo, where a mutiny in the Belgian-officered Force Publique at the time of Independence had spread very rapidly over the whole country.

The Action Group Plot of 1962

The Action Group was founded by Chief Awolowo in 1950, and for the first six years of its existence it was confined to the Western Region, where it was predominantly the party of the Yoruba élite. In the period from 1956 onwards Awolowo tried to turn it into a nation-wide organization, supporting the claims of minorities in the North and East to have their own separate states, though this strategy was not popular with all the party leaders. In fact this grandiose effort was a failure; the party won less seats in the 1959 Federal elections than either the NPC or the NCNC. These two parties formed a coalition government, and Chief Awolowo, who had resigned from the premiership of the West in order to stand for the Federal House, now found himself Leader of the Opposition there. The AG suffered further reverses in the Regional elections in the North and East in May 1961, and several of its successful candidates soon crossed the carpet to share in the patronage open to members of the government party. By the end of that year it was clear that the party had little hope of any electoral successes in the near future outside the Western Region, where the party still retained control of the government.

Under these circumstances, the most realistic strategy was to confine AG activities to its original base in the West, abandon the costly support of the minority groups in the North and East, and seek to enter the Federal coalition on the best terms available. This was the policy favoured by Chief Akintola, who had succeeded Awolowo as premier of the West when he made his bid for power at the centre. Previously, when Akintola had been a minister in the Federal government from 1957 to 1959, he had worked in co-operation with Sir Abubakar, who was known to favour such an all-party coalition again. The disadvantages of such a policy, from the point of view of Awolowo, were that he would have to abandon the AG allies in the North and East whom he had mainly been instrumental in recruiting

K

to the party, and accept a junior position in Sir Abubakar's government. Even this was not certain, since he was greatly disliked by many of the NCNC leaders, and had recently made himself obnoxious to the prime minister by betraying the confidential discussions on the Anglo-Nigerian Defence Pact.

Not surprisingly, Awolowo opposed this alternative and advocated a different course. Abandoning the moderate, pro-Western policies that the party had previously followed, he began to advocate 'democratic socialism' and the alignment of Nigeria's foreign policy with that of the 'Casablanca Bloc' of President Nkrumah, whom he visited in Ghana in June 1961. This appeal for the support of the radical young men of the South who were unhappy at the NCNC's coalition with the con-servative NPC might have been a winning strategy in the very long run, given rising discontent and disillusionment with the coalition government, but it certainly did not offer any swift road to power by constitutional means. Nigerian electors had frequently shown that they were most easily swayed by appeals to tribal loyalties and by the promises of tangible amenities to be provided by the government, rather than by ideological slogans. Consequently the Federal Government later alleged that Awolowo's advocacy of socialism was merely a façade, covering the fact that he was really engaged in a revolutionary conspiracy to achieve power by violence.[2]

This disagreement between Awolowo and Akintola finally came to a head in May 1962, when Awolowo secured the signatures of a majority of the Action Group members of the Regional Assembly on a petition to the regional governor, asking him to dismiss Akintola from the premiership and appoint a reliable supporter of Awolowo, Alhaji Adegbenro. The governor acted on this request, but Akintola refused to accept his dismissal; his supporters created an uproar in the legislature; Federal police, acting on the orders of Sir Abubakar, cleared the Western House of Assembly with tear gas and locked it up, effectively preventing any vote being taken; the Federal

parliament declared a state of emergency in the Western
Region, suspended the government, appointed an administrator and put most of the Action Group leaders under restriction.

When the state of emergency was lifted in January 1963,
instead of a general election being held, Akintola was installed
as premier by the Federal Government, at the head of a ministry composed of former AG members and also the NCNC, who
had until then formed the opposition in the Western House.
Akintola did not find it easy to secure a parliamentary majority,
and so the Regional House of Assembly was not summoned to
meet for three months, until a sufficient number of Awolowo's
supporters had been won over by bribery or coercion. Those
who still remained loyal to Awolowo continued to be known as
the Action Group and now formed the opposition.

Meanwhile, during the time he was held in restriction,
Awolowo himself had been arrested on a charge of treasonable
felony, accused of planning to stage a revolution. Thirty of his
supporters were also arrested on the same charge, including
several allies of the AG in the North, such as Joseph Tarka, the
leader of the Tiv. The trial began in November 1962 and eventually Awolowo and seventeen of the accused were found guilty
and sentenced to long terms of imprisonment. The case for the
prosecution was that a number of potential revolutionaries had
been sent to Ghana where they were trained for military
operations; that arms and explosives had been imported; and
that plans had been made to seize certain strategic points in
Lagos on the night of 22 September 1962, including the electric
power station, the army stores depot and the airport. It was
also intended to detain the prime minister, other members of
the government and the British commander of the Army. Chief
Awolowo would then issue a proclamation that he had taken
over the government.[3]

It is quite certain that there was some sort of plot afoot, since
a small quantity of arms was actually seized by the police. It is

also accepted by two of the accused, who have since published books on the trial, that men were sent to Ghana for military training, but they claim that this was arranged by certain extreme AG militants without the knowledge or agreement of Chief Awolowo. A discussion of the verdict of the court would take too long, and in any case it is immaterial to this study who the leading conspirators actually were. In what follows it will be assumed that the account of the conspiracy given by the prosecution was substantially correct and we shall only be concerned with the strategy of the conspiracy and the reasons for its failure.

Why did the Action Group conspirators plan a popular revolution and not attempt to initiate a military *coup d'état*? The obvious reason is that there were very few Yoruba officers (see table on p. 51) and only six of these held senior rank: Brig. Ademulegun, Lt.-Col. Ogundipe and four majors. At the time of the plot in 1962 five of these officers were not in places where they could have organized a coup, even if they had wanted to. Lt.-Col. Ogundipe and Major Fajuyi were in the Congo; Major Shodeinde was on a staff course in England; Major Banjo had just returned from taking a degree course at the Royal Military College of Science, Shrivenham, and was at the Army Workshops in Kaduna; Major Adebayo held a staff post at Army Headquarters in Lagos. But Brigadier Ademulegun was in a very strategic position: he was commander of 2 Brigade, which covered all of Southern Nigeria. Evidence was given at the trial that Awolowo had suggested that Ademulegun should be approached.[4] If this is true, he certainly refused to have anything to do with the plot; he was confirmed in his acting rank of brigadier soon after the trial began and continued to hold high posts in the Army until he was murdered in the January 1966 coup.

Nor could the conspirators hope for much assistance from the rank and file of the Army. There were only a few hundred Yoruba soldiers, and most of these were serving in the technical

units and hardly any in the battalions. It is just possible that
the infantrymen from the minority areas of the North might
have rallied to Awolowo, particularly if the Tiv leader, Joseph
Tarka, were associated with him in the revolutionary government and a Middle Belt State had been proclaimed. But the
conspirators would hardly expect that such soldiers would be in
a position to take the initiative in a plot to overthrow the gover-
ment.[5]

So the only possibility was a popular revolution from outside
the Army. To achieve this, external assistance to provide
arms and training was vital, and this was supplied by Ghana.
According to evidence given at the trial, three hundred men
had been sent there for military instruction. Since there was
not yet any widespread discontent with the government, the
plotters could hardly hope to wage a long guerrilla campaign,
but with the help of men trained in Ghana it might have been
possible to seize the airport at Ikeja, a few miles north of Lagos.
Once this had been done and the new revolutionary government proclaimed, it would have been open to Dr Nkrumah to
recognize the new regime and send in assistance by air, even
including troops. For obvious diplomatic reasons, this possibility
was not mentioned at the trial.[6]

It is just conceivable that the initial stages of the plot might
have succeeded, given complete surprise. In September 1962
there were only two infantry battalions in the country, 1
QONR and 2 QONR; as for the rest, 4 QONR and 5 QONR
were out in the Congo and 3 QONR had just been flown there
as a relief. 1 QONR was at its station at Enugu, 450 miles from
Lagos and on the other side of the Niger river, which could only
be crossed by ferry. There was only one battalion in the
Western Region, 2 QONR based at Abeokuta; but this battalion had just gone off to camp in bush at Tapa, forty miles
north of Abeokuta over bad roads. At an optimistic estimate it
would have taken four hours to assemble the troops and cover
the one hundred miles or so to Lagos. Thus on the night of the

projected revolution the defence of Lagos would have rested on the newly formed Federal Guards (a company of infantry on Lagos Island) and the clerks, mechanics, drivers and storemen at the military workshops and depots in Lagos and its northern suburbs. There were also the police, but, following the British pattern, Nigerian policemen on duty do not usually carry arms.

In fact the efficiency of the security forces was never put to the test. There was a leakage of information and Chief Awolowo was placed under house arrest on 22 September – the day the revolution was due to commence. The same day a company of infantry was hurriedly sent from Tapa to take up position in north Lagos, and the next day the whole battalion returned to its base at Abeokuta.[7]

Even if Lagos had been temporarily seized on the night of 22/23 September before 2 QONR could arrive, it seems probable that these troops would have obeyed the orders of their Northern commanding officer, Lt.-Col. Maimalari, and would easily have routed a motley throng of Lagos Yoruba, hastily armed with weapons taken from the army stores. The futility of the whole scheme was well summed up by Sir Abubakar in his last interview:

> The thing I don't understand and have never understood is how Awolowo could have been so childish. . . . I did not believe he could be so foolish. How could he think that he could give a man training in three weeks – just three weeks – and then expect him to overthrow the whole government?
>
> (*West Africa*, 29 January 1966)

Whatever the truth about the guilt or innocence of Awolowo, the final result of the trial was highly satisfactory to the NPC. Awolowo was in prison and the premiership of the West was once more held by Chief Akintola, who was indebted to the Federal Government for his restoration to power. Once the emergency was over many AG members of both the Regional and Federal Houses had decided it was in their interest to support him, so that the NPC now had an alternative ally in the South, if the NCNC should ever be unwilling to continue the Federal coalition.

The only difficulty was that a majority of the Yoruba never forgave Akintola for his treachery against his former leader. Even though he was in prison, Awolowo retained their allegiance in spite of all the pressures which Akintola's government brought to bear. Elected District Councils were dissolved and replaced by handpicked committees of management, chiefs had their salaries cut to a penny, laws were arbitrarily enforced, but all to no avail. Akintola had the support of the Western NCNC, his own home area and most of the Yoruba élite, who wished to share in government patronage and contracts; but most of the common people of the West still regarded Awolowo as their martyred hero, while Akintola was a puppet imposed on them by the North.

The 1964 Federal Election and Dr Azikiwe's Intervention

The NCNC profited at least as much from the crisis in the West as did the NPC. As a result of the Action Group split the Western branch of the NCNC entered the new ministry of Chief Akintola after being on the opposition benches in the Western Assembly for eleven years, and their leader, Chief Fani-Kayode, became deputy premier. In addition, the change of government in the West enabled the Federal Government to split off the Mid-West area to form a new region, the fourth in the Federation. This was where the non-Yoruba minority tribes lived, and it had long returned mainly NCNC members. There had been agitation here for a separate state for many years, on the ground that the area had been neglected by the Action Group, and as soon as the Western Government ceased to object to the excision of this area from its territory the necessary constitutional steps for creating a new region were soon completed. The first elections for the new Regional Assembly were held in February 1964. The opposition to the NCNC was no longer the Action Group, which had practically disappeared in this area, but a new party, the Mid-West Democratic Front, which served as a focus for all those in the new region opposed to the NCNC, and was backed by the NPC. The election thus turned into a trial of strength between the two partners in the Federal coalition, and the NCNC won by 53 seats to 11. As a result of its victory the NCNC now controlled two of the three Southern regions and made up half the government of the third (the West). Incidentally, it may be noted that the Mid-West election was the last reasonably honest election to be held in Nigeria.

Shortly after this success the NCNC held its annual convention in Kano. Party members were in a jubilant mood, supremely confident (on the basis of an unconfirmed report) that the new census results that were shortly due to be published would show that Southern Nigeria now had a higher population than the North. If the constituencies for the forthcoming Federal elections were then reallocated in accordance with these expected census figures, they were sure that the NCNC would win; for since they controlled three of the four Regional Governments (East, Mid-West and West), they believed that they had the means to influence or coerce the electorate to support them.

These hopes were shattered while the conference was still in session. The final census result showed that the North still had a majority of the population (approximately 55 per cent) and so would retain its majority of seats in the Federal parliament. The NCNC Federal ministers and the Eastern Region Government refused to accept the figures and a bitter fight ensued. At the height of the controversy the Western wing of the NCNC suddenly abandoned their party and formed a new party with the followers of Akintola, the NNDP (Nigerian National Democratic Party). They then bid for support on the basis of the need for Pan-Yoruba solidarity and began vitriolic propaganda tirades against the Ibo.[8]

After three months of vituperation the matter of the census was finally settled at a meeting of the regional premiers with Sir Abubakar in May 1964. Dr Okpara, the NCNC premier of the East, agreed to pursue his objections to the census result only through the law courts; and since, according to the constitution, Federal law overrode Regional law on the subject of the census, this was tantamount to tacitly abandoning the NCNC demand for yet another count of the population. In return the conference agreed that the projected iron and steel industry should be split between the North and the East.[9] This decision was economic nonsense, since Nigeria at that time had scarcely enough demand for one economically-sized steel mill, let alone two. Such political compromises, however, are necessary if dignity is to be preserved and nations are to remain united. But nationalists in the South remained convinced that the Northern Region had arranged to inflate its population figures by a vast amount in order to ensure that it would dominate the Federal Government in perpetuity.[10]

Faced with these two reverses – the result of the census and the loss of its Western wing – the NCNC did what best it could by making an electoral alliance with those members of the Action Group who were still loyal to Awolowo. These two parties, together with a number of other small groups, formed the United Progressive Grand Alliance (UPGA) and issued a militantly anti-Northern manifesto for the Federal election of 1964. The regions were to be divided into twenty-five states on the lines of the provinces used under the old British administration. As for the Army, the UPGA manifesto said:

UPGA will accelerate the training of Nigerian officers in the Armed Forces; it affirms its belief in the present arrangement whereby the Head of State is the Commander of the Armed Forces, and a civilian is in charge of Defence, as the best

arrangement for peace and orderly progress in the country.
. . . Recruitment and promotion of members of the Armed
Services will be divorced from tribalism and based strictly on
merit and qualifications.

(*Daily Express* (Lagos), 11 December 1964)

The head of state referred to was the president, Dr Azikiwe.
Though he was called Commander-in-Chief of the Armed
Forces, this was a nominal appointment only. The Army Act of
1960 made it clear that the Army was subject to operational
instructions issued by the prime minister and the Army
Council. The UPGA manifesto was deliberately misleading in
this respect.[11]

The emphasis on 'merit' in promotion and recruitment was
not the platitude that it appears to be. 'Merit' is most easily
measured by the possession of academic certificates and there
were far more Southerners with such paper qualifications than
Northerners (see table on p. 117). If the regions were broken up
into twenty-five states, as UPGA proposed, and 'merit' alone
was considered, Northern school-leavers feared that they would
lose the preferential treatment that they now enjoyed from the
Northern Regional Government over their more numerous
Southern competitors for jobs.

Such a manifesto appealed to the South, but it had few
attractions for Northerners. Yet the NCNC–AG alliance needed
to win at least thirty seats in the North to have any hope of a
parliamentary majority. There were only 145 seats in the South
compared to 167 in the North, and Chief Akintola's NNDP,
now a firm ally of the NPC, was bound to win a number of seats
in the West. However, in spite of these difficulties, the NCNC
leaders appeared to be full of confidence about the results of the
election.

The campaign was marked by a fair amount of thuggery by
'party stalwarts'. Conditions were so bad in Tiv Division that
the Army had to be sent in. But in most of the country it is

unlikely that this violence, which was not abnormal at election times, would have had much influence on the result. However, certain NPC officials in the North showed an excess of zeal when they forcibly prevented certain UPGA candidates in the far North from filing their nomination papers, and so secured the unopposed return of sixty-seven NPC candidates. None of these seats was likely to return UPGA members; all but one had been won by the NPC in 1959, and in that one case the sitting member had since crossed the carpet to join the NPC. But this irregularity gave the UPGA leaders an excuse to demand that the election should be postponed. When the Electoral Commission refused to do this the UPGA leaders called a boycott of the whole election. The news of this boycott was broadcast by radio and loudspeaker van throughout the South. In Lagos and some other towns mobs of thugs destroyed many of the polling booths. In the East electoral officers ignored the decision of the Electoral Commission that the election should continue in spite of the boycott, and failed to issue ballot papers, so no election took place there. But in the North, West and Mid-West the election took place as arranged, though most of the UPGA supporters in the West followed the instructions of their party leaders and stayed away from the polling booths. In the Mid-West the NCNC premier, Chief Osadebey, changed his mind halfway through polling day and ordered his supporters to vote. Thus at the close of voting, it was seen that there had been a normal election in the North and Mid-West (apart from the places where there had been unopposed returns) no voting in the East and most of Lagos (where thugs had destroyed the polling booths), and a partial boycott in the West which had allowed the NNDP to gain a majority of the Western Region seats. Not surprisingly, the NPC won all but five of the seats in the North, and so gained an overall majority in the new parliament, even without the help of its Southern ally, the NNDP.

Polling took place on 30 December, a Wednesday. By Friday morning, 1 January 1965, when results were in from almost all the seats, it was clear that the boycott had had the effect of turning an expected NPC victory into a landslide. Why, then, did the UPGA leaders perpetrate this lunacy? It appears from an examination of their statements and articles in the press that they believed, on a partisan interpretation of certain clauses in the constitution, that the general election was invalid (since they had persuaded three of the six members of the Electoral Commission to resign), and that therefore President Azikiwe was not obliged to recognize the results; and that he was entitled to assume 'executive powers', nominate a 'caretaker government' under a prime minister of his own choice (i.e. a member of UPGA) and hold a fresh election. The UPGA leaders naturally assumed that, with the machinery of government under UPGA control, they would be able to win. It seems that Dr Azikiwe accepted this point of view, since he prepared a broadcast for the evening of 1 January (which was not in fact delivered, but was afterwards published in the press) in which he claimed that the elections were unsatisfactory and declared that he had no intention of 'acting literally' on the results announced and reappointing Sir Abubakar as prime minister. Sir Abubakar then issued a reply in which he asserted that any complaints about the election should be settled in the law-courts, and not by 'some people who claim to be the sole judges of whether the elections are free and fair'; the election had been deliberately sabotaged by a Regional Government (i.e. the East).[12]

So far the disagreement between Dr Azikiwe and Sir Abubakar had been a difference of interpretation of the constitution. Why, then, did not the president act in accordance with the UPGA interpretation of the position, assume 'executive powers' and appoint his own prime minister? It seems that he had already been advised by a number of lawyers, including the Attorney-General, the Chief Justice of the Federal Supreme Court and the Chief Justice of Eastern Nigeria, that the president did not in fact possess such powers. So any attempt to

appoint a 'caretaker prime minister' would be immediately
challenged in the courts and be most unlikely to receive the
co-operation of the public service, particularly in the North.
This lack of legitimate authority would be fatal to any caretaker prime minister. So Dr Azikiwe decided on a much bolder
course; he summoned the heads of the Police, Army and Navy
to State House and announced that in view of the present
crisis he proposed to take control, and asked for their support
on the ground that he was both president and their commander-
in-chief.

The success or failure of Dr Azikiwe's attempted 'coup from
above' turned on two things: first, whether the heads of the
Army, Navy and Police would accept the president's view of
his powers; and secondly, whether their subordinate officers,
who were actually in command of troops and police would still
obey them, if they did side with Dr Azikiwe. In fact this attempt
to subvert the constitution from within was a failure. According
to the only account of this meeting which has been published,
Inspector-General Edet (Police), Commodore Wey (Navy) and
Major-General Welby-Everard (Army) all refused to recognize
the president's authority to command them. They had already
been in consultation with the prime minister and the Attorney-
General and were quite clear about the legal position.[13] So
the second question posed above did not arise. But it is interesting to speculate what Dr Azikiwe's chances would have
been, if the heads of the Armed Services had accepted his
authority.

The adhesion of the Navy could have had little practical
effect, except perhaps in Lagos, but the support of the Police
was vital. This had been recently shown in Ibadan in 1962 when
the Police, acting on the orders of Sir Abubakar, had prevented
the Western Region Assembly from voting on the question of
Akintola's right to continue to be premier. Almost three-
quarters of the Police were from the South and nearly half of
them were Ibos or Easterners and therefore likely to support

Dr Azikiwe (see table on p. 98). But three of the five regional police commissioners were Northerners (Kam Selem – North, Timothy Omo-Bare – Mid-West, Hamman Maiduguri – Lagos); the commissioner in the West was a Yoruba, Odofin Bello, who had recently been appointed to the post while Akintola was premier, and so was likely to be at least sympathetic to the NNDP point of view;[14] and the commissioner in the East was still an expatriate. So it is probable that the president's orders would never have been relayed to the rank and file of the Police Force.

As for the Army, it is extraordinary that Dr Azikiwe should ever have expected a British officer to co-operate in what was patently an attempt to involve the Army on one side in a political quarrel. But even if General Welby-Everard had been temporarily removed, there were enough Northerners or friends of the North in strategic positions to thwart such an attempt. In the North the brigade commander at Kaduna, Brigadier Ademulegun, had already shown his loyalty to the government at the time of the Action Group conspiracy and he was generally believed to be on close terms with the Sardauna. There were also two battalions in Kaduna; one was commanded by an Ibo, Lt.-Col. Ojukwu, but the other by a Northerner, Lt.-Col. Pam. Thus any attempt in the Northern capital by Ojukwu to support the president would most likely have been neutralized by the joint action of Ademulegun and Pam.[15] In the West the Regional Government was sure of the support of the battalion at Ibadan under the command of another Northerner, Lt.-Col. Largema. The only place where the president might possibly have been given Army support was in Lagos itself, where the brigade commander was Brigadier Aguiyi-Ironsi and the troops on Lagos Island were also commanded by an Ibo, Major Okafor of the Federal Guards. The nearest battalion to Lagos, 2 NA at Ikeja, was temporarily under the command of an officer from the Cameroons, Major Anagho.[16]

This listing of police and army commanders may seem rather

academic, but such calculations as these must have been made during the four days of the crisis, when the resolution of the confrontation between the president and the prime minister would depend on each side's estimate of its own strength and how far each of the protagonists was prepared to indulge in 'brinkmanship'. In fact the president's position was far weaker than has been set out above. General Welby-Everard was fully in control of the soldiers in Lagos and had sent round a circular to all officers setting out the constitutional position. So, when the heads of the Police, Army and Navy had refused to accept Dr Azikiwe's contention that the office of prime minister was vacant and continued to obey Sir Abubakar as the legal prime minister, it was then open to the NPC ministers to use the security forces to coerce the president. Plans for this eventuality were in fact made, but there was no need to put them into operation.[17] On 4 January Dr Azikiwe gave way and formally reappointed Sir Abubakar as prime minister. In his turn Sir Abubakar gave some vague verbal reassurances to enable the president to retreat from his exposed position with a few threads of dignity left.

Later, elections were held in the constituencies in the Eastern Region where no voting had taken place, and portfolios were once more found for the NCNC ministers in a renewed coalition government. This was an act of grace on the part of the NPC; they had an overall majority in the Federal House and did not need any Southern allies. The subordinate position of the NCNC was underlined by the inclusion in the government of an equal number of NNDP ministers, and by the complete exclusion of any representative of the Action Group, the NCNC's ally.

The resolution of the crisis was hailed by commentators as a triumph of conciliation and compromise. The reality was rather different. Faced with almost certain defeat in the elections the UPGA leaders had made a desperate gamble for power; they deliberately created a crisis by organizing a boycott of the

elections, and then used this boycott as an excuse to enable the
president to take over power on their behalf. But they grossly
over-estimated both the constitutional powers possessed by the
president, and also the support they could hope to receive from
those who actually controlled the instruments of coercion, the
Army and the Police. They also over-estimated, so it was said,
Dr Azikiwe's determination.[18] In the final result, the NCNC
found themselves in a much worse position than when they
started, and were forced to abandon their ally, the Action
Group, in order to maintain their membership of the coalition
government at the centre. But in the mythology of the average
Easterner blame was laid not on the foolhardiness of the
UPGA leadership but on the deceitfulness of the NPC who had
now won twice by trickery – first over the census and then over
the election.

The Possible Coup D'État, December 1964

After Lt.-Col. Gowon had taken over power in August 1966, the
Federal Government issued several pamphlets which alleged
that:

> As far back as December 1964 a small group of Army officers
> mainly from the Ibo ethnic group of the Eastern Region,
> dissatisfied with political development within the Federation,
> began to plot, in collaboration with some civilians, the over-
> throw of what was then the Government of the Federation
> of Nigeria and the eventual assumption of power in the
> country. . . .
>
> The 1964 Plan was designed to take place at Enugu during
> the shooting competition of the Army which is normally
> attended by all senior officers of the Army. The plan leaked,
> most senior officers kept away and the plan was temporarily
> abandoned.

(*Nigeria 1966*, 5 f.)

The publication then names exactly the same list of fourteen officers as those whom it subsequently accuses of complicity in the January 1966 coup.

There are certain difficulties in accepting this account. According to another Federal document:

> It is to the credit of the former civilian Federal Government that in the interest of peace, no Army officer or civilian was subsequently punished for the planned military coup of December 1964.
>
> (*Government Statement on the Current Nigerian Situation*, 2)

It is understandable that the Army should not wish to alarm the public and foreign observers by revealing such an attempted *coup d'état* at the time. But it is hardly likely that the conspirators would have been left in the strategic positions that they then occupied. This applies particularly to Major Okafor, who remained in command of Federal Guards on Lagos Island, and Major Ifeajuna, who was not removed from the post of brigade major of 2 Brigade. They could easily have been shifted elsewhere without exciting comment. Furthermore, it is somewhat surprising that exactly the same group of officers are alleged to have taken part in a plot centred on Enugu in December 1964, as took part in a plot in which action took place at Lagos, Kaduna and Ibadan – but not Enugu – in 1966.

A different version of this proposed military conspiracy has since been given by General Gowon.[19] He has told an interviewer that he was approached by Lt.-Col. Ojukwu and Lt.-Col. Banjo with a plan that these three colonels should take over the country. This proposal for a triumvirate to govern Nigeria, with one member from each region, does credit to the Army's commitment to the unity of Nigeria. But since General Gowon only revealed these details after Lt.-Col. Banjo had been executed in Biafra, exactly what Ojukwu and Banjo had in mind will probably never be known.[20]

L

The Promotion of General Aguiyi-Ironsi

Apart from the inclusion of the NCNC in his revived coalition government, Sir Abubakar seems to have decided that a further gesture was necessary to convince the Ibos that they would still enjoy their fair share of patronage from the Federal Government. An appointment had to be made in February 1965 of the Nigerian to succeed Major-General Welby-Everard as head of the Army. Four brigadiers were possible candidates for the post: Ironsi, Ademulegun, Ogundipe and Maimalari. Ironsi had been senior to Ademulegun up to 1962, when they had both been made brigadiers on the same day, but Ironsi had been employed as military adviser to the Nigerian High Commission in London since 1961 and with the UN Force in the Congo, and had only held a command position in the Nigerian Army for three months since his return from the Congo in 1961 (he was commander of 2 Brigade from November 1964 to February 1965). On the other hand Brigadier Ademulegun had commanded both 1 and 2 Brigades over the past two and a half years. Below these two were Brigadiers Maimalari and Ogundipe. Maimalari was the only Northerner of the four and had been the first Nigerian to pass out of Sandhurst. Ogundipe was the only one of the four to have served in action in the last war, in Burma, and was believed to be the officer recommended by the retiring British commander. Dr Mbadiwe of the NCNC described how Ironsi came to be chosen for the post in the course of his obituary tribute to Muhammadu Ribadu, the Minister of Defence:

> Ribadu had an unshakable belief in the unity of this country. Never before had the cause of Nigerian unity been so shaken as during that crisis. . . . Tribalism and separatism featured in their worst form. . . . Despite all the rumours, gossips, undercurrents and evil machinations, Ribadu came out in that heat to recommend to the prime minister the appoint-

ment of Aguiyi-Ironsi as the Officer Commanding the
Nigerian Army.

(*HR Deb*, 4 May 1965, col. 1923)

Thus the appointment of Ironsi was not only an acknowledg-
ment of his long-standing seniority in the Army; it was also a
political gesture of conciliation, a part of the package which had
resolved the 1964-1965 election crisis. The news was greeted
with exultant gratitude in the NCNC press, in practically the
first cheerful editorials these papers had carried since the
election.

Unfortunately this gesture was criticized by certain circles
in the North who believed that the NPC should have pressed
home its advantage in January 1965 and secured all the top
posts for the NPC and its ally, the NNDP, leaving the Ibos out
in the cold. A writer in the *Nigerian Citizen* (Zaria) commented:

Today I am weeping because the North has foregone all its
advantages brought to it by its natural position – majority
in population, expanse of land and majority in parliament.
. . . The head of the Police Force goes to Eastern Nigeria,
the Navy also goes East. Where is the Army now? Eastern
Nigeria has captured it too. . . . What has the Northern
Alliance gained from winning the election? Two UPGA men
who should not be ministers are there. Why? Dr Mbadiwe and
Chief Festus Okotie-Eboh are Sir Abubakar's personal
friends. The opinion of all élites in the country is that Sir
Abubakar should be recalled home to Bauchi if he cannot
carry out the great tasks devolving upon him.

(3 March 1965)

The spirit of reconciliation induced by Ironsi's appointment
lasted less than a month. At the beginning of March the
Council of the Federal University of Lagos decided not to
renew the appointment of Dr Njoku, an Ibo, as vice-chancellor
but to replace him by Dr Biobaku, a Yoruba. This decision

precipitated a crisis in the university which eventually led to the dismissal or resignation of all the expatriate and most of the Eastern members of the staff. The temper of the Ibos at this time can be judged from the following editorial published in a newspaper owned by the Eastern Regional Government:

> The immediate result of last December's election was a systematic and planned assault against Ibos holding public offices in the Republic. . . . We have always been prepared to give the Abubakar 'broadly based' government a fair trial, but are the present happenings in the country in the true spirit of President Azikiwe's broadcast of last January 4? . . . Anyone who fondly nurses the idea that Nigerian unity can only be sustained at the expense of the Ibos has got some more thinking to do. . . . It is to be hoped that no-one gets the stupid idea that the Ibos are going to stay like a punching bag for any group of mischievous but cowardly clots.
>
> (*Nigerian Outlook*, 4 March 1965)

The Western Regional Election, October 1965

The political parties were now all waiting for the Regional election in the West. The stakes were high for both sides. If the NNDP won, the AG would clearly collapse during five further years of opposition, and the NCNC would then be isolated in a Federation completely dominated by the North. If the AG defeated the NNDP all the three Southern Regions would then be held by parties opposed to the North; if they acted together they might be able to cause sufficient trouble to force a new Federal election.

The campaign was more violent than any previous one in Nigeria. The result was blatantly rigged to secure the victory of the NNDP. Electoral officers disappeared or refused to receive the nomination papers of opposition candidates and declared NNDP candidates elected unopposed; other officers had their appointments revoked after they accepted the nomination papers of opposition candidates; ballot papers were widely found in the hands of unauthorized persons on the election day; returning officers refused to declare the result of the poll after the count, enabling false returns to be broadcast from the regional capital, Ibadan; these and many other irregularities took place. The Chairman of the Electoral Commission subsequently resigned in protest and all these items are listed in his letter of resignation.[21] Even more lurid accounts can be found in the press. In several constituencies the AG candidate secured a certificate from the returning officer that he had won, but the victory of the NNDP candidate was later announced from Ibadan. The result of this so-called election gave 73 out of 94 seats to the NNDP.

After the first demonstrations against this result were over, the NNDP hoped that the AG leaders would accept the *fait accompli* and join a coalition government in the West under Chief Akintola. The votes in the constituency of the acting leader of the AG, Alhaji Adegbenro, were deliberately left uncounted to leave this possibility open. But instead of submitting, the supporters of the AG launched a campaign of riot, arson and murder against the NNDP government and their supporters which continued for two and a half months right up to the coup. Quite apart from the rigging of the election, cocoa farmers were also enraged by the cut in the guaranteed price for cocoa from £120 to £65, which was one of the government's first acts after the election.[22] Throughout the region houses were burnt, NNDP leaders were macheted and on several occasions the police were forced to open fire on mobs which refused to disperse. There were also attacks on council offices, court houses and similar buildings. One popular method was to fill flit guns, usually used for spraying cocoa trees, with petrol and drench the house or car before setting it alight.

As a result of this orgy of destruction there was an increasing number of conversions of local dignitaries to the support of the

AG. Even two recently elected NNDP members of the Regional
Assembly declared their change of allegiance 'at the request of
my constituents'. By the end of November and increasingly
in December the *West African Pilot* was daily reporting the
recantations of former NNDP customary court judges and
members of local management committees appointed by Akintola's government. Others fled from outlying areas to more
secure places of refuge in Lagos or Ibadan.

The leaders of the AG and NCNC wanted the Federal
Government to declare a state of emergency in the West, as had
been done with far less cause in 1962; an administrator or interim government could then be put in power in order to hold
fresh elections. Sir Abubakar did not accept these helpful
suggestions. He took refuge in the excuse that the Federal
prime minister had no power to intervene in a regional matter,
and that only parliament, and not the prime minister, could
declare a state of emergency. This was technically true; but
the NPC had the necessary parliamentary majority to do this,
if it wanted to, even over the objections of the NNDP. The real
point was that Sir Abubakar could not command this majority
against the wishes of the president of the party, the Sardauna.
And in December the Sardauna went off with a retinue of 124 to
perform the *hadj* to Mecca. Until he returned no decision could
be taken. Meanwhile, to distract public attention, Sir Abubakar
had arranged a Commonwealth Conference in Lagos for early
January 1966, to discuss the recent Rhodesian Unilateral
Declaration of Independence. Until this was over the government was inhibited from taking any extreme measures to
restore law and order in the West.

There was now a more sinister development in the con-
tinuing murder and mayhem in the West: the growth of
inter-tribal violence between the Yoruba and the Hausa. Most
Yoruba towns had a small community of Hausa merchants who
organized the trade in kola nuts, beef and other products
between the West and the North. There was also a seasonal

migration of Hausa labourers to the West to help with the cocoa harvest. These Northerners naturally supported the party of the Sardauna's ally, Chief Akintola, and their property suffered from the indiscriminate attacks on all followers of the NNDP. Drivers of large trucks which brought produce down from the North to Lagos found it necessary to assemble in convoy before crossing the Western Region border in order to avoid being individually waylaid and murdered on the road. Cars with Northern Region number-plates were liable to be stopped and burnt. These excesses against their fellow-Northerners caused some circles in the North to doubt the wisdom of the NPC policy of supporting the NNDP at all costs. On 10 January 1966, the *New Nigerian*, a newspaper owned by the Northern Regional Government, made this comment in an editorial entitled 'The North Cannot Sit Back':

> When Sir Ahmadu Bello returns from a pilgrimage to Mecca today, he will find many urgent problems awaiting him, and among them none will be more urgent than the situation in the West where killings and lootings have become a daily occurrence. . . . Facts must be faced . . . and the facts are that thousands of people in the West are convinced that the last elections there were not fairly conducted. They remain convinced that Chief Akintola has no right to be in power. . . . Force is having to be used to prevent the violence in the West from spreading. . . . In the North we cannot sit back doing nothing while *our kinsmen* are being killed in other parts of the Federation.

(italics added)[23]

It was not only Northerners who found themselves attacked on the road. By early January even on the main Lagos–Ibadan road, the busiest in the country, travellers, both Nigerian and expatriate, were being stopped by thugs demanding money on threat of damage to the car.[24] Thieves, ruffians and party thugs dissatisfied with their pay were eager to cash in on the situation.

The police were quite unable to guarantee safety on the roads, in view of the prevailing antipathy towards the government.

The Commonwealth Prime Ministers' Conference ended on the evening of Wednesday, 12 January. The same day the Federal parliament met for an extraordinary session. The following day the Sardauna and his entourage returned from Mecca. Sir Abubakar was clearly anxious for a peaceful solution. On the evening of 14 January he gave an interview, just six hours before he was kidnapped and assassinated:

Question: Do you envisage a political solution of the Western Region crisis?

Prime Minister: Yes, I do. I have tried to bring about a settlement and I have the solution at my fingertips – I could solve it in five minutes.

Question: Do you see the solution as taking the form of a coalition government in the West?

Prime Minister: Yes, it would have to be that. . . . The Action Group has accepted my mediation, but the NNDP has asked for more time. . . . If I used real force in the West – and make no mistake about it, I haven't yet – then I could bring the people to their knees. But I don't want to use force like that. Force can't bring peace to people's hearts.

Question: Would you consider the release of Chief Awolowo as part of a political solution of the West's troubles?

Prime Minister: I think that might be part of it; yes, obviously we would have to see.

(*West Africa*, 29 January 1966)

But the final decision was not in the prime minister's hands. Chief Akintola was inflexibly determined not to give way, and on the same day as Sir Abubakar gave his interview, Akintola flew to Kaduna for a conference with the Sardauna.[25] Something clearly had to be done to arrest the deteriorating situation in the West. The government had to act or abdicate.

IX · The Military Coups of 15 and 16 January

At the end of September 1965 detachments of troops from the battalions at Ibadan and Ikeja (4 NA and 2 NA) were posted out to a number of towns in the Western Region to stand by if needed over the election period. On polling day (11 October) they had to open fire in Mushin, a northern suburb of Lagos, and also in Ibadan, after the disputed results were announced. During the next months there were reports in the press of troops patrolling in troubled areas and particularly in the parts of the Western Region bordering on Lagos. But by about mid-November most soldiers had returned to their barracks. Demonstrations against Chief Akintola were becoming increasingly like a guerrilla struggle with UPGA supporters striking suddenly at night to commit arson and to murder prominent members of the NNDP. The Army was competent to deal with a large riot, but not with such 'hit and run' attacks which could only be handled effectively by the police on the spot. So it was usually the Police Mobile Force (riot squads) who opened fire when disturbances got out of control, as at Isho, where thirty demonstrators were killed on 7 November.[1]

Since the Army had not intervened in previous crises, such as the General Strike of June 1964 or the Federal election, the possibility of a military coup seemed remote in the first months of the Western Region disturbances. But when General Mobutu seized power in the Congo on 25 November 1965 and this was followed by General Soglo's coup in Dahomey on 29 November, the possibility of a similar event in Nigeria was openly discussed in the press for the first time. On 4 December the

Nigerian Outlook (published by the Eastern Region Government) said in an editorial:

> The Federal Government has neglected its duty. It is unable or unwilling to provide security for the people. The present chaos in the West could very easily spread, if not checked, to other parts of the Republic. . . . That is why I feel that the armed forces should now intervene in order to save our country from ruin.
>
> By this I do not mean that there should be a coup. All I am saying is that *the Federal Government should invite the armed forces to take over* in Lagos and Ibadan and restore law and order and public confidence, while at the same time organizing fresh elections in the West.
>
> (italics added)

There is also evidence that certain intellectuals were looking to the Army as the only means of bringing about political change in Nigeria. In May 1965 a lecturer in Law at Lagos University, Dr Ohonbamu, was prevented from delivering a lecture at the army barracks in Enugu. He subsequently published his views as a pamphlet after the coup; it advocated that the Army should be loyal to the government of the day only so long as that government was 'impartial, honest, progressive and incorrupt'.[2] At about the same time Chinua Achebe was completing his novel *Man of the People* (published in January 1966), which describes the last days of a corrupt West African government and ends with the military taking over to cleanse the country.

The military interventions in Congo and Dahomey were followed by the coups of Colonel Bokassa in the Central African Republic on 1 January 1966 and of Colonel Lamizana in Upper Volta on 4 January 1966. But the NPC government in Lagos could feel reasonably confident that nothing similar would happen in Nigeria. General Ironsi at the head of the Army was an Ibo, and therefore likely to be sympathetic to UPGA, but

he was surrounded at Army headquarters by Northerners or
officers reputed to be sympathetic to the NPC. The exact dis-
position of the senior commands on the evening of Friday 14
January was as follows:[3]

Army Headquarters, Lagos

Chief of staff	Col. Kur Muhammed	(North)
i/c 'G' Branch	Lt.-Col. Ejoor	(Mid-West)
i/c 'A' Branch	Lt.-Col. Pam	(North)
i/c 'Q' Branch	Lt.-Col. Unegbe	(Ibo, East)
Federal Guards (Lagos Island)	Major Okafor	(Ibo, East)

2 Brigade, Southern Nigeria

Brigade Commander	Brig. Maimalari	(North)
2 NA Ikeja	Major Igboba	(Ibo, Mid-West)
4 NA Ibadan	Lt.-Col. Largema	(North)
Abeokuta Garrison	Lt.-Col. Fajuyi	(Yoruba, West)
1 NA Enugu	Major Ogunewe	(Ibo, East)

1 Brigade, Northern Nigeria

Brigade Commander	Brig. Ademulegun	(Yoruba, West)
3 NA Kaduna	Lt.-Col. Kurobo	(Ijaw, East)
Commandant, Defence Academy, Kaduna	Brig. Varma	(Indian Mission)
Deputy Commandant	Col. Shodeinde	(Yoruba, West)
Regimental Depot, Zaria	Lt.-Col. Bassey	(Efik, East)
5 NA Kano	Lt.-Col. Ojukwu	(Ibo, East)

It is clear from this list that most of the key positions below
Ironsi were held by Northerners. The only other senior Ibo
officer at Army Headquarters, Lt.-Col. Unegbe, was loyal to the
government, as was shown by his death at the hands of the
conspirators. He had just been promoted substantive lieutenant-
colonel over the head of Lt.-Col. Kurobo. Both brigade commands were in safe hands. There were two battalions in the
troubled area of the West; 4 NA at Ibadan was already com-

manded by a Northerner, and 2 NA at Ikeja was just about to be. The retiring commander, Lt.-Col. Njoku, had already been 'dined out' of the battalion and his second-in-command, Major Igboba, was temporarily in charge awaiting the arrival of the commander designate, Lt.-Col. Gowon. On the night of the coup Gowon had just returned from a visit to Pakistan and had not yet reported for duty; this probably saved his life.

Unlike Ghana where a detailed account of the military coup was published shortly afterwards by one of the leading conspirators, the Nigerian public was given no authoritative account of the events of 14–17 January 1966 at the time. Until it was clear that General Ironsi had taken over the government the Nigerian newspapers said as little as possible, awaiting the outcome; and once he had been installed as Supreme Military Commander there were no further references to the events which had brought him to power.

But after the counter-coup of July 1966 both the Federal Government and the Eastern Region Government (later Biafra) issued a series of propaganda documents on the events of 1966, and these were supplemented by less restrained private pamphleteering. According to Federal and Northern sources, the coup of 15 January was part of a long-laid Ibo plot to dominate the country, to which General Ironsi was privy. According to Eastern (Biafran) sources Major Nzeogwu and his fellow-conspirators only acted to cleanse the country from corruption and to forestall an imminent usurpation of power by the Sardauna, who intended to take personal control in Lagos and elevate Sir Abubakar to the dignified but powerless office of president.[4] The evidence of the activities of the Sardauna will be examined first.

The Sardauna's Alleged Plot

This story first appears in a series of articles by *The Guardian*'s commonwealth correspondent, who was in Lagos at the time of the coup. According to this account the Sardauna was planning an immediate take-over in Lagos in the same way that the communists took over Prague in 1948. He intended to make himself prime minister and to elevate Sir Abubakar to the presidency.[5]

No evidence is adduced for this account; perhaps none could be. But the allegation presents several difficulties. The Sardauna disliked Lagos and rarely visited it; when Sir Abubakar wished to confer with him, he had to go to Kaduna. Sir Abubakar was certainly thinking of resigning from the prime ministership.[6] But Dr Azikiwe showed no inclination to step down from the presidency. The constitutional procedure for removing a president was extremely complex; and though the NPC could probably have mustered enough votes to carry it through, it would have taken several weeks. Similarly, it would have taken at least three weeks, if not more, to arrange a by-election so that the Sardauna could enter the Federal parliament, as was necessary before he could be Federal prime minister.[7]

The alternative is that the Sardauna was proposing to disregard the constitution and set himself up as a sort of dictator without any delay. This is not credible. The NPC had achieved its victory in the 1964–1965 election crisis by scrupulous adherence to the letter of the constitution, and by so doing had been able to thwart President Azikiwe. Provided that the constitution remained substantially unchanged the power of the North in the Federation was unshakable. Why should the Northern leaders put themselves irretrievably in the wrong when they could get all they wanted with the constitution as it was? There is no evidence that Sir Abubakar, whom the Sardauna had once described as 'his lieutenant in Lagos', had ever gone against his wishes in any important matter. The story of the 'Sardauna's plot' seems to be on a par with other rationales produced by successful conspirators. The Greek generals in 1967 acted 'to prevent a communist takeover'; and the Russians invaded Czechoslovakia 'to suppress counter-revolutionary forces'.

But though there is no evidence so far produced that the Sardauna was contemplating any unconstitutional move himself, there are some indications that he was intending sterner measures to deal with the situation in the Western Region. He returned from Mecca on 13 January, and on the 14th he held a meeting at Kaduna attended by Brig. Ademulegun, Lt.-Col. Largema and Chief Akintola. According to one account, 'the decision was taken to go ahead with a ruthless blitz on opposition activities in the West, using the Army'.[8] This had been the decision of the NPC leaders in 1964 when faced with similar trouble in Tiv Division, and the remedy had proved reasonably successful. Lt.-Col. Largema, who had come from Ibadan, would be able to give the meeting an up-to-date military appreciation of the situation. Brigadier Ademulegun may have been present at the meeting merely to advise on the affairs of his home region; or his presence may indicate that plans were being made to send Ironsi on leave and put Ademulegun, who was the next senior officer, in charge of the Army. This possibility had been rumoured for some time.[9]

Whether this was to take place or not, the planning of any repressive operations in the West would be entirely under Northern control, since the Army chief of staff, the brigade commander and the two battalion commanders in the West would all be Northerners (Col. Kur Muhammed, Brig. Maimalari, Lt.-Col. Largema and Lt.-Col. Gowon).

If this reconstruction of the Sardauna's plan and the decisions of the Kaduna meeting is correct, he may have been *politically unwise* to act in this way, by force rather than by conciliation, in the Western Region. But there was nothing *unconstitutional* about it. In a sense, the constitutional basis of the government in the West had been breached already by the flagrant rigging of the October elections there, but there was nothing unconstitutional about deploying the Army to

maintain law and order. The Sardauna officially had no authority to take decisions on the dispositions of the Army, but
in fact he knew the Federal Government would carry out his
wishes, whether he was prime minister in Lagos or not. Once
the decision to back Chief Akintola had been taken, swift
action was essential to prevent any further erosion of NNDP
support under threats of arson and murder. No government, of
whatever complexion, could ignore the deteriorating internal
security situation in the Western Region without completely
abdicating from its responsibilities to maintain law and order.

Major Nzeogwu's Coup

Whatever plans the Sardauna may have made, they were
anticipated by the action of the conspirators. Major Nzeogwu,
an Ibo from the Mid-West who had been born in Kaduna, was
an instructor at the Military Academy, Kaduna. On the night
of 14–15 January he took some soldiers out on a 'training
exercise'. When they reached the vicinity of the Sardauna's
house, they found they had been issued with live ammunition
and were told the full details of the plan. The soldiers then
accepted their role, the residence of the Sardauna was stormed
and he and his wife were murdered. Later, Brig. Ademulegun
and Col. Shodeinde were also killed. The governor of the
Northern Region and a number of Northern ministers were
arrested. On Saturday Major Nzeogwu broadcast over Kaduna
radio, proclaiming martial law, 'in the name of the Supreme
Council of the Nigerian Armed Forces'. He then issued ten
proclamations, making 'looting, arson, homosexuality, rape,
embezzlement, bribery, corruption or obstruction of the revolution, sabotage, subversion, false alarm and assistance to
foreign invaders' punishable by the death penalty. Major
Nzeogwu was clearly in control of the situation. On Sunday he
appointed a government of civil servants in place of the deposed
Northern ministers.[10]

After the deaths of Ademulegun and Shodeinde, the senior officer in Kaduna was officially Lt.-Col. Kurobo, but he seems to have accepted Major Nzeogwu's authority. Lt.-Col. Bassey at the Training Depot at Zaria was uncertain what to do and eventually disappeared for a few days. Similarly Lt.-Col. Ojukwu at Kano seems to have awaited the outcome of events; in Lagos at the time a government spokesman claimed that his battalion was 'loyal' to the government.[11]

The success of the conspirators in the North was not repeated elsewhere. At about the same time as they struck there, soldiers from the Armoured Car Squadron arrived in Lagos to join up with other groups led by Major Okafor of Federal Guards, Lagos Island, and by Major Ifeajuna from 2 Brigade HQ, Apapa. These bands succeeded in killing Brig. Maimalari, Col. Kur Muhammed, Lt.-Col. Pam, Lt.-Col. Largema and Lt.-Col. Unegbe.[12] They also kidnapped the prime minister and the minister of finance, Chief Festus Okotie-Eboh, and later murdered them. Some public buildings in Lagos were temporarily occupied by the rebels and a broadcast was made announcing that the military had taken over. But this success was short-lived. According to Major Nzeogwu, General Ironsi was one of the 'bigwigs' and 'compromisers' whom the conspirators had decided to kill.[13] Ironsi managed to escape the men sent to assassinate him in his house on Lagos Island and slipped out through north Lagos to the battalion at Ikeja. Until the arrival of Lt.-Col. Gowon this battalion was temporarily under the command of the second-in-command, Major Igboba. Lt.-Col. Njoku, the retiring commander, was still in his house near by. Both these officers were Ibos who had been with Ironsi at Bukavu in the Congo.[14] With their aid, and that of the senior (Northern) warrant officers, Ironsi rallied the battalion to his support. Troops from Ikeja were moved into Lagos and took over control of the capital from the conspirators.

Meanwhile Chief Akintola had been assassinated in Ibadan by another group of conspirators. But they did not get control of the town, and their only other achievement was a temporary interruption to the electricity supply. No action took place in the Mid-West capital, Benin, as there were no troops there. Nor did anything happen in Enugu; possibly any conspirators there were inhibited by the presence of Archbishop Makarios, who was staying with the governor after the Commonwealth Prime Ministers' Conference.

General Ironsi's Coup

The situation in the Northern Region on the morning of Saturday 15 January was that the main army units (one infantry battalion and the Recce Squadron) were under the control of Major Nzeogwu at Kaduna, while the training depot at Zaria only contained a few regular troops and could not have resisted any move against it from Kaduna. The loyalty of the other battalion in the North, at Kano, was doubtful, but it was 150 miles away. There were reports that Nzeogwu was proposing to march on the South with the troops under his control to complete the task which had been bungled by his fellow-conspirators in Lagos.[15]

In the South, as a result of the murders that had been committed, the three battalions were under the control of Ibo officers:

2 NA Ikeja   Lt.-Col. Njoku and Major Igboba.
4 NA Ibadan   Major Nzefili (2 i/c to Lt.-Col. Largema).
1 NA Enugu   Major Ogunewe (Lt.-Col. Ejoor was sent by
              Ironsi to take over command of this
              battalion on Saturday).

Northern officers had also been eliminated from 2 Brigade at Apapa and Army Headquarters.

According to the communiqué broadcast by the Nigerian Broadcasting Service on Saturday afternoon, 'The General Officer Commanding the Nigerian Army and the vast majority

M

of the Army remain loyal to the Federal Government, and are taking all effective measures to bring the situation under control.' But the question was, what constituted the Federal Government? The Minister of Defence, Inuwa Wada, was away in Europe for medical treatment, and the Defence portfolio was temporarily held by Chief Festus Okotie-Eboh, who had been kidnapped. According to the Army Act the operational use of the Army was vested in the army commander, but the prime minister was entitled to give directions to him with respect to the operational use of the Army in Nigeria for the purpose of maintaining and securing public safety and public order. But there was no prime minister to give Ironsi any such directions. The NPC cabinet members recommended to the acting president that Zanna Dipcharima, the senior-ranking NPC minister, should be appointed acting prime minister until the whereabouts and fate of Sir Abubakar had been established.[16] At this moment Dr Azikiwe was having medical treatment in England and the acting president was another Ibo, Dr Orizu. Dr Orizu refused this request. The situation was thus very like that in January 1965 when President Azikiwe had refused to reappoint Sir Abubakar as prime minister. But there was a crucial difference: the head of the Army was now General Ironsi, an Ibo and not an expatriate, and the main army commands were now in Ibo hands.

From the point of view of the NPC and their Western ally, the NNDP, the situation could hardly be worse. In the North the NPC ministers were in the hands of Major Nzeogwu, a self-proclaimed murderer, and the Regional Government was clearly under his control. In Ibadan there was no government at all after the murder of Chief Akintola; many ministers had fled to Dahomey and mobs were happily engaged in burning the houses of NNDP supporters while the police looked on, uncertain whom to obey. It was only in Lagos that the NPC government still retained some semblance of control, and that was only by leave of General Ironsi. He was clearly the only

man whose orders stood a chance of being obeyed over the
whole country, and if he had chosen to complete the unfinished
plans of the conspirators and turn out the rump of the cabinet
by military force, there would have been nothing to stand in his
way.

The only recourse left to the NPC leadership to regain control of the situation was to ask for the help of British troops.
The British High Commissioner was certainly consulted by the
NPC. Naturally the British denied that any request for military
assistance had been made.[17] If it was, it was refused. Quite
apart from the military difficulties, there was no one competent
to make the request, as a result of Dr Orizu's refusal to appoint
an acting prime minister. Every intervention in Africa by a
former colonial power since the Belgian reoccupation of the
Congo in 1960 has been validated by a request from the African
prime minister. When there was a *coup d'état* in Gabon in 1964,
and the prime minister was held by the rebels, the French
took the precaution of securing an 'invitation' from the vice-
president. Probably one reason for the murder of Sir Abubakar
was to prevent any possibility of such a request being made.[18]

Once the question of foreign intervention was ruled out,
there was very little that the cabinet could do except hand over
to General Ironsi with the best grace that they could muster.
The cabinet met on Sunday and General Ironsi gave a survey
of the position. He insisted that power must be handed over to
him in order to save the situation and the ministers had
perforce to agree.[19] Dr Orizu announced the decision in a
broadcast to the nation late on Sunday night, 16 January. As
far as is known, power was handed over to Ironsi to use at his
unfettered discretion. According to Dr Orizu's broadcast, the
decision of the cabinet was 'unanimous and voluntary'. There
was no provision in the constitution for such a hand-over to the
Army; but no one worried about such a technicality.

General Ironsi's first task was to secure the surrender of
Major Nzeogwu to his authority. On Monday morning (17

January) Major Nzeogwu announced that he was offering his sword and command to the new supreme commander. But he made it clear that this had been done only when General Ironsi had agreed by telephone to five conditions which he had proposed. These were: safety for himself and the other conspirators; freedom from legal proceedings; release of those officers arrested in the Western Region; compensation for the families of the officers and men killed in the revolt; and assurance that 'those whom we fought to remove would not be returned to office'.[20] Although Major Nzeogwu claimed that these conditions had been accepted by General Ironsi this was never stated by the General; nor was it ever denied. Ironsi could hardly admit that he had bargained with a self-confessed rebel. But, whatever he may have promised Nzeogwu, not all the conditions were fulfilled. The conspirators in the South who had been arrested were not released. Major Nzeogwu came from Kaduna to Lagos under safe-conduct, brought by a fellow-Mid-Western Ibo Officer, Lt.-Col. Nwawo. He seems to have been left free for a few days in Lagos, and was then arrested, and remained in custody in the East until 1967.

Nzeogwu's surrender to Ironsi, whom he had originally marked down for death, is a little surprising. But he had only one battalion of troops and the Kaduna Recce Squadron under his control, and he could not be certain of their loyalty if it came to actual fighting. As he said in 1967 after he was released:

I was being sensible. The last thing we desired was unnecessary waste of life. If I had stuck to my guns there would have been civil war, and as the official head of the Army, he would have split the loyalty of my men. Again, you must remember that the British and other foreigners were standing by to help him. Our purpose was to change our country and make it a place we could be proud to call our home, not to wage war.

(*Africa and the World*, May 1967)

Once Major Nzeogwu had surrendered the first phase of the military take-over was complete. It is now necessary to try to identify the conspirators and to discern their motives.

Who Were the Conspirators?

According to a pamphlet issued by the Eastern Region (Biafran) Government, thirty-two officers and more than a hundred other ranks were imprisoned by Ironsi's government for their part in the conspiracy. There is no reason to doubt the Biafran assertion that the NCOs and privates who were arrested included men from all the main tribes. Major Nzeogwu himself claimed that most of the infantrymen who took part in the assault on the Sardauna's residence in Kaduna were Northerners.[21] But these troops knew nothing of the purpose of the 'night exercise' on which they had set out until they were actually ordered to open fire; it would have been amazing if they had questioned their orders at such a crisis after being trained to instant obedience since entering the Army. So the composition of the rank and file proves nothing about the origins of the conspiracy. To discover that we must seek information about the thirty-two officers involved.

Thirty-one of the thirty-two officers arrested are named by the Eastern Region pamphlet, *January 15 – Before and After*. The Federal Government document, *Nigeria 1966*, lists fourteen officers whom it claims were in charge of the operations at Kaduna, Ibadan and Lagos. Thirteen of these names agree with those given by the East, and the last name – Major Ademoyega – supplies the only name missing from the Eastern list.

Five of the thirty-two officers (16 per cent) have Yoruba names, and even the Federal List has two Yoruba among the fourteen conspirators which it names (14 per cent). This alone shows that the conspiracy was not an all-Ibo affair, as Federal

TRAINING AND REGIONAL/TRIBAL ORIGIN OF
OFFICERS DETAINED FOR ALLEGED COMPLICITY
IN THE COUP.

A. Federal List (all with regular combatant commissions at date of coup)

Maj. Nzeogwu	Ibo/Mid-West	Sandhurst	1959
Maj. Ifeajuna	Ibo/Mid-West	*Mons	1961
Maj. D. O. Okafor	Ibo	Mons	1959
Maj. Anuforo	Ibo/East	Sandhurst	1961
Maj. Chukuka	Ibo	Sandhurst	1960
Maj. Ademoyega[1]	Yoruba	*Mons	1962
Maj. Onwuatuegwu	Ibo	Sandhurst	1961
Capt. Gbulie	Ibo/East	Sandhurst	1962
Capt. Nwobosi	Ibo	Sandhurst	1963
Capt. Oji	Ibo	Mons	1961
Lt. Oyewole	Yoruba	Mons	1962
2/Lt. Azubuogor	Ibo	?	1965
2/Lt. Nwokocha	Ibo	Mons	1963
2/Lt. Ojukwu[2]	Ibo/Mid-West	Canada	1963

B. Additional Names on Eastern List only

(i) with regular combatant commissions at date of coup

Lt.-Col. Banjo	Yoruba/West	*Sandhurst	1956
Capt. Udeaja	Ibo/East	Sandhurst	1960
Capt. Ude	Ibo	Mons	1962
Lt. Adeleke[3]	Yoruba	U.S.A.	1963
Lt. Ezedigbo	Ibo	India	1964
2/Lt. Onyefuru	Ibo	India	1964
2/Lt. Igweze	Ibo	Mons	1963
2/Lt. Egbibor	? East	India	1964
2/Lt. Olafimihan	Yoruba	India	1964
2/Lt. Ngwuluka	Ibo	U.S.A.	1964
2/Lt. Nweke	Ibo	?	1964
2/Lt. Ikejiofor	Ibo/East	Australia	1963

(ii) five officers with direct short service commissions

Maj. Aghaya	Ibo	*NA Mech. and Elect. Engineers
Lt. Okafor	Ibo	*NA Engineers
Lt. Okaka	Ibo	*NA Ordnance
Lt. Anyafulu	Ibo	* ?
Lt. Okocha	Ibo	* ?

(iii) one Nigerian Air Force officer

Lt. Amuchinwa.

Notes: * denotes an officer with a degree or professional qualification.

1. Major Ademoyega is the only officer on the Federal List who is not also
   named by the East; this seems to be because he was not imprisoned in
   East Nigeria.

2. This officer is from the Mid-West and is not related to Lt.-Col. Ojukwu.

3. See note 24, p. 262, for a possible muddle over this officer.

propagandists have claimed. However, this list also gives no support to the Biafran assertion that the conspiracy was an all-Nigeria affair.[22] There are no obviously Northern names on the list. The only connection with the North seems to be that Major Nzeogwu himself was born at Kaduna in the North, and this may also be true of one of the Ibo subalterns.[23] Apart from the five Yorubas all the other names seem to be Ibo or Eastern (see table opposite).

This is hardly surprising. As has already been shown, three-quarters of the Majors and Lt.-Cols. were Easterners (see table on p. 123). Any conspiracy that was to have a hope of success was bound to include some of the officers at this level. Furthermore, almost all the Easterners were united in support of the NCNC against the NPC-dominated government; but the Yoruba were divided between those who supported Chief Akintola's NNDP with its pro-Northern policy, and the AG followers of Chief Awolowo. It would only be common prudence to exclude any Yoruba officer from the initial stages of the conspiracy, for fear that he might reveal the plot or be acting as an *agent provocateur*.

Only one of the thirty-two officers arrested had served a long period in the ranks before commissioning.[24] This was Major D. O. Okafor, the commander of the Federal Guards, who joined the Army in 1951 and was commissioned in 1959 after a short course at Mons OCS. He commanded the only troops on Lagos island and his participation was essential to the plot. A contrast can be drawn between officers such as Okafor, who had come up through the ranks and had been given 'short service' or 'executive' commissions after spending many years in the somewhat restricted life of a regular army NCO, and those officers who had completed a normal secondary school or university course with their civilian contemporaries and who began officer training immediately they entered the Army. All the remaining thirty-one belonged to this group, and it is reasonable to assume that many of them would share the enthusiasm for radical changes in society that was common among Nigerian students in the South.

Among the senior officers arrested, officers with degrees and officers who had spent at least two years in England at Sandhurst were prominent. Of the fourteen captains and officers of higher rank, eight had been to Sandhurst. Although there were only six graduates in the Army who held combatant commissions, three of these were accused of taking part in the plot (Lt.-Col. Banjo, Major Ifeajuna and Major Ademoyega).

Major Nzeogwu said that five majors were the original nucleus of the conspiracy, though he did not name them. From his own account, it appears that one was Major Onwuatuegwu, who worked with him in Kaduna, and that another was Major Ifeajuna, the brigade major at the headquarters of the southern brigade at Apapa, near Lagos. Like Nzeogwu, Ifeajuna was an Ibo from the Mid-West.[25] The fourth major was probably Major Anuforo, who commanded the Recce Squadron at Abeokuta. He was in the same company as Nzeogwu at Sandhurst, Normandy Company. The fifth was probably one of the three Majors Chukuka, Okafor and Ademoyega – probably the first-named, who was at Sandhurst with Anuforo and Onwuatuegwu.[26]

Nzeogwu claimed that he was the originator of the conspiracy and that no more senior officers were involved. As against this, Federal spokesmen since 1966 have claimed or implied that Ironsi was privy to the conspiracy from the beginning. Although Ironsi was certainly quick to take advantage of the vacuum created by the partial success of Nzeogwu's plans, it seems unlikely that this was the original intention of the plotters. According to Nzeogwu's own account, Ironsi was one of the 'compromisers' who were marked down for death and he only escaped because the conspirators were not ruthless enough (see p. 262, note 13). Nzeogwu never troubled to conceal his low opinion of Ironsi's competence, even at a time when Eastern propagandists were trying to build him up as a man of heroic stature. In his final interview in May 1967 he said of Ironsi, 'He joined the Army as a tally clerk and was a clerk most of the time.'[27]

The only direct piece of evidence linking Ironsi with the original conspiracy is the account of Ironsi's last moments of life current among Northern soldiers of the Ibadan battalion, 4 NA, some of whom were responsible for his murder in July 1966; according to this story, he confessed his guilt before they executed him.[28] But this statement is of doubtful value: the soldiers would naturally wish to exculpate themselves from the guilt of killing their commander-in-chief.

To set against this, there is Ironsi's own behaviour after he had taken over power. He seemed to be in genuine fear for his life. During the first hundred days of his regime he never appeared in public, and left State House every night to sleep on a ship of the Nigerian Navy on Lagos lagoon. His A.D.C. was a Northerner, Lt. Bello, and the troops guarding State House were also Northerners.[29] He seems to have been more afraid that some sympathizer with Major Nzeogwu might try to complete the unfinished task of 15 January, especially after he had put Nzeogwu and his followers in prison, in spite of his promise to him, than of any Northern plot against him.

It is just possible that Ironsi might have been warned by one of the Ibo conspirators at the last moment, so that he might be able to escape assassination. But, as far as present evidence goes, it seems unlikely that he knew more of the conspiracy than this.

Were any politicians involved in the conspiracy? According to the first Federal document: 'The army officers plotting to seize power were assisted by some prominent civilians, including politicians' and the theme is repeated in subsequent Federal and Northern publications.[30] General Ironsi's road to power was certainly made easier by the action of Dr Orizu, the acting president, in refusing to appoint Zanna Dipcharima as acting prime minister after Sir Abubakar had disappeared.

Dr Azikiwe tried to climb on to the band-wagon as soon as the news of the coup was announced. He was then convalescing in England, and immediately told the press that he was ready to fly home as soon as possible to help restore peace – an offer that was not accepted.[31]

But the fact that the results of the coup *coincided* with the aims of UPGA politicians does not mean that they *collaborated* in the plotting of the coup. The eagerness of Dr Azikiwe to take advantage of the military intervention and the opportunistic way in which Dr Orizu turned the events of the night 14–15 January to Ironsi's advantage does not mean that they necessarily had any *foreknowledge* of these events.

Most army officers had little respect for politicians, and this sentiment was particularly prominent in both Ironsi and Nzeogwu. When Nzeogwu was in power in Kaduna he had appointed a cabinet of civil servants and he introduced them to the press with the remark, 'We have got experts to do the job now, and not profiteers.'[32] One of the conditions he made with Ironsi when he surrendered was that 'the people that we fought to remove will not be returned to office'. Similarly, when Ironsi was supreme commander, he never considered setting up any political advisory body, even after the disastrous riots of May 1966. When the need for some sounding board of public opinion was patent, he preferred to set up a nation-wide conference of chiefs and natural rulers rather than consult with the politicians of the former civilian regime.

As far as Dr Azikiwe was concerned, he was considerably discredited in radical circles as a result of his failure of nerve during the Federal election crisis, and he had avoided all public engagements in the East thereafter. Lt.-Col. Ojukwu, who might be thought the nearest in sympathy to the radical aims of the conspirators of all the regional military governors, deliberately snubbed Dr Azikiwe by removing him from the chancellorship of the University of Nsukka, which he had founded, and by ordering the students to leave the hostels that were rented from him.[33] This was despite his father's long-standing business connections with Dr Azikiwe.

Personal Motivations of the Plotters

Was the coup carried out by officers who were aggrieved over promotion or because they felt that their pay was too low? The pay of officers had remained unimproved for six years. But officers received yearly increments and most had recently achieved rapid promotion. There can have been little real dissatisfaction in the Army as a whole over pay, since the regime of General Ironsi did not increase the pay of officers or other ranks, though this is the normal sequel to the installation of a military regime. Ironsi could easily have effected this by a stroke of the pen, without any great outcry, in the first months of the new regime.

It is certainly possible for a coup to be carried out purely for motives of personal self-advancement. There is the evidence given by Lt. Arthur at his court-martial in Ghana for the failed coup, 'Operation Guitar Boy', that he felt that there were too many senior officers, some of them young, who were preventing the promotion of others.[34] But it has already been shown that there were few, if any, grounds for the claim that Ibos were subject to discrimination in army promotions. As regards the majors involved in the coup, four had been promoted sub-stantive majors and three had not. These three had no reason-able ground for complaint, since their contemporaries had also not yet received promotion. None of the officers involved in the coup had been superseded in the army list by an officer who was formerly his junior. A particularly interesting case is that of Majors Anuforo and Onwuatuegwu. Both these officers had been commissioned from Sandhurst at the same time as Northern officers Bissalla, Haruna, Shuwa Muhammed and Muhammed Murtala. But at the time of the coup, only Major Anuforo had achieved promotion to substantive major, while

the others were all still temporary majors, substantive captains
(see table on p. 122). So Major Anuforo, though an Ibo, had
been promoted above four Northerners.

In any case, it is unnecessary to postulate the motive of self-
advancement in order to explain why the seven senior officers
were murdered on the night of 14-15 January. The seven
officers murdered (four Northern, two Yoruba and one Ibo)
seem to have been killed as a necessary part of the plot, in
order to remove hostile holders of command positions, or to
eliminate officers who might have served as rallying points for
any army reaction against the conspirators. The action was
bloody and treacherous, but, given the aims and dangers of the
enterprise, it is hard to see how such deaths could have been
avoided.[35]

Thus it would seem that the plotters had no reason to be
disappointed on pecuniary grounds, nor is there any evidence
that they were, up to the time of the coup, frustrated in their
careers.

But even if the plotters had no justifiable complaints about
their treatment in the past, they did have grounds for appre-
hension about the future. At this time many Ibos had become
convinced that they were the victims of a systematic campaign
to remove them from prominent posts in the civil service and
public corporations. In April 1965 Dr Njoku had not been
reappointed to the vice-chancellorship of Lagos University,
despite the recommendation of the university senate in his
favour. Later, Dr Ikejiani was removed from the chairmanship
of the Nigerian Railways; and in January 1966 it was learnt
that Francis Nwokedi was resigning his post of permanent
secretary to the Ministry of External Affairs, to take up a
position with an oil company. The *West African Pilot*, 10
January, commented on this: 'Nwokedi is only the most important first member of his kin to be shanghaied out of the
service by perfectly legal means. More will follow. . . .' On the
very day before the coup an NCNC member of the House of

Representatives, Professor Kalu Ezera, interjected a supplementary question:

Ezera: Could the minister clarify the rumours that certain police officers from a particular region are being contemplated to be eliminated because of their numerical strength?

Minister: This supplementary is irrelevant.

(*HR Deb*, 13 January 1966, col. 2870)

In the particular case of the Army, Eastern officers were well aware that places would have to be found for about fifty new officers when the first entrants to the Nigerian Military Academy had completed their three-year course of training and were commissioned at the end of 1966. Since the Army was not to be expanded, room could only be found for them by thinning out officers in the higher ranks. There were fears that this would give the NPC Minister of Defence the opportunity he needed to adjust the regional balance in the senior ranks of the officer corps, just as the quota system of officer cadet entry had already altered it among the subalterns. It is possible that fears about such an abrupt end to their careers may have nerved some of the conspirators to action.

Ideological Motivations of the Plotters

A fine selection of ideological inspirations have been suggested. Let us begin with the ludicrous and work towards the more credible. The CIA is often given the credit for secret machinations all over the globe. But it seems incredible that they could have been behind a plot to remove such a firm supporter of the Western Powers as Sir Abubakar. Nigerian foreign policy had taken an independent line on several matters, but it was likely to be more inclined to the American point of view than that of any alternative radical Southern-dominated regime.[36]

Another humorous suggestion is that the whole affair was

another 'Popish Plot'. The Roman Catholic Church has a strong following among the Ibo, and several of the assassins, including Major Nzeogwu, were Catholics. He is said to have been a very pious church-goer, attending Mass every day. It is a further curious consequence of the coup that under the Ironsi regime four of the five military governors were Roman Catholics: Ironsi himself, Fajuyi (West), Ejoor (Mid-West) and Ojukwu (East). But it would seem that this is merely the result of an unlikely series of coincidences, in spite of the fact that, statistically speaking, the chance of a random sample of officers producing so many Roman Catholics would be very low.[37]

Some observers whose main interest is in the Middle East have described the whole coup as a 'Jewish–Zionist plot', since it eliminated the Sardauna and other Muslim leaders. The Sardauna had always been a militant supporter of Islam and had achieved the 'conversion' of 350,000 Nigerians to the true faith of the Prophet on his last tour of the North before his death.[38] He was reputed as saying that for him 'Israel does not exist', and on another occasion he was said to have favoured the membership of Nigeria in some Islamic alliance. However, such a suggestion of a Jewish conspiracy seems a little far-fetched. The Nigerian Army had no links with Israel for training or equipment and it is difficult to imagine Nigerians risking their lives for the sake of the borders of the Middle East.

A more likely possibility is the influence of Ghana. The attitude of many radical nationalists in Nigeria to Ghana was ambivalent. The pretensions of Dr Nkrumah to be the leader of Africa were resented in view of the minute size of Ghana compared to Nigeria. On the other hand, radicals admired the supposed dynamism of his regime as compared with the apparent tribalistic inertia and corruption of Nigeria.

It is possible that someone in Ghana had prior knowledge of the plot. Dr Ikoku, a former member of the Action Group who had been convicted in his absence of participating in Chief Awolowo's plot and who was now employed by Dr Nkrumah,

is said to have travelled to Dahomey on the night of the coup
with a supply of arms. Nkrumah is said to have boasted later
that he was behind the plot, though this hardly proved that he
was. The most solid piece of evidence that Ghana had something to do with it is the fact that Major Ifeajuna fled to Ghana
after the rout of the conspirators in the South by Ironsi, and
was received there as a hero.[39]

There are, however, objections to giving Ghana any of the
credit or blame for the January 15 coup. Ghanaian help was
essential to the Action Group conspirators in 1962 because they
needed a source for arms and ammunition and a place where
revolutionaries could be trained. Major Nzeogwu's plotters had
access to as much arms and ammunition as they needed; and the
success of the plot would depend on as few as possible knowing
of it beforehand. It seems plausible that Nkrumah's strong
centralized regime may have served as a model to the plotters,
but there is no reason to believe that Ghana had a greater part
in the plot than this. The arms that Ikoku brought to Dahomey
on the night of the plot were possibly intended for the use of
some of the UPGA thugs active in the Western Region riots
at this time.[40]

According to the conspirators themselves they were moti-
vated by the desire to put an end to corruption, inefficiency and
anarchy. Major Nzeogwu said, 'We wanted to get rid of rotten
and corrupt ministers, political parties, trade unions and the
whole clumsy apparatus of the federal system. We wanted to
gun down all the bigwigs in our way.' The same theme was
struck in the first and only broadcast made by the conspirators
over Lagos Radio: 'The Military has taken over to bring an end
to gangsterism and disorder, corruption and despotism. My
compatriots, you will no longer need to be ashamed to be
Nigerians.'

Similar rhetoric is quite normal in the proclamations issued
after a military take-over, but in the case of Nigeria it was
somewhat more justified than in most cases. Although Sir

Abubakar was personally free from any taint of corruption, the peculations of his colleagues were notorious and went quite unchecked. It may be that some measure of corruption is inseparable from a democratic government, but the blatant extravagance of Nigerian ministers at the same time that they were urging the people to accept austerity for the sake of economic development, deprived the government of any moral authority among the masses, and particularly in the towns and among the more mobilized sectors of the community.

Coupled with this was the increasing reliance of the government on force to secure its perpetuation in office and its refusal to allow any possibility of the opposition coming to power by constitutional means. Until fourteen months before the coup, the Army, when on internal security duty, had never been called upon to give more than a token display of force in support of the Police. But in November 1964 military units had been deployed in strength to pacify Tiv Division. This commitment had lasted throughout 1965. At least three of the majors in the plot – Anuforo, Ademoyega and Onwuatuegwu – had been involved in the suppression of the Tiv, and the distaste that soldiers would feel in the employment of the Army on such tasks may well have been one of the reasons which led them to take part in the conspiracy. Now in January 1966 it seemed that a similar operation on a wider scale was to be mounted in the Western Region. Law and order had completely broken down and travellers could not be sure of passing in safety on the main roads without molestation. Clearly a concentrated military effort would be required to bring the situation under control, and the Army would be forced to suppress, and probably kill, their fellow-countrymen who were protesting against the refusal of the government to allow them to exercise their right to vote Chief Akintola's discredited regime out of office.

In my opinion, the plotters genuinely believed that they were acting in the interests of all Nigerians to end a corrupt and discredited despotism that could only be removed by violence.

But it also seems likely that the perception of this need for action may have been sharpened, for at least some of the rebel officers, by fears for their own military careers if the North remained in power. But this is only a personal guess, of no more worth and as unsubstantiable as anyone else's.

X · The First Four Months of the Ironsi Regime

'E ku new era – o,' said the government clerks to each other as they arrived to work on the morning of Monday, 17 January 1966 – 'Greetings to you on this new era.' The sense of relief that the uncertainty of the last few days was over and the joy at the end of the political regime was obvious all over the country. Such happiness is quite usual at a country's first military *coup d'état*. The East rejoiced at the end of the rule of the North; the West exulted at the end of Chief Akintola and hoped for a halt to the rioting and burning of the past three months; the Middle Belt, and particularly the Tiv, looked to receive fairer treatment from the new regime; and even in the far North (in Kano, Katsina and Zaria) ex-ministers of the former Northern Regional Government were molested and jeered at on their return to their provinces.[1] Political parties and trades unions hastened to declare their support for the new regime with fulsome praise for the military leaders and insults to the corrupt politicians who were now deposed. It seemed like a second Independence Day as undergraduates at the University of Ibadan ceremonially buried a mock coffin of the 'First Republic' with rejoicing such as had greeted the lowering of the Union Jack five years earlier.

But in spite of this general goodwill, the Military Government faced serious problems. One of these was the situation in the West where the supporters of the Action Group now took their revenge on the NNDP. But this mob violence was soon brought under control by the firm measures taken by the new military governor, who quickly dismantled the NNDP political machine. Much more serious was the situation in the Army and the dangers of a counter-revolution in the North.

Unrest in the Army

The abdication of power to General Ironsi by the former Federal government gave his commands some semblance of legitimacy, but it did not convey effective power. In fact, his control of the Army was threatened on two sides: by the supporters of Major Nzeogwu who believed that Ironsi had aborted the true birth of the revolution by his actions on 15 January when he gained control of Lagos from Major Ifeajuna and his fellow-conspirators; and on the other side by those Northern soldiers who were furious at the slaughter of the senior Northern officers and were about to take the law into their own hands. Dodan Barracks in Lagos, where the Federal Guard was stationed, was effectively under the control of angry soldiers for several days. At Ibadan, Ibo officers were driven out of the barracks and one Yoruba officer, Major Adegoke, was killed on suspicion of complicity in the coup. Another officer, Lt. Odu, was killed in Kaduna.[2]

Meanwhile, what government there was in the regions was exercised by the *de facto* military commanders, Major Nzeogwu in the North, Major Nzefili in the West and Lt.-Col. Ejoor in the East.[3] They proceeded to issue orders and act as military governors, deriving their authority not from appointment by General Ironsi but because they were in real, or at least nominal, control of the troops on the spot in the regional capitals.

This was the situation on Monday morning, 17 January. By the time of his midday press conference Ironsi was able to announce that Major Nzeogwu had submitted to his authority. But the names of the new military governors were not announced until Tuesday morning. To the militant followers of Nzeogwu it must have appeared that tribalism and regionalism had triumphed once more: a Yoruba for the West, Lt.-Col.

Fajuyi; an Ibo for the East, Lt.-Col. Ojukwu; an Urhobo for the Mid-West, Lt.-Col. Ejoor; and a Fulani for the North, Major Hassan Katsina, son of the Emir of Katsina.

Meanwhile the rebels were being rounded up. Major Ifeajuna escaped to Ghana, but the others were placed in protective custody, including those who were only suspected of being privy to the plot. Among these was Lt.-Col. Banjo, who was summoned to General Ironsi to explain how it came about that he, a lieutenant-colonel, was still alive, and was then arrested because he was carrying a revolver with him – a not unreasonable precaution in view of what had just occurred.[4] This search for the conspirators was much exaggerated in foreign press reports and fantastic stories appeared of fifty or more officers killed in a gigantic witch-hunt. In fact it seems that thirty-two officers and about a hundred other ranks were finally kept in prison, and that the only officers killed were the two named above, in addition to the seven killed on the night of the coup.[5]

But if no further officers were killed, a number of Northern officers seem to have decided that it would be safer for them to leave barracks for a while, until the situation became clearer. Directive No. 1. of the Military Government ordered that 'all military officers who have left their posts must return thereto immediately and resume their normal duties' or be dealt with under the provisions of the Army Act. Probably the absence of these Northern officers made it easier for the remaining officers to assert control of their units in the crucial first days of the regime.

But the restoration of discipline was not an easy task. Col. Adebayo had to be summoned back from a course at the Imperial Defence College in London for a short time to assist.[6] The appointment of Lt.-Col. Gowon as Chief of Staff also helped to reconcile the Northern soldiers and officers to the new regime. However, Major Nzefili was not able to regain complete control of 4 NA at Ibadan and four weeks after the coup he handed over command to a Northern officer, Major Akahan, a Tiv. It is not surprising that 4 NA had to be placated in this way: two of the four Northern officers killed had been commanders of this battalion, Col. Kur Muhammed (1963) and Lt.-Col. Largema (1963–1966).

The result of the murders of 14–15 January and the subsequent imposition of military rule was to accentuate the predominance of Easterners in the top ranks of the Army. Of the fifty-three majors and officers of higher rank in the Army at the beginning of the year (listed on p. 123) eight were killed in the coup and its aftermath, five were in prison and five were now military governors; in addition, Lt.-Col. Kurobo was transferred to head the Air Force and Col. Adebayo was on a course in England. This left thirty-three senior officers to fill the top posts in the Army; twenty-four of these were Easterners or Ika-Ibo (73 per cent). Only two senior Northerners were left, Lt.-Col. Gowon and Major Akahan. This preponderance of Easterners was fortunate for Ironsi. Prudence dictated that all the important units and garrisons should be under commanders loyal to himself, and this could now be achieved without any obvious injustice. The position in March 1966 was as follows:

2 Brigade (Southern Nigeria)

Brigade Commander	Lt.-Col. Njoku	(Ibo, East)
2 NA, Ikeja	Major Igboba	(Ibo, Mid-West)
Abeokuta Garrison	Lt.-Col. Okonweze	(Ibo, Mid-West)
4 NA, Ibadan	Major Akahan	(Tiv, North)
Federal Guards, Lagos	Major Uche	(Ibo, East)
1 NA, Enugu	Major Ogunewe	(Ibo, East)

1 Brigade (Northern Nigeria)

Brigade Commander	Lt.-Col. Bassey	(Efik, East)
3 NA, Kaduna	Major Okoro	(Ibo, East)
Depot, Zaria	Major Akagha	(Ibo, East)
5 NA, Kano	A/Major Shuwa Muhammed	(North)

It can be seen that the only units commanded by Northerners were the battalions at Ibadan and Kano. The reasons why a

Northerner was needed at Ibadan have already been explained.
The Kano battalion was the only one commanded by an officer
from the far North. But Kano was far enough away from any
crucial centre of government to be given to an officer whose
loyalty was in doubt. The command was held by Lt.-Col.
Ojukwu under the previous regime. In addition to these two
Northerners, Lt.-Col. Gowon was Army Chief of Staff, but the
other senior officers at Army Headquarters were Easterners, so
there was little danger in this.

But the tribal loyalty of the commanders could not guarantee
the adherence of the rank and file. There are a number of
indications that the government and those in sympathy with it
were anxious about the attitudes of the soldiers. For example,
the *West African Pilot* protested against slanted reporting on
the B.B.C.

> This gives the world the false impression that the Army
> take-over was sectional and that it would not be long before
> discontent and disloyalty started to burst out in the open.
> These tirades are to foster disloyalty in the rank and file of
> the Army.
>
> (2 February 1966)

The plainest indication of the regime's anxieties was a secret
order that for the present no unit was to be issued with live
ammunition for range practices.[7] An army that cannot be
trusted with live ammunition for fear of the targets it would
choose would not be much help in any internal security crisis.
But it does not appear that those who were advising General
Ironsi realized what limits this placed on their plans.

The Northern Region

It was widely feared that the whole of the North would rise in
revolt when the news of the deaths of the Sardauna and Sir
Abubakar was made known, so the new regime took great care

to respect the wishes of the Northern leaders. In place of Major Nzeogwu the son of an emir, Major Katsina, was made Regional military governor and immediately promoted lieutenant-colonel. The ministers detained by Major Nzeogwu were released and were not subsequently rearrested, although NCNC and NNDP ministers were imprisoned in the East and West. After some delay the death of Sir Abubakar was announced and he was buried with full honours in his home town of Bauchi, after the proclamation of national mourning. A Northerner, Alhaji Sule Katagum, was confirmed for a further three years in office as chairman of the Federal Public Service Commission. Another Northerner, Mallam Howeidy, was placed in charge of the Electricity Corporation, and a distinguished Northern academic, Dr Audu, replaced an expatriate as vice-chancellor of Ahmadu Bello University, Zaria, in spite of a campaign by certain lecturers for another (i.e. Southern) choice, to emphasize, as it was claimed, the non-regional character of the universities.

In the Army there was no attempt to purge Northern officers who might be expected to be divided in their loyalty. On the contrary, when a series of army promotions was announced in May, the regime reached down the Army List to promote three substantive captains who came from the far North, A/Majors Shuwa Muhammed, Muhammed Murtala and Haruna, to be acting lieutenant-colonels superseding at least eight Southern officers.[8] All these actions, great and small, suggest an attitude of extreme caution in dealing with the North.

In fact, many emirs and other Northerners were not entirely heartbroken by the end of the Sardauna. The correspondent of *The Times* commented:

The Sardauna had been unpopular with the emirs, as well as with the Army and the Southern intellectuals. He ran his party autocratically and his administration as a personal court. To the younger generation he was feudal emir writ large. To the emirs, he was British interference carried to extremes. His spiritual pretensions (especially his proselytizing) were a sour joke. When he fell dead, there was the same relief that pervaded the South. For the emirs it meant that colonial control instituted by Lord Lugard was at last ended. . . . Power went to the native authorities, generally to the emir's government.

(30 May 1966)

The progress of education in the Middle Belt meant that many senior posts in the Northern public service were held by the products of Christian schools, who were unhappy at the Sardauna's conversion tours, on which tens of thousands, so it was claimed, were turned to the true faith of Islam by the offers of material favours here below.

There were obvious fears for the future of the North under a government in Lagos headed by an Ibo, but Lt.-Col. Katsina energetically toured the region, reassuring the people and denying rumours that arose against the government, such as the story that pilgrims would no longer be allowed to make the *hadj* to Mecca. For at least the first four months the North seemed remarkably placid on the surface. The military governor was personally popular and his style of government was a complete contrast to the elaborate pomp and clientage with which the Sardauna had surrounded himself. On one occasion he played in a charity football match in a team of top civil servants against a team of local businessmen.[9] He seemed to retain the confidence of the people in spite of his reiteration of the 'One Nigeria' message of the new regime and his emphatic repudiation of the policy of Northernization formerly practised. To all outward appearances, Ironsi's policy of conciliation appeared to be working very well.

The New Structure of Government

It has been said that it is easy for an army to seize power, but difficult for it to govern, since it lacks the expertise necessary to run a modern state.[10] The Nigerian officers never tried to do this. As soon as he had taken over power, Major Nzeogwu appointed the Northern Region permanent secretaries to act as ministers in their departments, reserving to himself merely the concern with internal security.[11] Ironsi's government followed this example. At the centre and in each region a small council was formed, consisting of the governor, the military commander in the region and one or two civil servants, to give general directions; otherwise the permanent secretaries in each Federal and Regional Ministry were left in charge, and decisions, it was said, were now taken with much more despatch than formerly.[12] There was no attempt to inject army officers into the civil service at either the permanent secretary level, or lower down.

There were two reasons for this. The first was the shortage of senior officers to fill the top posts in the Army, let alone the public service as a whole. The second reason was the lack of qualifications and useful administrative experience. There were no officers available who had commanded anything larger than an infantry company or an engineers squadron or a motor transport unit of perhaps 150 men. They would hardly have contributed very much to the complex tasks of modern government planning.

Ironsi was advised or instructed on what policies to pursue by a small group of advisers in State House. These included Francis Nwokedi (recently permanent secretary of external affairs), Dr Okigbo (the government economic adviser) and several other Ibos. At least one officer, Lt.-Col. Okwechime seems to have been attached to this grouping for a time, as the member of the Military Government responsible for the affairs of the Nigerian Railways. He was later employed reorganizing the country's athletics for the Commonwealth Games. A former army transport officer, Lt.-Col. Nzefili, was made general manager of the railways. Also, in the last months of the regime Lt.-Col. Anwunah was made chairman of an eleven-man

National Orientation Committee which was to make surprise checks on civil servants in order to end inefficiency and absenteeism.[13] But apart from these three officers, and the activities of the military governors in the regions, the Army seems to have interfered hardly at all in the normal processes of the administration.

The new constitutional arrangements were set out in a decree issued on 4 March. The main points were that 'the Federal Military Government shall have power to make laws for the peace, order and good government of Nigeria or any part thereof with respect to any matter whatever'. So much for regional reserved powers. The regional military governors could legislate by issuing an edict, but decrees of the Federal Military Government, signed by General Ironsi, could override them. Executive authority of the Federal Republic was entirely vested in the head of the Military Government, but he was permitted to delegate this at his discretion. The decree set up a Supreme Military Council and a Federal Executive Council; but no specific powers or functions were assigned to these bodies. It seems from the decree that they were more in the nature of advisory bodies that the head of the Military Government could disregard at will. General Ironsi thus wielded powers that were as great as those of a British governor before 1946. In fact they were greater, since Ironsi was not responsible to a colonial secretary and parliament in Britain; and the courts of law were specifically forbidden 'to entertain any question of the validity of this or any other decree'.

Though this decree formally set up a completely unified and centralized administration of Nigeria under the supreme commander, decisions continued to be made and implemented through the old Federal/Regional apparatus. This could only be altered gradually, but a start was made by a number of minor executive decisions taken during the first months of the regime. Regional agents in Britain were abolished (28 January). A central Ministry of Agriculture was established (1 February).

Nwokedi was appointed as sole commissioner to report on the establishment of administrative machinery for a united Nigeria and the unification of the public services (12 February). The Regional governors were made members of the Federal Executive Council, 'to underline the fact that there is now only one government in Nigeria', and this council jointly approved the Federal and Regional budgets (31 March). All labour ministries were centralized under the Federal Ministry of Labour (11 April). There could be no doubt about the developing strategy of transforming the government machinery into a new unified pattern.

Local government also turned back to an earlier model. The colonial governor had been supported by a hierarchy of provincial commissioners (known in Nigeria as Residents) and district commissioners. When local councils came to be elected after the war, these officials in the West and East were redesignated 'Local Government Advisers' and 'Senior Local Government Advisers' with certain inquisitorial duties in connection with the new councils. Occasionally, when the peculations and inefficiency of a democratically elected council became too notorious, the Minister of Local Government had power to dissolve the council and appoint a management committee or the district adviser as 'Sole Administrator' to put the matter right before fresh elections were held. Now the Regional military governors promptly promulgated edicts abolishing all elected provincial assemblies, local and urban councils and management committees. Their powers were transferred to the local government advisers. The colonial system of administration had returned. This was the pattern in the East, West and Mid-West.

In the North there was a slight difference. Governor Katsina ordered the removal of all elected members of native authorities. He explained that this was 'a consequence of the removal of the former legislators and is designed to remove political influences in the local government of Northern Nigeria'.[14] But the effect of this action in the North was to increase the power of the nominated members of the native authorities, that is to say the powers of the emirs, most of whom had been compelled to accept a majority of elected members on their councils. However, the native authorities lost control of their local police forces, which were now brought under the authority of the Inspector-General of Police.

The Regional governors set an example of vigorous activity. They all toured extensively in the provinces, speaking bluntly about the need for hard work and honesty. When greeted by local spokesmen with effusive compliments and requests for government grants they were accustomed to point out that the government would be most ready to assist those who first made an effort to help themselves. Enquiries were set up into the peculations of the old regime, politicians and senior civil servants were put on trial, ministries were amalgamated and new schemes pushed ahead. Lt.-Col Ejoor ordered the doors of all government offices to be locked at the time when the day's work was due to begin, and then harangued the tardy civil servants who found themselves locked out on the vice of unpunctuality in the New Nigeria. Lt.-Col. Ojukwu later followed his example. It seemed that the governors were vying with each other to show which was the most vigorous 'new broom'.

In contrast to this show of activity the Federal Government of Ironsi seemed less dynamic. Most of the decrees published in the first few months were routine legislation drafted under the previous civilian regime. One exception was the 'Suppression of Disorder Decree' of 16 February, which contained such draconian provisions for the proclamation of military areas and the setting up of military tribunals able to inflict the death penalty that the government found itself unable to make use of these powers when disorders actually broke out in May, for fear of exacerbating the rioters further. Another decree (5 April) imposed a minimum penalty of ten years' imprisonment for smoking Indian hemp and a minimum of twenty-one years or the death penalty for planting or cultivating it. But apart from these matters it seemed that the centre was following the regions rather than setting an example to them. For instance, Ojukwu, followed by Ejoor, had already abolished the office of Regional Agent in London before Ironsi announced the general abolition of these posts. Fajuyi promulgated an edict for preventive detention in the West before the Federal Government acted, superseding his edict by a general decree which incorporated the Western list of detainees. The Lagos City Council was the last elected council in the country to be dissolved.

Ironsi's government not only followed the regions, it also showed itself eager to take advice from other quarters. There was no censorship of the press and attention was paid to journalists considered to be sympathetic to the policies of the new regime. Thirty days after the military take-over the *Daily Times* complained that no moves had yet been made to work out a new constitution to follow the Military Government. Four days later Ironsi announced that a series of groups would be set up to study the problems and draft a new constitution.[15] On 28 February the *Daily Times* complained that civil servants in the North were still required to pass an examination in Hausa, which was a hardship to those from the Middle Belt. Within twenty-four hours the government abolished this requirement. In April, during the food shortage when prices were soaring, the same newspaper suggested a ban on food exports, and one was imposed the following day.

Achievements and Criticism of the Regime

By the end of its first hundred days of power, the Military Government could congratulate itself on a successful beginning. Peace had been restored to the Western Region; the North appeared to have acquiesced in the end of its predominance; the first steps had been taken towards reshaping the Federal/Regional structure. The only place where there had been any show of resistance to the new government was, oddly enough, in the Eastern Region, where Isaac Boro, a former undergraduate of Nsukka University, had proclaimed 'The People's Republic of the Niger Delta'. He had gathered a band of supporters, briefly seized control of the town of Yenagoa in Rivers Province, and sabotaged a number of oil installations in that area. But Boro and his followers were captured by the Army within a fortnight and he was later convicted of treason and sentenced to death.[16] Otherwise, the whole of Nigeria was more free of internal strife than at any time since the beginning of 1964.

The regime appeared to be so stable and realistic in its economic planning that it attracted considerable development aid from friendly countries and from the AID bank, and negotiations were successfully concluded for the association of Nigeria with the European Common Market; the treaty was actually signed in July, just before Ironsi's downfall.

But within Nigeria itself increasing criticism of the regime was being heard. These complaints were most vigorously put by the columnist of the *Daily Times*, Peter Pan, on 28 and 29 April. He denounced the soldiers for 'dilly-dallying', for 'appeasement', for 'behaving like politicians in the spirit of compromise'. This was not good enough:

> The Army should take the bull by the scruff of the neck and grip its horns. . . . Ban tribal unions. . . . Instil harsh discipline into corrupt officials. . . . Reshuffle the military governors away from their areas of ethnic origin. . . . This country can never become a nation until special privileges are withdrawn. . . . Those who will not move with the times should be dragged, kicking and screaming – but dragged all the same. . . . To the battlements, my general.

Similar advice was given to Ironsi by the correspondents of the British press, such as the *Financial Times* and *The Times*.[17] According to the latter, 'The inability of the military regime to make up its mind on vital questions is becoming dangerous.'

The government did not only have to contend with such criticisms as these. In Northern newspapers, and particularly in the vernacular paper *Gaskiya Ta Fi Kwabo*, an increasing number of letters and articles were appearing, complaining of the murders of Northerners by which the regime had been inaugurated, and casting doubt on the practicability of transforming Nigeria into a unitary state. The Military Government was well aware of these grumblings; some were reproduced in the Lagos newspapers.[18] But it dismissed them as the work of an unrepresentative minority, since they did not chime in with its own views.

A third problem was the rising prices of staple foodstuffs over the whole country and particularly in the South, where the aftermath of the troubles in the Western Region at the end of 1965, which interfered with planting, was now being felt.

In order to satisfy its critics in the South and silence the growing volume of dissatisfaction in the North at one blow, the Military Government produced the disastrous miscalculation of the May Decrees. These decrees, in conjunction with the rising cost of living, sparked off the May riots in the North, which marked the beginning of the end of the Ironsi regime.

XI · The May Decrees, the Riots and the July Counter-coup

The two decrees issued on 24 May mark the watershed of the Ironsi regime. Up to that date a purposeful pattern can be seen in the actions of the Military Government, leading towards the setting-up of a single unified central government for the whole of Nigeria. But so far, the cumulative administrative actions and decrees of the Supreme Military Council had been a series of small steps, taken covertly, one at a time. Decrees 33 and 34 which abolished all political parties for a period of three years and formally unified the Federal and Regional civil services, were intended to set the seal on this gradual process, set a clear and irreversible course for the future, and psychologically unify the country. Quite the contrary result followed. General Ironsi's speech was followed within a few days by bloody riots in the North; the regime was forced to backtrack hastily on the decrees and seemed to be in a state of indecision for the next two months. Then, at the end of July, when it seemed that a new firm line of policy had been decided upon, the regime was overthrown by a Northern counter-coup.

The advocates of unitary government were influenced by a number of factors – ideological, economic and personal. In common with all the other radical mass parties of West Africa the NCNC had long proclaimed the merits of a strong central government with the minimum concessions to tribal or regional particularisms. Such a government, it was believed, would serve to build up a strong sense of solidarity and common citizenship throughout the country, and, by fostering rapid economic progress, would free the Negro race from the stigma of backwardness while providing 'life more abundant' for all.

This policy was first clearly formulated at the 1951 party conference. In its manifesto for the 1957 election the NCNC advocated the splitting of Nigeria into fourteen states. These views were soft-pedalled in 1959 when the NCNC had some sort of tacit alliance with the NPC, but once this inhibition was removed the NCNC entered the 1964 election with a programme to divide the four regions into twenty-five states.

This ideological commitment was bolstered by a number of political myths. According to this view, federalism was a product of the old British imperial policy of 'Divide and Rule'. The British, it was said, had suborned tribalist politicians such as Awolowo and the NPC leaders to break up the original unity of the nationalist movement. Once in power, these tribalists had secured their continued supremacy by appeals to ethnic chauvinism, and deliberately exacerbated inter-tribal and inter-regional antagonisms for political advantage. It was argued that, when the power-base of these politicians had been removed by the abolition of the regions, they would be forced to make their appeal on a national and not a tribal basis, and so strengthen the unity of the country instead of contributing to its disintegration. Thus the end of the federal structure would at one stroke complete the annihilation of the political system of the First Republic and lay a healthy foundation for the future. Arguments such as these are frequently to be found in the columns of the *West African Pilot* and similar publications in the months before May 1966, coupled with the assertion that the great majority of Nigerians supported the government of General Ironsi and would welcome strong measures against the surviving politicians of the old regime.[1]

Quite apart from such appeals to the emotions, there were strong economic arguments in favour of unification. The expense of five parliaments and five sets of ministers with all their generous salaries and allowances was excessive. Each region competed with the others in setting up industries. The latest example of this was the decision taken in March 1964 to split the plans for one barely viable iron and steel industry into plans for two plants, with a third to follow.[2] It was wasteful to employ expatriates, on inflated salaries, in the North in preference to qualified Southern Nigerians. In theory, Nigeria was working to an integrated six-year economic development programme; in fact, Federal civil servants did what they could to harmonize decisions taken as a result of inter-regional bargaining. This necessary process of political accommodation was very frustrating for academic economists in Nigeria – not only Ibo ones – and also for international development experts. A recent FAO report on agricultural development in Nigeria had emphasized the need for 'a central co-ordinating authority at the federal level to perform certain generally recognized functions and duties of a national government, which are being carried out either ineffectively or not at all'.[3]

However, the case for rational economic planning was also argued from less disinterested motives. The North suffered from serious economic disadvantages. It lacked natural resources, had a more scattered and less wealthy population, poorer communications and was farther from the sea. (This last factor was important since most new industries have to import their machinery and often a proportion of their raw materials.) The sources of fuel – oil, natural gas and coal – were all to be found in the South, at least until the hydro-electric scheme at Kainji would be completed in 1968–1969. So any national plan for siting industry could not fail to favour the Southern Regions, if calculations were made on purely economic considerations of maximum profitability.

This point was further reinforced by calculations of more personal economic advantage. In the public services of the Federation and the Southern Regions there were now few expatriates left in the senior posts. Those Nigerians who had been lucky enough to join the service in the 1950s were now firmly ensconced in 'superscale' posts that they seemed destined to occupy for the next twenty years, forming a complete blockage to hopes of promotion for those below them. After the rapid promotions of the early 1960s this was deeply frustrating to those who had come out of the universities a few years too late to get on the escalator to the top, and it had led to demands that additional promotion posts should be created in the service to 'raise morale' or to 'improve promotion prospects'. This extraordinary suggestion that the public service exists for the benefit of its members had just been indignantly turned down by a grading commission.[4] But if there was to be *one* staff list instead of five, senior posts in the North, where there were still a large number of expatriates, would be open on 'merit'. And for most civil servants 'merit' was most easily measured by years of seniority.

However, the reasons which made unitary government a very rational policy for any southern politician, administrator or soldier to follow, so long as the levers of power were in southern hands, were equally reasons against unification when viewed from the North. Writing on the 1953 constitutional crisis the Sardauna of Sokoto had said:

> We were not only educationally backward, but we stood at that time far behind the others in material development. This was due largely to our great size and rather scattered population, but also to the simple fact that we were a long way from Lagos. If the British administration had failed to give us the even development that we deserved and for which we craved – and they were on the whole a very fair administration – what had we to hope from an African administration, probably in the hands of a hostile party? The answer to our minds was, quite simply, just nothing, beyond a little window dressing.

> (*My Life*, 111)

This equally represented the fears of the North in 1966. And these fears were not confined merely to the Northern ruling élite or to the northernmost, predominantly Muslim, provinces.

If anything, the threat to the North was more keenly felt in the Middle Belt than in the Holy North, since education was more advanced there and the need to find jobs more acute. It was a member of a minority tribe from Kabba who dared to say openly in February 1966:

> If ever the new government is to succeed in eradicating tribalism in the country the foremost task of the new regime would be to do all within its power to prevent one tribe trying to dominate the others and trying to portray others as inferior people who are only good for the odd jobs in a united Nigeria. It was on this fact that the foundation of tribalism was founded. Political leaders may be guilty of various moral offences through the game of politics, but the fact shall remain that these leaders fought at the altar of tribalism to save their tribe from being oppressed or victimized through the ambitious domination from a section of the country under the pretext of one united country.[5]

The Decrees and the Riots

Decrees 33 and 34 were discussed by the Supreme Military Council (which included the Regional military governors) on 12 May. There seems to have been some opposition in the council, and the final drafts may have been somewhat watered down. But from his previous speeches, Lt.-Col. Katsina seems to have been in general agreement with the national and unitarian policy of the government, and the depth of feeling against any alteration in the status of the Northern Region may not have been properly represented on the council.[6] But whatever the views expressed, Ironsi was not legally required to obtain the council's agreement before issuing the decrees; and the Ibo advisers on whom he relied seem to have been convinced that they knew what was best for the country and regarded any opposition in the North as that of a small minority. The

press was informed that vital decisions for the future of Nigeria
had been taken at the meeting and there was a considerable
build-up of publicity for the announcement to be made by
Ironsi on 24 May. His speech was carried on television and by
all radio channels.

The broadcast began with a lengthy introduction dealing
with national economic planning over the next twenty years.
He then went on to the gist of the announcement:

It is time that the Military Government indicates clearly
what it proposes to accomplish before relinquishing power . . .
The former regions are abolished, and Nigeria grouped into
a number of territorial areas called provinces. . . .

The grouping of the provinces has been made to coincide
with the former regional boundaries. This is entirely a
transitional measure, and must be understood as such. The
present grouping of the provinces is without prejudice to
the constitutional and administrative arrangements to be
embodied in the new constitution in accordance with the
wishes of the people of Nigeria.

The public services of the former federation and regions
become unified into one National Public Service Commission.
There is a Provincial Service Commission for each group of
provinces to which is delegated functions in respect of public
officers below a given rank. . . .

Political parties and tribal societies and organizations
are dissolved and the formation of new ones prohibited until
17 January 1969. . . .

We propose as a last act to give the country an accurate
count. . . .

A formula for identifying backward areas will be worked
out and measures taken to bring about improvement of such
areas.

The decrees published the next day added very little to the
broadcast. Decree 33 listed the eighty-one political societies

and twenty-six tribal and cultural associations that were to be dissolved and ordered that all their assets should be registered with the police. Decree 34 listed the thirty-five provinces into which Nigeria was henceforward to be divided, and made all civil servants members of a single unified civil service, subject to a National Public Service Commission. This commission was to deal with all appointments carrying a salary of over £2,292 a year, with immediate effect. Officers of lower rank would be dealt with, as a temporary measure, by Provincial Service Commissions, but this delegation could be revoked at any time by the National Commission.

This point was rather tactlessly underlined by Lt.-Col. Ojukwu. Speaking the next day to civil servants in the Eastern Region, he told them that there would be in future one National Public Service Commission and a common national roll with seniority commensurate with each civil servant's length of service; and that they would in due course be transferred to various parts of the country and especially to Lagos.[7]

Taking the decrees and the explanatory broadcast together, a Northerner could be easily induced to believe that, in the next three years, the Military Government proposed to remove control of appointments to Lagos and pack the public service in the North with Southerners, who had longer years of service; that a census would be held which would 'discover' a Southern majority in the country; that this Southern majority would then ratify a new constitution in which the Northerner would be for ever a second-class citizen in a 'backward' area of the country.

Quite apart from the May Decrees there were reasons enough for discontent in the North. In the first place, there was the provocative behaviour of many Ibos. After the murder of the Sardauna, Ibos in the North held parties to celebrate their victory, displayed photographs of the Sardauna and his 'conqueror', Major Nzeogwu, in the markets and gave great offence by continually playing a particular gramophone record which simulated the sound of machine gun fire.[8] Their boasting and derogatory remarks about the Northerners are, perhaps, understandable, now that they had achieved relief from years of threats and increasing economic discrimination. But it did not convince the indigenous Northerners of the genuineness of the Military Government's good intentions.

Secondly, the early months of the Ironsi regime coincided with sharp increases in the price of foodstuffs. The main cause of this was the disturbances in the Western Region from October 1965 to January 1966, which prevented many farmers planting their crops. Price rises in the West were quickly taken advantage of by traders elsewhere in the country; and in the North, where much of the retail trade was in the hands of the Ibos, resentment at rising prices would be directed against them.[9]

These two factors had produced a general feeling of discontent throughout the North. This could be used by certain classes of people who had been put at a disadvantage by the overthrow of the NPC government. They included former politicians and ministers; local petty contractors and party functionaries who were beneficiaries of party political patronage; debtors of the Northern Marketing Board and the Northern Development Corporation who were pressed to pay their arrears by the new regime; civil servants who feared for their promotion prospects under unification; and university students who feared that posts in 'their' public service would now be open to graduates from other regions.[10]

After the initial shock of the coup had worn off, these discontented elements had begun to agitate against the new regime, and particularly against the threat to the North posed by unification, by writing letters to the press and by circulating pamphlets. Unlike the Eastern and Western Regions where politicians of the old regime had been placed in preventive detention, NPC ministers in the North who had been imprisoned by Major Nzeogwu had been released by Lt.-Col.

Katsina and were even allowed to take up posts in their native authorities. Inuwa Wada, the former NPC Federal Minister of Defence who had been in Europe at the time of the coup, returned to run a transport business in Kano. He had been treasurer of the NPC and still had the use of substantial party funds for political purposes. Overtures were made to leaders of the NEPU and UMBC such as Aminu Kano and Joseph Tarka, who had previously been allied with UPGA but were now becoming increasingly disaffected towards the policy of Ironsi.[11] Ironically, it was the actions of the Military Government in ending the suppression of the Tiv and abolishing the compulsory qualification in Hausa in the Northern Region public service which now allowed this rapprochement between former political enemies. The old NPC slogan 'One North, one people, irrespective of religion, rank or tribe' was truer now than it had ever been under the rule of the Sardauna, since the educated class of the Middle Belt now had far more to lose in terms of employment opportunities if the Northern Region was broken up.

Thus there was a large amount of latent discontent and a number of individuals with every reason and opportunity to take advantage of it. The May Decrees served as a catalyst. Ironsi's broadcast was on Tuesday evening. For three days the North appeared quite peaceful and the military governor left Kaduna on Friday to go on tour, apparently expecting no trouble. But over the weekend there were riots and mass murders of Ibos in most of the urban centres of the North.

According to Northern sources, the riots were an unplanned outburst by an oppressed people; according to the East, they were deliberately organized by the co-ordinated action of emirs, district heads and students. It is naturally difficult to find proof of organization, but there is a limit to the possibilities of spontaneous coincidence. Although there were some demonstrations on Saturday, 28 May, in most towns which suffered violence over that weekend the riots, arson and murders began on Sunday morning, when Southerners were in church. This is not usually a time of great activity. As an example, at this time in Sokoto the mob set to work deliberately to break the goods and chattels of all Ibos living there, beat them up and drive them out of town. As each house was pillaged, the ringleaders of the mob reported to the elders of the town, who then directed them to the next house to be cleared. The police made no attempt to interfere. No Ibos were killed. In Gusau, a hundred miles south of Sokoto, a similar plan seems to be have been put into operation; but here the Ibos attempted to defend their property with firearms, and many were murdered.

It seems likely that there was some rudimentary organization of the rioting, but that once violence started it quickly got out of hand. As a Northern pamphleteer himself admits, 'In the absence of any effective constitutional means of expressing their legitimate and genuine feelings, therefore, the people were forced to resort to violence.'[12] Thirteen years previously, the British Government had been forced to concede a federal system to Nigeria after the Kano riots of April 1953, and no doubt this parallel was remembered by the Northern leaders. As the news of the riots spread, in spite of the censorship which Ironsi's government had hastily imposed, towns which had previously been untroubled felt that they should follow the example set elsewhere. For instance, Katsina had no disturbances over 28–30 May, but was badly affected the following weekend.

These outbursts seem to have taken the Military Government entirely by surprise. This was a remarkable failure of intelligence, perhaps because the internal security apparatus in the North was still in Northern hands. But whatever the reason, the Army was well trained in the techniques of riot control and should have been able to suppress the trouble, at least in Kano, Kaduna and Zaria, where there were military garrisons. However, soldiers were not used in force, though small patrols were sent out in Zaria, and in Kaduna three days after the original outbreak.[13] Evidently the authorities feared for the loyalty of the troops if they were ordered to fire on Northern rioters in defence of Ibos, and the police made no attempt to intervene. So in most places the riots were left to take their course of arson and murder. According to the government, only one fatal casualty was inflicted by the security forces in the whole of the North. This was in Sokoto where armed Ibo police were flown in. After the pillaging was over they opened fire unnecessarily on a demonstration by senior secondary school pupils, killing one of them.

Accurate figures of the Eastern dead are not available. The Ironsi regime, which at that time wished to minimize the extent of the disaster, claimed that 92 people were killed and 506 injured. Mr Loshak, a staff reporter of *The Daily Telegraph*, who toured the North immediately after the riots and made extensive enquiries at hospital mortuaries, estimated the number of dead as at least 600.[14] Large numbers of Ibos fled from the North in the following week, causing a massive dislocation of commercial activity. Atrocities continued through to the following weekend, 4–5 June, and sporadically for some while thereafter. The riots extended widely throughout the North, though some parts of the Middle Belt, such as Ilorin and Makurdi, were unaffected. Another surprising exception was Bornu. Three of the four Northern officers who had been murdered in January came from this province – Maimalari, Kur Muhammed and Largema, but this area remained completely unaffected.

The Reactions of the Military Government

The first reaction on the night of 29 May was to blame 'some Nigerians in collusion with certain foreign elements'. By this was meant British expatriates. Ibo suspicion that the British favoured the North had been of long-standing. It was noted that the British High Commissioner had been visiting the North a few days before the riots. A retired British officer, Major

Boyle, and two British correspondents, Mr Schwarz and Mr Loshak, were deported.

Another excuse put forward to explain the riots was the failure of the government to inform the people properly of its intentions. Statements from the governor of the North and from Lagos emphasized that the May Decrees were 'interim and temporary measures' until civilian government was restored, and that 'massive assistance' would be given to the less developed areas to enable them to catch up with the rest of the country as soon as possible. It is true that Ironsi's speech had referred to the arrangements made by Decree 34 as 'entirely a transitional measure without prejudice to the new constitution'. But this proviso was not emphasized in the broadcast, and when looked at in its context, it could equally well have referred to greater measures of centralization to be taken later. So the government was wise to arrange for films to be shown and for loudspeaker vans to be sent around to explain its intentions in the vernacular.

Measures were also taken to curb the tactless behaviour of Ibos. Three days after the first riots Ironsi warned the public against singing provocative political songs or selling or playing records that contained them. A decree imposed a fine of £50 or three months imprisonment, or both, for displaying photographs, publishing pamphlets or playing recordings 'in a manner likely to provoke any section of the community'. The threat was not idle: on 3 June the editor of the *West African Pilot* and its political cartoonist were arrested for publishing a cartoon of a cock, labelled 'Military Government' crowing over the defeat of Tribalism and the new dawn inaugurated by the May Decrees. The cock was formerly the symbol of the NCNC, and this was an interpretation of events which the government did not appreciate. But such severity to its own supporters was now too late.

The only way to stabilize the situation in the North was to enlist the support of the emirs to calm their people. Peace committees of elders were formed in the main towns, and a conference of emirs and chiefs met Lt.-Col. Katsina on 1 June. This despatched a memorandum to General Ironsi for consideration by the Supreme Military Council, 'on the grievances of our people and our recommendations on how to bring about peace in Nigeria'. The memorandum was not published, nor was Ironsi's reply. But it seems clear that the emirs demanded that there should be no further interference with the autonomy of the Northern Region, and that no new constitution should be imposed on the country without the consent of the North. For the moment the Military Government had no alternative but to accept these demands. The statement issued by the Supreme Military Council claimed that the May Decree was 'designed to meet the demands of the Military Government and to enable it to carry out its day-to-day administration. . . . *It has in no way affected the territorial divisions of the country*'[15] (italics added). It also reiterated the promise of a Constituent Assembly and a referendum on permanent arrangements for a new constitution after the various study groups had reported. With these concessions the Sultan of Sokoto, acting as the leader of the emirs, professed himself satisfied, broadcast a renewed appeal for peace and asked those who had left the North to return. The success of the riots, from the emirs' point of view, was underlined by a speech made by Lt.-Col. Katsina to the resumed session of the conference of emirs and chiefs. He assured them that they were the government's main source of knowledge about public feeling and that their representatives would be invited to go to Lagos regularly for consultation.

However brave a face might be put upon the facts in official handouts – (official notices still referred to the Northern Group of Provinces and Decree 34 was never repealed) – the Military Government had clearly suffered an overwhelming defeat for its policies. So far it had been able to proceed by small steps towards its goal of unification, claiming that its policies enjoyed the support of the bulk of the people. The May

Decrees had been intended as a culminating step in the abolition of the Regions so that they could never be revived. The
statement issued after the riots pledged that the Military
Government would *safeguard* the Regions. No further encroach-
ments were possible; the North was now alerted, and any new
moves would invite a fresh explosion.

Two alternative strategies were now open to the Military
Government. In the first place it could accept this limitation
to its field of action and continue to govern by a process of
consultation and compromise with the existing power groups.
In other words, it could start to act just like the civilian political
government that it had overthrown. If this course was to be
chosen, then it followed that the January conspirators, who
had been kept in prison for the past five months, must be
brought to trial, as an earnest of good faith to the North and as
the Northern leaders had requested.

Alternatively, the Military Government could attempt to
recover its freedom of action by imposing its will on the North
by force. Advocates of this point of view claimed that the riots
were caused not so much by the May Decrees as by the feeble-
ness of General Ironsi in dealing with opposition elements
there; if the government would act boldly, arrest the leaders of
the NPC and make a determined show of force, then the opposition would collapse. If this was the course to be followed, then
the rebel majors might well be set free, as radical opinion had
long been requesting.[16]

By the time he was overthrown, General Ironsi had not yet
made clear which course he had chosen. He was not naturally
given to decisive action. Even at the time of the counter-coup,
it was strongly rumoured in Lagos that the conspirators were
to be executed while he was away in Ibadan, as a move to
conciliate the North. However, there were a number of actions
at the end of June and in July which suggest that the government was now inclining to the second line of policy, i.e. imposing its will by force. On 24 June it was announced that

military courts would be set up in the major towns to combat nepotism and corruption. Nine Northerners were placed in preventive detention, including a former NPC minister, a former provincial commissioner of Sokoto and the editor of the Northern newspaper, *Gaskiya Ta Fi Kwabo*. A company of infantry under an Ibo commander was sent to garrison Sokoto. This gave great offence as no army unit had been stationed there for many years. On 13 July Ironsi announced that military 'prefects' would be appointed at local level, responsible for seeing that government policy was carried out. He also announced that the four military governors would rotate every six months and that a military presence would be established all over the country.[17] Northerners immediately assumed that this meant that Lt.-Col. Ojukwu would be posted to Kaduna.

Taken all together these moves suggest that a new, tough policy against the North was about to be implemented. How far Ironsi was prepared to go will never be known. On 29 July he was murdered in the counter-coup while he was attending the first All-Nigeria Conference of Chiefs held at Ibadan.

Discontent in the Army

Seen in retrospect, it was madness for the Military Government to attempt to impose far-reaching changes when it could not rely on the loyalty of the Armed Forces, the ultimate guarantee of public order. The government was under no illusions about the reliability of its troops. This was shown particularly by the fear of issuing live ammunition to the soldiers, and by the unwillingness to commit soldiers to suppress the riots in the North.

Within the units even an occasional visitor would not fail to notice the tension between officers. For example, at the barracks in Lagos the Northern captain, who was second-in-command, did not trouble to conceal his bitter contempt for the Ibo major commanding the unit. Other officers commented in private conversation on the tension that was now felt in the officers' mess in contrast to the pleasant atmosphere that had prevailed before the coup.

One complaint in particular was made against Ironsi by the Northern officers and other ranks: that he did not order the trial and punishment of the original conspirators of 15 January. Ironsi had been elevated to the supreme power by the Army to suppress the original coup, and it was naturally expected and demanded that those officers who had so offended against all military tradition and honour by murdering their fellow-officers in their beds should be made to pay the penalty for their crimes.[18]

This was not a demand that Ironsi could satisfy. It would give great offence to radical opinion in the South which regarded the rebel majors as patriotic heroes; and Ironsi had given his word that the conspirators would be safe from any criminal proceedings when he needed to secure the submission of Major Nzeogwu on 17 January. General Ironsi was no Machiavelli; he kept his pledged word and deferred any decision by asking the new Army Chief of Staff, Lt.-Col. Gowon, to carry out a full investigation of the coup. This report was not submitted before Ironsi's own death. He was accustomed to reply to questions about the fate of the conspirators with the enigmatic remark, 'Justice will be done.'[19]

Another complaint concerned the treatment of the arrested conspirators. It was alleged that they were still being paid their salaries and allowances. This was in fact unexceptional. The officers had not been tried and convicted, so, according to the Army Act, they could not suffer any deduction or stoppage of pay.[20]

It was also alleged that some of the conspirators had been promoted while in custody. This was true of only one of the arrested officers: 2/Lt. Ojukwu was promoted lieutenant among a large batch of promotions of subalterns on a time basis. This looks like an administrative oversight; it was

certainly not a particular act of favouritism. It is possible that
the soldiers confused the conspirator Major D. O. Okafor
(N/73) who was not promoted, with Major D. C. Okafor (N/74),
the military attaché in London, who was promoted A/Lieu-
tenant-Colonel. The latter officer had nothing to do with the
plot.

However, the main complaint against the Ironsi regime was
the list of army promotions announced in May: eleven majors
were promoted substantive lieutenant-colonel and fourteen
others were given the acting rank of lieutenant-colonel.
Eighteen of the twenty-five promoted were Easterners or
Mid-West Ibos, along with five Northerners, one Yoruba and
one Mid-Westerner. In fact, there was no injustice to Northern
officers in this list. The one Northerner who was made a substantive lieutenant-colonel was the most junior of the eleven
so promoted; and three of the four Northerners given the acting
rank of lieutenant-colonel were still only substantive captains.[21] If one wishes to trace the matter right back, the reason
why so many 'Eastern' majors were promoted at this time was
because Easterners had predominated among the cadets taken
for officer training in the period 1955–1958, when selection was
entirely in the hands of British officers. In Ibo eyes, these
promotions were an elementary act of justice to officers whose
advancement had been deliberately held back by the NPC
Minister of Defence. For example, Gowon had been one of five
officer cadets who passed out of Sandhurst in December 1956.
He was promoted substantive lieutenant-colonel in April
1964. One other of the five, Unegbe, was promoted lieutenant-
colonel in July 1965. But the other three officers, Majors
Anwunah, Okwechime and Madiebo had to wait until May
1966.

But even if this list of promotions was justifiable in terms of
army seniority, it was an outstanding blunder in public
relations. The Nigerian Army List was not generally available;
it was a confidential document. The summary given above can

only be discovered by many hours of burrowing through back copies of the *Federal Gazette*. To the government, these were simple examples of promotion on 'merit'. But to the Northern rank and file it appeared that an Ibo government was doing what it was expected to do – promote Ibos to the senior posts – and they naturally assumed that this pattern would be followed for promotions in the lower ranks in future.

What could Ironsi have done to conciliate the Northerners in the Army? He might have increased it in size, thus opening up more opportunities for promotion. Something of this sort seems to have been contemplated; an Ibo lieutenant-colonel spoke in conversation of a future army of three divisions, though nothing was done on this before the regime was overthrown and there was no increase in the military budget in the April 1966 estimates. Soldiers' pay might have been increased. In April, Ironsi told troops he inspected at Kachia that their rates of pay were under active review; but nothing was done before the counter-coup. It is doubtful, however, if any conceivable rise in pay could have bribed the Army into support of what was believed to be an Ibo-dominated regime.

A more practical suggestion is that moves could have been made to set up a Middle Belt State, carved out of the southern part of the Northern Region. This had long been the ambition of the tribal groups in this area and it was they who still formed the largest element in the infantry. If the government had taken this step at any time before May 1966 it would have both divided the Northerners and given the Army a strong incentive to support Ironsi's regime. Unfortunately, such a policy ran completely counter to the long-term plans of Ironsi's advisers. Their aim was to unify the country, not to create further regions with their wasteful duplication of ministries and another independent civil service. They may also have realized that a Middle Belt Public Service Commission would be just as discriminatory against Southerners, and particularly Ibos, as the Northern Region itself had been. So no Middle

P

Belt State was contemplated. If one single cause had to be
nominated for the overthrow of the Ironsi regime, this would
seem to be a good candidate.[22] Instead, the Military Government united all Northerners against it by issuing the May
Decrees.

Two events in July seem likely to have spurred the hostile
elements in the Army to action. In that month a new draft
of army recruits was enrolled at the depot in Zaria. A large
number of potential recruits from the North were turned
away and preference seemed to be given to Southerners. It had
been customary for each province in the North to send a pre-
selected batch of recruits to the depot for their medical examination and intelligence test. In July the squad sent by the provincial office in Sokoto were practically all rejected on the tests,
a thing which had not happened before.[23] If the same thing
happened to the recruits sent by the other Northern provinces
it is easy to understand the fears that, in the name of 'merit',
the former regional recruitment quotas were to be disregarded
and the Army packed with Ibos.

Then, a week before the counter-coup, Ironsi told the men
of the 4th Battalion in Ibadan that they were to rotate in the
same way as the military governors, and that they would
shortly change places with the 1st Battalion at Enugu. Rotation of the battalions had been normal practice up to 1961,
when it had been discontinued because of the Congo operation; but it may be surmised that the main reason for its re-
introduction now was to move the 4th Battalion out of Ibadan.
This unit had been out of control after the January coup, was
bitter over the deaths of two former commanding officers and
was now commanded by a Northerner, Lt.-Col. Akahan. On
the other hand, 1 NA was commanded by an Ibo, Lt.-Col.
Ogunewe, and had been based in the East for seven years, for
three of which it had been under the command of Lt.-Col.
Fajuyi, the present governor of the Western Region. Presumably it was therefore thought to be more reliable. However,

this totally unexpected change of station was bound to create domestic problems for the troops, particularly in relation to the schooling of their children.

The Counter-coup of July 1966

The end of the Ironsi regime came as suddenly as the January coup which inaugurated it. On the night of 28–29 July Ibo officers were murdered in the units at Abeokuta, Ibadan and Ikeja, and General Ironsi and Lt.-Col. Fajuyi were seized at Ibadan and afterwards assassinated. The next day loyal troops from Lagos who attempted to retake Ikeja airport and the army barracks there were ambushed and fled. Negotiations then began between the rebels and Brigadier Ogundipe, the senior member of the Supreme Military Council left in Lagos. Meanwhile rebel officers had also taken over the army units in the North, with the slaughter of more Ibo officers and soldiers. But Lt.-Col. Ojukwu had been able to remove the weapons from the soldiers at Enugu into police control before they heard what was happening elsewhere, thus frustrating any move in the East.

The facts given above are undisputed, but as with the January coup, the detailed accounts put out by Federal and Eastern (Biafran) sources differ widely. According to the Eastern propagandists, the above sequence of events was the result of a long-laid plot in which most Northern officers were involved, master-minded by Lt.-Col. Gowon who abused his position of trust as Army Chief of Staff to co-ordinate all arrangements. As against this, Federal and Northern sources allege that the Ibo garrison commander at Abeokuta accidentally triggered off the first killings on the night of 28 July by issuing arms to some of the Southern rank and file; that Northern soldiers feared that this was the prelude to a massacre and struck first, killing the Eastern officers and NCOs in the garrison; and that their action was then followed in other units. The Northern account claims that there was an Ibo plot 'designed to annihilate completely certain categories of Northern Nigerians, including the chiefs, commissioned and warrant officers of the Nigerian Army and senior civil servants'. This plot, it is said, was only frustrated by the prompt action of the Northern soldiers.[24]

At first sight, this story of an 'Ibo plot' seems on a par with the story of the 'Sardauna's plot' which was claimed as a justification of the January coup. As with that story, it is possible that it is true, but it would be extraordinary folly if a plot on these lines had been seriously contemplated. The senior non-Eastern officers in the Army were remarkably few, as has already been shown, and they were all appointed to their posts by Ironsi himself. Brigadier Ogundipe had been recalled from London by Ironsi, and Lt.-Col. Gowon, Lt.-Col. Katsina and the other Northern colonels had been promoted or appointed especially to mollify the Northern soldiers. Any plan to massacre them would certainly have renewed the state of open mutiny that several units had experienced after the January coup, and such a situation would not have been easy to control. If the Military Government had wished to remove any Northern officer, he could easily have been posted to a sinecure position abroad. Murder was quite unnecessary. Similar objections apply to the story of a plot against the emirs and chiefs. Lt.-Col. Ojukwu and others had just been advising the Ibos who had fled from the North to return there; any attempt at a wholesale slaughter of the natural leaders of the North would have removed any restraining influence over the mob and have brought about a renewal of the violence of May on an even more murderous scale. So, unless some more concrete evidence of this alleged plot can be produced, such a plan must be judged *prima facie* unlikely. But the Northern officers and NCOs who carried out the counter-coup may well have believed that this story was true, and that their own lives would be endangered unless they acted resolutely. One might hazard a guess that such a story could have been deliberately spread by those opposed to the Ironsi regime in order to spur the Northerners

in the Army to action, since it was obvious that there was no
other way of displacing him except by an army mutiny.

If Ibo officers were hatching a plot, it is much more likely
that this was directed against General Ironsi himself, rather
than against the Northern officers. Among the more radical
young officers there was considerable dissatisfaction with
Ironsi's 'moderate' policies, and some *may* have wished to
replace him in the supreme command by a more dynamic
leader such as Lt.-Col. Ojukwu, or Major Nzeogwu who was
still held in prison. Certainly, when the news of the army muti-
nies first reached Lagos many people assumed that a coup of
this sort was taking place, and not a Northern reaction.[25]
But it is difficult to believe that any such conspirators, if they
existed, would have complicated their tasks by attacks on
Northern officers. However, in the highly charged atmosphere
produced by the bloody events of January and May, any story
of a plot was likely to find easy credence. The January coup
came like a bolt from the blue. Now both sides were on edge
and prepared to see conspiracy round any corner.

It is impossible to say how much plotting, if any, was done
by the Northern officers and soldiers who executed the counter-
coup. They certainly had every incentive to overthrow the
Ironsi regime, as both the Northern Region and their own
careers seemed to be threatened by the new emphasis on 'merit'
instead of regional quotas. *Prima facie* some planning had been
done or, at the very least, preliminary soundings had been
taken, from the speed with which the first killings at Abeokuta
were initiated in other garrisons. There is no evidence that
Lt.-Col. Gowon was involved in any plotting. He was sent to
Ikeja by Brig. Ogundipe to parley with the mutineers and was
then forced to act as their spokesman.

After the attempt to retake Ikeja airport had failed on
Friday evening (29 July), negotiations began between the
Military Council and the rebels. Brig. Ogundipe was urged by
the council, and by Lt.-Col. Ojukwu on the telephone from

Enugu, to assume the office of supreme commander now that Ironsi was in rebel hands, but he refused, on the compelling grounds that the soldiers would no longer accept his authority; he had just given an order to a sergeant who had refused to obey it until it was confirmed by his captain. In these circumstances Lt.-Col. Gowon was perforce persuaded to take over as supreme commander. The constitutional decrees of the Ironsi regime had made no provision for filling such a vacancy, and Ojukwu never acknowledged Gowon's assumption of power. However, his right to it was as good, or as bad, as General Ironsi's had been on 17 January. There was no alternative to his elevation if complete anarchy was to be avoided.[26]

In the first flush of victory some Northern officers, who now found themselves in a position to determine the future of Nigeria, appear to have demanded the instant secession of the North.[27] But international pressure was quickly applied, and they were soon led to realize that the landlocked North had a greater interest than any other region in the unity of Nigeria, provided the North retained a dominant position in the central government. When Gowon made his first broadcast as supreme commander on Monday, 1 August, he acknowledged the severe strains to which Nigerian unity had been subjected, but made no mention of a break-up of the country.

While these negotiations were taking place, Eastern officers and other ranks were being systematically hunted down and massacred in the army units where Northern soldiers had seized control. In a few units Northern officers were able to keep their authority and there was little bloodshed, but in other cases officers who tried to stop the killings were threatened by Northern NCOs and told to keep away while the troops dealt with those who had abused them. Even after Lt.-Col. Gowon was installed as supreme commander, he was unable to prevent further murders, as that of Major Ekanem when he had been summoned to Military Headquarters. Within a few days all Easterners in the Army were either dead, in prison or had escaped to the East. Those still alive were later returned to Enugu, in exchange for the Northern soldiers who had formed part of the battalion there. In all, according to a list issued by the Eastern Region Government, at least 43 officers and 170 other ranks were murdered during the counter-coup.[28]

Ironically, most of the actual conspirators of 15 January escaped unharmed. Two of them (Majors Anuforo and Okafor), who were held in the Western Region, were removed from prison and shot, but Major Nzeogwu and other leading figures were imprisoned in the East, and so survived. Those who died had had nothing to do with the conspiracy. Quartermasters, education officers and army clerks were slaughtered for no other reason than that they were Ibo.

There is no difficulty in fathoming the motives of the Northern soldiers involved in the counter-coup. A few days afterwards a Northern corporal explained the events very simply to me: 'The Ibos killed our leaders in January; they were taking all the top jobs; we had to get rid of them. Now we have only got Northerners in this barracks; all the Southerners have run away.'[29] Envy of Ibo success, fear for their own future and the desire for revenge give a complete explanation.

The Northern officers seem to have expected that their troops would return to their customary obedience once all Ibos had been eliminated. But the officer corps had lost 40 per cent of its numbers when almost all the Eastern officers had been murdered or had fled, and this fact alone made the restoration of normal discipline very difficult. In addition, when once the mystique of instant obedience to orders has been breached, it is not an easy task to re-establish the authority of superior officers. In October the troops at Kano mutinied and killed one of their own Northern officers when ordered to patrol the city to protect Ibo civilians who were being massacred; the mutinous troops then took the lead in the slaughter. There were many occasions where an order now became merely a

'basis for discussion', as the army phrase puts it.[30] Discipline
was not properly restored until the battalions were stiffened by
the recall of reservists at the outbreak of the Civil War.

Outside the Army, the Lagos population greeted the news of
the overthrow of General Ironsi and the substitution of Lt.-Col.
Gowon with apparent apathy. There was no sign of popular
rejoicing, such as had greeted the news of the January coup.
The prevailing feeling was one of anxiety as to what crimes the
soldiers would now perpetrate; the assassinations of 15 January
had been carried out secretly at night, but in July murder was
committed in daylight in the crowded streets of Lagos, as
when Major Ekanem and two Ibo soldiers with him were shot
down on Carter Bridge.[31] The initial enthusiasm for Ironsi had
long since evaporated; the Yoruba were disappointed at the
failure to release Chief Awolowo and many of them shared the
fears of the North about 'Ibo domination'; but at the time of his
elevation to the post of supreme commander, Lt.-Col. Gowon
was quite unknown to the public and memories of the re-
pression in the Western Region in 1965 by the NPC government were still fresh. It was not until a week later, when Gowon
freed Awolowo and the other Action Group prisoners, that he
achieved the status of a popular hero and Lagos and the West
enjoyed a night of delirious rejoicing.

An Assessment of General Ironsi's Military Government

When the Army took over on 17 January it stood at a pinnacle
of popular esteem. In contrast to the politicians, it appeared
remote, unsullied and efficient. All Nigerians were proud of its
long service in support of the United Nations' action in the
Congo, and when it was called upon to save another African
state, Tanganyika. When engaged on internal security operations in Tiv Division the soldiers had a much better reputation
than the Police. Also, unlike the Police, the Army was relatively
uncorrupt. It stood apart from politics. On national occasions

it symbolized the sovereignty of the nation in a way that no other person, group or institution was able to do. It was smart, modern, efficient and, once General Welby-Everard had left in 1965, it was entirely run and commanded by Nigerians. As every other hope faded, nationalists looked more and more to the Army for the salvation of Nigeria from the politicians of all parties who had betrayed the nationalist ideals and aspirations.

However, this favourable image of the Army was already tarnished by the manner of its coming to power. Once the initial public rejoicing at the end of the politicians had subsided, the conviction began to grow that the soldiers had not been impartial saviours of the state, but rather that the Army had been used by a sectional interest – by the Ibos – to serve tribalistic ends. The names of the officers killed on 15 January were not officially published until after the counter-coup, but it was well known that four Northern officers, two Westerners, but only one Ibo had been eliminated. In spite of the efforts made to conciliate the North, such as the appointment of Lt.-Col. Hassan Katsina as military governor there, the impression that the regime was Ibo-dominated was confirmed by a number of blunders in public relations, in particular by the appointment of Francis Nwokedi, an Ibo, as sole commissioner to advise on the unification of the public services, and by the list of army promotions announced in May.

This political ineptitude was coupled with a blindness to the signs of rising discontent. This was not because the press was gagged. On the contrary, once the regime was consolidated in power, there was no ban on the criticism of government policy, and censorship was not imposed until the outbreak of the May riots. During the first four months of the regime, the fears of the Northerners that they would be put at a permanent disadvantage in a unified Nigeria were voiced in the Northern newspapers, moderately in the English language paper, the *New Nigerian*, and more virulently in the vernacular newspaper,

Gaskiya Ta Fi Kwabo. There was a lively debate in all news-papers on the virtues of unitary government, with the case against being fully aired. Soldiers in government are commonly accused of stifling the channels of communication between the ruled and the rulers, so depriving administrators of necessary information about the functioning and effects of the govern-ment's policies to enable them to be modified or corrected.[32] This was certainly not true of General Ironsi's government.

Another channel of communication available to the govern-ment was consultation with the chiefs and emirs. But little attempt was made to tap this source of information before the May riots. The former regional governors were made advisers to the new military governors, and on one occasion the Sultan of Sokoto, the senior emir in the North, was officially enter-tained by General Ironsi in Lagos, but there is little sign that much attention was paid to their views. It was only after the riots that the Military Government attempted to erect a formal structure for consultation with the natural rulers, by summon-ing regional meetings and finally a national conference of chiefs and emirs. (It was while attending the first of these gatherings that Ironsi was assassinated in July.) There was never any attempt to seek the views of the deposed political leaders, whom both Ironsi and his civil service advisers thoroughly despised.[33]

The trouble was not so much that the soldiers suppressed views that they disliked, but that they completely misjudged, until it was too late, the strength of the feelings against their policy. The messages of rising Northern anxieties and dis-affection, relayed to the government by the press and by those representatives of the old order that were consulted, reached the 'receiver', but there was then an inappropriate 'feedback' to deal with the situation revealed by the message, because it failed to agree with the regime's preconceived views on what 'the real' sentiments of the Northerners were. Ironsi's advisers preferred to listen to those journalists who shared their own sympathies for a centralized Nigeria, such as 'Peter Pan' in the *Daily Times*.

In this respect the failure of the military regime was exactly on a par with the failure of the previous civilian government to assess correctly the strength of the opposition to its policies in Tiv Division in 1964 and in the Western Region in 1965. The soldiers were no worse than the politicians in this respect.

The fundamental reason why the military is commonly said to be unfitted to rule a country is that soldiers tend to regard government merely as a process of efficient administration; but the main task of any government is to choose between different courses of action and mediate between conflicting pressure groups; in other words, to engage in the *political* activity of conflict resolution; and it is claimed that politicians are better at this than soldiers 'accustomed as they are to the blind obedience of their inferiors, the dry voices of command and the narrow horizon of their profession'.[34]

The Nigerian officers themselves did not share this point of view. When Lt.-Col. Gowon, Lt.-Col. Ojukwu and other military leaders met at Aburi in Ghana in January 1967 in a final attempt to achieve a compromise and halt the drift to civil war, they began their meeting by deploring the tendency of politicians to inflate all disagreements for political advantage, and congratulated each other that when soldiers met they would be sure to settle any disagreements easily in a spirit of harmony.[35]

Before considering the truth of this in relation to Nigeria, a general point needs to be made. Conflicts can only be resolved within a single political system when each contestant feels that he has a greater stake in the continuance of the system than in the complete achievement of his own objectives. Where one of the contenders is prepared to destroy the political system rather than accept less than the fulfilment of his demands, then there is no possibility of 'resolving' the conflict except by the total surrender of the other party.

In the case of Nigeria, it might seem obviously true that government by politicians is preferable to government by soldiers. Whatever other faults may be imputed to the government of Sir Abubakar it succeeded in keeping Nigeria together as a single political unit, whereas seventeen months after Major Nzeogwu's coup Nigerians were fighting a bloody civil war. Sir Abubakar was well aware of the political necessity to make tactical concessions in the interest of unity, as when part of the iron and steel industry was allocated to the East after the publication of the census results in 1964, and when Ironsi was made G.O.C. after the defeat of Dr Azikiwe's attempt at a revolution in January 1965. In similar fashion, the political leaders of all parties showed a remarkable suppleness of principle in their frequent realignments of parties against each other.

But the Sardauna and Sir Abubakar were only prepared to make tactical concessions to their opponents *within the framework of continued Northern dominance of Nigeria*. When it seemed that this was in danger, such as in Tiv Division, in 1960 and 1964 and in the Western Region in 1965, opposition was ruthlessly crushed by force. No concessions could be made which imperilled the hegemony of the NPC. In 1962 the Federal Government of Sir Abubakar was quite prepared to stretch the constitution to its limits in imposing a state of emergency on the Western Region in order to make sure that the potential ally of the NPC, Chief Akintola, won his contest for the leadership against Chief Awolowo. In none of these cases did the NPC leadership show any willingness to accept any true compromise. There is no need to doubt that Sir Abubakar himself would have preferred not to use force in this way, as he said in his final interview, but the final decisions on NPC policy were made by the Sardauna, and he had no such qualms. When Northern dominance was imperilled the Northern leaders preferred to consider secession, as in the crises of 1953 and in July 1966, or at the very least to turn Nigeria into a sort of 'Common Market' rather than an effective modern state, as was shown by their first proposal at the Constitutional Conference of September 1966.[36]

The record of the NPC may be compared with that of General Ironsi's government. When he was faced with the riots in the North after the May Decrees he did not use force, but compromised with the representatives of the North, the emirs, to the extent of backtracking almost completely on the plans for unification already announced. It may be argued that Ironsi had no alternative in view of the unreliability of the internal security forces available to the government; it is also possible that this was merely a tactical retreat until he was in a better position to impose his will on the North by force. These questions cannot be answered since Ironsi was assassinated within two months, before he had an opportunity to show his hand clearly. But two comments may fairly be made. In the first place, the military government showed itself far more willing to compromise over the May Decrees than the NPC government had shown itself willing to climb down over the disputed result of the Western Region election. Secondly, the military regime had a far greater incentive to seek a compromise with the North, because of the number of Ibos who were living there and who were likely to suffer for any blunders of the regime, than the NPC government had to compromise with the South in 1965. It seems just possible, therefore, that Ironsi's government might have been forced by these facts to meet the North halfway over the future form of government in Nigeria – a solution which the NPC was never prepared to concede to the South in the days when it was in power.

But this is probably too favourable an assessment of the possible future evolution of the military regime. From what little is known of the attitudes of Ironsi's advisers, it appears that they, like the politicians before them, viewed the possession of political authority as a weapon to be used to crush the opposition, and in spite of the experience of the May riots they still seem to have believed that they could impose their blue-

print for the future on the whole country. As far as can be
discerned, they aimed to restore the political institutions of the
old colonial era, re-creating in a new guise the hierarchy of
governor, residents and district officers, united in a single public
service and advised by subservient natural rulers. Certainly,
this was to be the pattern for at least the first three years of the
military regime, until political parties were to be allowed to
function again after the interim of 'corrective government'.

This nostalgia for the certainties of the past, when the administration decided what was best for Nigeria and the people
obeyed, was quite unrealistic in the conditions of 1966. It might
have been possible for a British governor in the heyday of the
colonial era to impose his will on Nigeria, relying on the loyalty
of the British-officered Army and the fact that, in the last
resort, additional troops could be found from a neighbouring
colony or the Imperial Reserve.[37] But in 1966 the North was no
longer an inert mass, ready to accept whatever decisions were
taken in Lagos, any more than the West in 1965 was prepared
to acquiesce in the attempt by the NPC to impose their ally,
Chief Akintola, on it as Regional premier. Such policies only
made political sense if the government possessed forces which
were both strong enough to crush utterly all opposition, and
also completely loyal to those in power. This was not the case,
either for the politicians or for the regime that replaced them.
Both the civilian government of Sir Abubakar and the military
government of General Ironsi were overthrown when a section
of the Army made common cause with the opposition.

The logic of sectional domination of a country requires a
sectional army. If the Army is multi-tribal, then it cannot be
used to enforce policies which appear to be predominantly
designed to favour one tribe or one section. If such an army is
used on internal security duties to coerce the government's
opponents, it is likely to be an unreliable instrument of re-
pression, a constant threat to its nominal master. This obvious
truth has been most clearly acted upon in Uganda, where Presi-

dent Obote purged the Uganda Army of Buganda officers when he overthrew the Kabaka, and he now relies on a force almost wholly composed of soldiers from the Northern part of the country, his own political base.[38] In Nigeria, the NPC government at Independence was very conscious of the threat posed by the fact that two-thirds of the Nigerian Army officers were from the East. For five years they deferred complete Nigerianization of the Army, preferring to retain the services of British officers on secondment and contract until enough Northern officers had been trained. It seems likely that one contributory cause of the January 1966 coup was the fears of some Eastern officers that the NPC Minister of Defence intended to retire a number of Ibo officers now that he would soon have sufficient Northern officers to replace them.

When General Ironsi came to power he might have thought that his government was much better protected than the NPC had been six years before, since three-quarters of the senior officers were Ibos or Easterners and they held practically all the strategic positions in the Army. But the disorders in barracks after the January coup had shown the temper of the rank and file; the Eastern officers might be able to keep the soldiers under control, but they were not prepared to trust them with loaded rifles in an emergency. The multi-tribal nature of the Army held a more effective veto over the policies of Ironsi's government than any elected parliament could have achieved. It was obvious to both sides that this deadlock would not be allowed to continue. Unless the regime was prepared to allow its plans to be dictated by the Northern rank and file, it would have to alter drastically the tribal composition of the Army, to 'Easternize' the infantry battalions. Clearly something on these lines was being planned, as was shown by the rejection of Northern recruits in July. Warrant officers and subalterns from the North did not wait to see what the new order had in store for them. They feared that they would be purged, and so they acted.

Without any counterweight to oppose to the soldiers, the Military government of General Ironsi collapsed over most of the country. Tribal and sectional loyalties had disintegrated the old Nigerian Army. The counter-coup of July 1966 marks a more violent break with the past than any which occurred at the time when the Army passed from British to Nigerian control.

Postscript

Ojukwu never recognized Gowon's elevation to the post of supreme commander. He claimed that General Ironsi's death had not yet been confirmed and that therefore the post was not vacant; another reason was the fact that Gowon was not the senior surviving officer. Quite apart from Commodore Wey (the head of the Navy), Brig. Ogundipe (the High Commissioner in London) and Col. Adebayo (the military governor of the West), there were three other lieutenant-colonels who ranked above Gowon in terms of military seniority – Bassey, Imo and Njoku. There was also an element of personal rivalry. Gowon had been commissioned from Sandhurst in 1956 and Ojukwu from Eaton Hall OCS in 1958, but Ojukwu's commission had been backdated to take account of his university degree. At Nigerian Independence Lt. Gowon was two weeks senior to Lt. Ojukwu, but then Ojukwu was promoted captain and major with effect from a few days before Gowon, and he was also the first to be made an acting lieutenant-colonel. They were both promoted substantive lieutenant-colonels with seniority from exactly the same day.[1]

In the first two months after the July counter-coup it was possible that a future Nigerian constitution might have been agreed on the basis of a loose confederation of the four existing regions. There were still large Ibo communities in the cities of the North, and, as in previous crises, fears for their safety put the Northern leaders in a strong position to influence the actions of the East, and inhibited those Ibos who were already advocating secession.[2] A constitutional conference was convened in September 1966, and delegations from the West, North and East all tabled draft proposals which would have confined the central government in Lagos to a narrow range of activities in such matters as external affairs, currency, postal services and air transport, leaving all matters of substance to the regions; it was only the Mid-West, the smallest region, which advocated a strong centre, on the lines of the Federal Government as it had existed before the January 1966 coup. But a confederal arrangement, as proposed by the North, West and East, which would have left the Northern region intact, was quite unacceptable to the officers from the Middle Belt who were now largely in control of the Federal Army.

Q

They insisted that the Northern delegation should alter its stand, so that it now advocated the breaking-up of the North into a number of separate states, and consequent similar fragmentation of the East and West. Ojukwu was not prepared to consider such a proposal: break-up of the Eastern region would isolate the Ibo heartland from the main oilfields on the coast; and the splitting of Nigeria into a number of small states would inevitably lead to increased concentration of power in Lagos. But, before the conference could get down to detailed discussion, wholesale massacres of Easterners began all over the North, and the meeting adjourned, never to be resumed.

Biafran sources have claimed that these riots, like the ones in May, were deliberately instigated by Northern leaders in an attempt to frustrate a constitutional settlement of which they disapproved.[3] This is quite possible; but the riots could equally well have begun spontaneously. Since the army killings in July it had been difficult to restore normal standards of military discipline, and there were reports of soldiers molesting and murdering Ibos in the North throughout September. The massacres at Kano seem to have been sparked off by an incident at the airport, when the troops on duty there became incensed at the sight of Ibos departing with their belongings on a flight to Lagos, and then proceeded to murder them and other Ibo customs officers and airport staff that they could find.[4] Whatever the cause, the massacres very quickly spread throughout the North. Thousands of Easterners were killed and the survivors, more than a million refugees, abandoned their homes and businesses and fled in panic to the East. These traumatic events strengthened the hand of those Ibo leaders who were advocating Eastern secession.

In January 1967 the military leaders met for two days at Aburi in Ghana, in an effort to bridge the widening gulf between Lagos and Enugu. From the records of the meeting it seems to have been a happy reunion, with the soldiers united in hymning the incompetence of politicians. Ojukwu was the only participant who knew exactly what he wanted, and he secured the signatures of the Supreme Military Council to documents which would have had the effect of turning Nigeria into little more than a customs union. After the conference had ended Gowon retracted his agreement, when the full implications of the accords were pointed out to him by Federal civil servants, but Ojukwu refused to renew the negotiations. In the subsequent exchanges he appeared to be more anxious to be able to convict Gowon of bad faith than to achieve an agreed solution. On his side, Gowon did in fact make substantial concessions to the Eastern point of view, in order to avert the looming threat of civil

war. By Decree 8 of March 1967 the Regional governors were given a
veto on any territorial changes in their regions, on any law which
affected their regions and even on the capital expenditure of the
Federation. But the government in Lagos still retained the right to
declare a state of emergency in any region, provided the governors
of the other three regions agreed. This was quite unacceptable to the
East, but Ojukwu made no attempt to bargain for better terms, and
preparations for secession continued to go ahead. The Eastern leaders
optimistically expected that if they seceded they would gain diplomatic recognition within a few weeks. If they were then able to throw
back the first assault of the Federal Army it was believed that
Gowon would be forced to accept the *fait accompli*. There was even
the hope that the rest of the Federation would soon fall apart after the
East had left, since Awolowo had already shown considerable sympathy with the Eastern point of view. On 26 May 1967 a conference
of Eastern Leaders of Thought gave Ojukwu a mandate to secede.
A few hours later, in the hope of forestalling secession by appealing to
minority groups in the East, Gowon decreed the division of the four
regions of Nigeria into twelve new states, dividing the North into
six and the East into three.[5] Three days later, on 30 May, Ojukwu
proclaimed the birth of the new nation of Biafra.

The Federal Government immediately accelerated recruitment into
the Armed Forces and called up all reservists. Anyone who had
served in the Army at any time since 1939 and who was under fifty
was asked to re-enlist, and as a result the Federal forces were
strengthened by many veterans of the Burma campaign, a number of
whom were given emergency officer commissions.[6] These veterans
produced an immense improvement in military discipline which had
been severely shaken by the Army-led killings of July and September.
Immediately after the purge of Eastern soldiers in July 1966 the
Federal Army numbered about 7,000 men. By the end of the war,
in spite of heavy casualties, its strength had been built up to at least
120,000.[7] All this increase has been achieved by voluntary recruitment, particularly among the tribes of the Middle Belt, who now
make up 80 per cent of the Army. The main weakness of the Federal
forces at the outbreak of the war was in the technical arms, which
had been largely staffed by Easterners. Only about two hundred of
these Easterners, mainly those from the minority tribes, remained on
the Federal side, and a particularly vigorous recruiting drive to enlist
technicians had to be launched.[8]

On the Biafran side the outbreak of war was greeted with widespread popular enthusiasm. Graduates of Nsukka University en-

rolled for officer training and the mass of young men were eager to take their revenge on the Hausas for the recent massacres in the North. Those too old for service trained in the local Home Guard. By September 1967 Ojukwu was able to claim that his Regular Army numbered 50,000 men, but these were supplemented by large numbers in the popular militia and camp-followers who went into battle with the Army and took part in the fighting as soon as they could pick up a rifle from one of the fallen. However, as the war dragged on from month to month, war-weariness increased and voluntary recruitment had to be supplemented by what almost amounted to press-gang methods. There were reports of children of fourteen or even younger fighting in the Biafran Army.

The Federal Army had far more officers than Biafra. Only eight had been killed in the January coup, leaving about 180 officers from the North and the West who had been given combatant commissions before 1966. In addition, the first intake of the Kaduna Military Academy was commissioned in March 1967, providing a further forty officers for the Federation. In contrast, far fewer officer cadets had been accepted for training from the East after 1961, as a result of the policy of regional quotas, and in the murders of July 1966 the Biafrans had lost more than a quarter of their combatant officers. In July 1967 Ojukwu probably had less than seventy such officers who had been commissioned before 1966, when Mid-West officers of Ibo origin are excluded; and, unlike the Federation, there were very few experienced infantry WOs and NCOs in the East who could be given emergency commissions.

However, the Federal Army suffered from a shortage of *senior* officers. Of the fifty-seven commissioned before Independence only five were available for military duties on the Federal side – Ekpo (an Efik from Calabar), Olutoye, Obasanjo and Sotomi (Yorubas) and Akahan (a Tiv); and one of these, Col. Akahan, the Army Chief of Staff, died in a helicopter crash in the early days of the war. In contrast, the Biafrans started the war with eighteen majors and colonels who had been commissioned before Independence. In addition there were eight Ibo lieutenant-colonels in the Mid-West. At the outbreak of the civil war, the Mid-West officially took a neutral position, but five weeks later, when the Biafrans invaded that region, these officers fought on the secessionist side.[9]

There was a particular weakness in the Federal Army Medical Services. There were only twelve medical officers – (one of whom, Major Okonkwo, was later to be appointed Biafran governor of the Mid-West) – and these were mainly located in the base hospitals and

headquarters. So the few Northerners who were qualified doctors
were all drafted in the first few months of the war. But these were
quite insufficient to cope with the massive expansion of the Army
that followed the Biafran invasion of the Mid-West. Doctors from the
Western Region were reluctant to enlist, and since conscription there
was politically impossible, the Federal Public Service Commission
had to recruit medical officers and surgeons from Egypt and Algeria.
Surgical teams were also supplied by the Red Cross. Even so there
was frequently only one doctor to a Federal brigade and many of the
wounded had to be left unattended. Biafra started the war with four
medical officers who had been in the Nigerian Army, but it had the
advantages that there were a large number of civilian Ibo doctors
ready to serve and that the front lines were close to the main centres
of population.

With the exception of Obasanjo all the divisional commanders on
the Federal side were commissioned after Independence. Notable
among them are a group of four Northern colonels who were all commissioned from Sandhurst in July 1961 – Shuwa Muhammed,
Muhammed Murtala, Haruna and Bissalla. These were all substantive
captains, acting majors in 1966, and the first three were promoted
acting lieutenant-colonels by General Ironsi.

Shuwa Muhammed comes from Bornu in the North-East, the province which produced the three senior Northern officers killed in the
January 1966 coup. Like them he entered the Army after being
educated at Government College, Zaria, where he was a member of
the school cadet unit with Muhammed Murtala. At the time of the
July counter-coup he was in command of the battalion at Kano, and
then took over 1 Brigade in Kaduna. At the outbreak of the war the
bulk of the old Nigerian Army and the recalled reservists were concentrated on the northern border of Biafra, forming the First
Division. Col. Shuwa Muhammed commanded this division for two
years during its steady advance southwards into the heart of Biafra.
Then in September 1969 Col. Bissalla, who comes from Plateau Province in the Middle Belt, took over command of the division for the
final push which ended the war in January 1970.

Muhammed Murtala was in charge of Army Signals in Lagos at the
time of the counter-coup, and is credited by Biafran propagandists
with using this strategic position to co-ordinate the overthrow of the
Ironsi regime. After the sudden Biafran thrust into the Mid-West in
August 1967 he was put in command of the hastily formed Second
Division. This force, composed at first of garrison troops from Lagos
and Ibadan and Yoruba recruits from the training depot in the West,

was able to halt the Biafran drive at the battle of Ore and then force them back out of the Mid-West by the end of September. Second Division then tried to capture Onitsha by a frontal assault across the River Niger and were twice beaten back with heavy casualties. The city was eventually taken in March 1968 by crossing the Niger higher up and attacking from the landward side, but Col. Murtala was relieved of his command shortly afterwards and returned to his post in Signals. His successor was Col. Haruna, but the badly mauled division made no significant advance to the south in the next eighteen months, and was mainly occupied with the task of keeping the road from Onitsha to Enugu open, and also with dealing with Biafran infiltrators into the Mid-West. In September 1969 the command passed to Lt.-Col. Jalo (a Northerner from the Middle Belt, ex-Mons OCS 1961), and the operations of the division were thereafter confined to the Mid-West for the remaining months of the war.

On the Southern front the first commander was Col. Adekunle. He is the son of a Yoruba father and a Northern mother while his wife comes from an Eastern minority tribe, so he has been able to claim that he is a truly inter-tribal Nigerian. He was educated at the Provincial Secondary School, Okene, in Kabba Province of the Middle Belt, and was commissioned from Sandhurst in December 1960. He was already a substantive major by 1966, but was ignored for promotion by General Ironsi. At the outbreak of the war he was promoted lieutenant-colonel and commanded the successful assault on Bonny in July 1967. Then, after the Biafran invasion of the Mid-West, he was put in command of the Third (Marine Commando) Division. His fiery temper was probably an asset in disciplining this hastily formed division into an effective fighting force, though it did not endear him to foreign newspaper correspondents. He was promoted substantive colonel and transferred to a staff post in charge of training in May 1969 after the Biafran recapture of Owerri in the previous month. His successor was Col. Obasanjo, also a Yoruba, who had been commissioned from Mons OCS in 1959. Under his command Third Division recaptured Owerri and finally linked up with Col. Bissalla's First Division to end the war.

The war opened the way to swift promotions at all levels in the Federal Army. Officers who were not yet substantive captains at the beginning of the war are now lieutenant-colonels and command brigades; even two officers who were commissioned as second lieutenants from Sandhurst in 1964 became brigade commanders, Innih and Musa Yaradua. At the first assault on Onitsha across the Niger one battalion was commanded by an education officer directly com-

missioned from the university in 1964 who had never had any training as an infantry officer. Because of the extreme shortage of
commissioned officers, platoons and companies were often commanded by sergeants and warrant officers.

On the Biafran side almost all the senior commanders had held
high rank in the Army before 1966. The first Biafran Chief of Staff,
Hilary Njoku, an Ibo, was commissioned from the ranks in 1956
after a short course at Eaton Hall OCS. In 1965 he had been a
lieutenant-colonel commanding 2 NA at Ikeja.[10] In the last year of
the war the Biafran Army was commanded by Phillip Effiong, an
Anang (a small tribe in Calabar province). He joined the Army in
1946 and was a CSM at the Zaria recruit training depot in 1955 before
he went to England for officer cadet training. In 1965 he had been a
lieutenant-colonel, director of Army Ordnance Services. The one new
man at the top of the Biafran Army was Col. Hannibal Achuzia, who
gained a reputation as a dogged fighter and tough disciplinarian in
the battles for Onitsha and later outside Port Harcourt. He is said to
have served with the British Army in Korea and joined the Biafran
Army at the outbreak of the civil war.[11] Most of the other Biafran
divisional and brigade commanders that have been named in newspaper reports were already officers before 1960, for example, Madiebo,
Nwawo, Eze, Kalu and Ivenso. Only a few of those commissioned
after Independence held senior commands; one such was Uwakwe,
ex-Sandhurst 1962, who commanded a Biafran brigade near Aro-
Chukwu in 1968.

Hardly any of the conspirators of the January 1966 coup now sur-
vive. According to Federal reports, Major Nzeogwu was killed in
August 1967, trying to stem the Federal advance north of Enugu,
and Capt. Oji died in action in 1968. In October 1967 Major
Ifeajuna was court-martialled by the Biafrans and shot for conspir-
ing against Ojukwu, together with Lt.-Col. Banjo, the Biafran
divisional commander in the Mid-West. Since Majors Okafor and
Anuforo were shot in the July 1966 counter-coup the only senior
member of the conspiracy who may still be alive is Major Onwuatuegwu, who was with Nzeogwu in Kaduna.

The events that followed the January coup were far different from
what the conspirators had expected, but it is possible that now the
war has ended the most important of their original aims have been
achieved. Nzeogwu repudiated the idea of secession, and the breaking-up of the large regions of the Federation, leading inevitably to
greater powers for the central government, is a result that he would

have welcomed.[12] He would not have been so happy at the return of the politicians in the shape of the twelve commissioners appointed by General Gowon at the outbreak of the war to take part in the government; but this partial return to civilian rule became almost unavoidable because of the disillusionment of many Nigerians with the performance of the Army in power.

No one now believes in the incorruptibility of military men. One lieutenant-colonel has been court-martialled and reduced in rank, and at least eight other officers have been imprisoned for various offences involving the misappropriation of public funds. The permanent secretary of the Ministry of Finance has claimed that the country has been cheated of millions of pounds through fraudulent contracts for military supplies.[13] The prolongation of the war throughout 1969, in spite of the Federal advantages in manpower and equipment, made it difficult to believe in the superior efficiency of the Army, and there was even speculation that the commanders were deliberately holding back from the final destruction of Biafra in order to retain their enlarged spheres of authority. Moreover, the behaviour of some troops with weapons in their hands has not always endeared them to the civilian population. Surprisingly, it seems likely that the reputation of the police is now somewhat higher than that of the military, since the Police Force generally retained its cohesion and discipline at a time when the Army disintegrated into its regional components.

However, it is fortunate that the convulsions of 1966 brought to the supreme command a soldier of the quality of Yakubu Gowon. During the war he endeavoured to moderate the ferocity of the conflict by the Code of Conduct which he issued to the Federal troops, and he was so anxious to alleviate the sufferings of non-combatants that he allowed Red Cross supplies to be flown into the Biafran enclave, even though he was well aware that they were partially used to succour the enemy forces. Now that the war is over he has shown an almost unparalleled magnanimity in seeking reconciliation with the Ibos and their reintegration into the national community. The new twelve-state structure seems likely to provide a more substantial basis for future stability than the rivalries of the overmighty regions of the past. This drastic political reorganization was inaugurated by a soldier – a soldier who exemplifies a devotion to the unity of Nigeria in the best traditions of the Nigerian Army.

Appendix

COMMISSIONINGS OF NIGERIAN OFFICERS AND DEPARTU
COMMISSION.   1959 to 1965.

| | Newly commissioned Nigerian Officers during year | | | |
	Combatant	Executive	Direct	Nursing
1959	12	–	2	–
1960	21	8	3	–
1961	42	31	4	8
1962	37	10	6	9
1963	96	13	36	7
1964	59	5	27	3
1965	35	1	18	5

Source: *Federal Nigeria Official Gazettes*. 1959–66.
NOTE 1.
The departure dates of 25 British officers are accidentally omitted
from the Gazette and have been guessed from the date of arrival
and the normal length of tour.

Nigerian Officers left, died etc. during year	Total Nigerian Officers Dec. 31st	Expatriate Officers remaining at end of year			Total All Officers Dec. 31st
		Contract	Seconded	Total	
−1	50	23	214	237	287
–	82	37	206	243	325
−7	160	39	171	210	370
−2	220	35	91	126	346
−5	367	28	51	79	446
−3	458	9	10	19	477
−10	507	1	0	1	508

NOTE 2.
In all, 27 Nigerian officers left the army between 1960 and 1965. 12 of these held combatant commissions (see p. 255, note 20). Of the rest, 3 held executive commissions and 12 direct commissions (5 nurses, 3 doctors, 1 lawyer, 1 chaplain, 1 engineer, 1 pay officer).

Notes

CHAPTER I

1. cf. the remarks in R. O. Tilman and T. Cole (eds.), *The Nigerian Political Scene* (Duke University Press, 1962) 244: 'I would add that the Army is not a factor in Nigerian politics. Fortunate is the democracy where such a reference can be treated as an after-thought.' One observer who did foresee trouble was S. E. Finer, *The Man on Horseback* (Pall Mall, 1962) 240.
2. Anthony Enahoro went to prison in 1948, but he was a minor figure at that time.
3. This simile comes from H. O. Davies, *Nigeria, the Prospects for Democracy* (Weidenfeld & Nicolson, 1961) 92.

    The distinction between 'mass parties' and 'élite parties' is drawn in Thomas Hodgkin, *African Political Parties* (Penguin, 1961).

    As Independence approached, parties of different types merged, and modernizing political leaders were willing to come to terms with the traditional rulers. However, the two broad categories are still useful.
4. *My Life: The Autobiography of Alhaji Sir Ahmadu Bello, Sardauna of Sokoto* (Cambridge University Press, 1962) 63, 87, 210.
5. *HR Deb*, 27 March 1962, col. 326, and 19 November 1960, col. 109.

CHAPTER II

The early history of the regiment is largely taken from A. Haywood and F. A. S. Clarke: *The History of the Royal West African Frontier Force* (Gale & Polden, Aldershot, 1964). See also the articles by A. H. M. Kirk-Greene and S. C. Ukpabi in *Journal of the Historical Society of Nigeria* (1964) 129–47 and 1966, 485–501.

1. The fourth battalion traced its origin to 'Glover's Hausas' and celebrated its centenary in 1963, when it was given the freedom of the city of Ibadan (*West African Pilot*, 10 June 1963).

2. For the Egba War, see also M. Perham, *Lugard, the Years of Authority* (Collins, 1960) 438–56.

3. Stanhope White, *Dan Bana* (Cassell, 1966) 50.

4. *Nigeria Handbook 1953* (Crown Agents) 245 and *Nigeria Government Gazette*, 3 June 1948.

5. 'The Development of West African Forces in the Second World War', *Army Quarterly* (October, 1947) 68. On the use of 'moral pressure' see the Sardauna's description of how the government's request for help in recruiting miners for the tin mines at Jos during the war was fulfilled: 'The people were naturally reluctant to leave their neighbourhood. . . . We had to allocate quotas to each village and hope for the best. Force was not to be used and I don't think it was, but no doubt some form of moral pressure was involved' (*My Life*, C.U.P., 1962, 53 f.).

6. Chief A. Enahoro, *Fugitive Offender* (Cassell, 1965) 68–70. The boys were protesting about conditions in their living quarters, caused by the Army's requisitioning of part of the school buildings. One of those conscripted died while on service.

7. Recruiting advertisements in the press stressed such themes as: 'Cpl. Bello will have a trade when victory is won.' Such appeals were only directed to the literate. In fact 32,502 qualified as Army tradesmen out of the 121,652 (*Daily Times*, 18 August 1953).

8. List of benefits in *HR Deb*, 31 July 1958, col. 1784, from which the calculation in the text was made.

9. *West African Pilot*, 3 June 1957, quoting Brigadier Browne. Detailed figures are only available from April 1958 when they were published in the *Annual Estimates of the Federal Government*.

10. *The West African Forces Conference 1953*, Cmnd. 6577 (Stationery Office, 1954) 3.

11. *Empire and Commonwealth*, Vol. XXXV (September 1960) 23.

12. Estimate made by the Chief Secretary, *HR Deb*, 21 March 1955, 420.

13. Sir Abubakar made the pilgrimage to Mecca and became *Alhaji* in 1957; he was knighted in 1960. In 1952 he was Minister of Transport in the central government at Lagos, and was government spokesman in a debate on Nigerianization in the Army, *HR Deb*, 19 August 1952, 215.

14. *HR Deb*, 16 February 1959, col. 534.

15. A complete list of British officers serving in Nigeria is only available from 1958, *Federal Government Gazette*, 18 December 1958, and subsequent issues. But there were few changes between 1956 and 1958.

16. *Notes on the Royal West African Frontier Force and the Stations in which it normally serves.* Author not stated, copy in War Office Library. A note inside states, 'This is not an official War Office publication. It has been prepared from accurate but unofficial sources.' Calculations on British service pay in Nigeria below have been made from this document.

17. *Final Report of the Parliamentary Committee on the Nigerianization of the Federal Public Service* (Lagos, 1959) 35.

18. *HR Deb*, Written Answer, 30 August 1955, 537.

19. In 1954 there were only seven schools in Nigeria maintained exclusively for white children; five of these were Army schools; the other two were maintained by the tin mines at Bukuru and the Sudan Interior Mission. *HR Deb*, 13–23 August 1954, Written Answer W. 183.

20. Release from prime minister's office, quoted in *West African Pilot*, 5 January 1959. The usual engagement was for six years, but certain tradesmen were required to serve for nine years once they had qualified.

21. Army pay, *Daily Times*, 11 June 1957. Police pay, *Daily Times*, 12 July 1955. Daily paid labour, *Daily Times*, 30 November 1955. Army privates' pay, *HR Deb*, 21 March 1955, 413.

22. *HR Deb*, 8 April 1963, col. 707.

23. *HR Deb*, 6 August 1959, 67; written answer by prime minister.

24. Brig. Clarke, 'The Development of the West African Forces', *Army Quarterly* (October, 1947) 60.
    Gen. Sir George Gifford, 'The RWAFF and its Expansion', *Army Quarterly* (July, 1945) 194.

25. *Nigerian Citizen*, 26 August 1961. *West African Pilot*, 21 October 1957, advertisement for recruit enlistment at Enugu: 'Applicants should have good physique and Standard VI Certificate. Limited vacancies for men without Standard VI for enlistment as non-tradesmen.'

26. *Daily Times*, 20 May 1952. *West African Pilot*, 20 and 21 May 1952. *HR Deb*, March 1953, Written Answer, 15 (details of the court-martial sentences). Haywood and Clarke, *op. cit.*, 478.

27. Army statistics from *HR Deb*, 7 February 1959, Written Answer. Police from *HR Deb*, 28 March 1955, 700.

28. Army spokesman quoted by *Daily Times*, 5 June 1959.

29. *The Observer*, 23 October 1966.

30. Haywood and Clarke, *op. cit.*, 254.

31. *Royal Nigerian Army Magazine* (1962) 91. See also the complaints about the sons of 'French' soldiers being admitted to the Boys'

Company, *HR Deb*, 14 March 1957, cols. 804 f. and 18 March 1957, col. 900.

32. Taken from the published biographies of Eastern members of the Federal parliaments of 1955 and 1959 and the Eastern Assemblies of 1952 and 1961 (*Eastern Region and Federal Government Information Services*).

33. This is the estimate by B. Dudley, *Round Table* (January, 1968) 30. On Yoruba soldiers, see below, p. 98.

34. See *House of Commons Hansard*, 10 March 1952, cols. 1036 ff. and *1953 Conference Report* (*Cmnd 6577*), 4.

35. *Daily Times*, 3 and 5 November 1956.

36. *HR Deb*, 19 August 1952, 216.

37. *Senate Debates*, 18 October 1965, 490.

38. *HR Deb*, 14 April 1960, col. 1266.

39. *West African Pilot*, 31 January 1956. For the meaning of the epithet, cf. 'Young men ridicule an old man who gets his work done thoroughly in my language as "abobaku", one whose loyalty to the government is so much that he would work and work even to the point of death' (*HR Deb*, 2 April 1963, col. 372).

40. *HR Deb*, 21 March 1955, 422.

41. Names taken at random from the full list in Haywood and Clarke, *op. cit.*, 490–1.

CHAPTER III

1. The account of this proposal and why it was turned down is taken from *HR Deb*, 18 March 1953, 519 and *HR Deb*, 12 March 1954, 216.

2. *Daily Times*, 12 July 1949 and *HR Deb*, Written Answer, 18 August 1952, 184. The details about the first Gold Coast officers are taken from W. F. Gutteridge, *Armed Forces in New States* (Oxford, 1962) 43.

3. This list of the stages towards a commission is taken from an interview with a Nigerian cadet at Sandhurst in *Eastern Outlook*, 20 October 1955. The Eaton Hall course was omitted after 1960.

4. *HR Deb*, Written Answer, 30 August 1955, 549. *West African Pilot*, 2 September 1956. This is a long, bitter article, apparently by one of the cadets at Teshie who had been failed, denouncing the prejudice of British officers against Southern candidates for a commission.

5. Sir John Smyth, *Bolo Whistler* (Muller, 1967) 199, quoting an interview with Sir John Macpherson.

6. Sey came originally from the Gold Coast, as is shown by his original army number recorded in the *London Gazette* at the time of commissioning, but he was made an officer in the Nigeria Regiment. Lt. Otu Amoo Kwa Wellington originally joined the Army in 1942, and was an RSM at the time of his commissioning (*Daily Times*, 17 February 1953). Details of the resignations of Sey and Umar Lawan are recorded in the *London Gazette*, but there is no notification of when or why Ugboma and Wellington left the Army.

7. 'Ironsi's father was a railwayman from Sierra Leone and his mother an Ibo', *West Africa*, 21 January 1967 – his obituary.

The details of the career of RSM Maigumeri in the next paragraph are taken from an appendix in Haywood and Clarke, *op. cit*, 502.

8. For a history of the school, see the article by Vivian Jones in *Nigeria Magazine* (1962) 26–34, 'Pioneer of Northern Education'.

On the Army's efforts at this school, see *HR Deb*, 19 August 1952, 205, and a letter by H. W. Ridley, a former member of the staff, on Gowon's schooldays, in *Daily Telegraph*, 10 August 1966.

9. Mallam Munir, *HR Deb*, 19 August 1952, 212.

10. *West Africa*, 27 August 1966; *Nigeria Magazine*, December 1966, 304; *Nigerian Citizen*, 25 January 1961.

11. For previous lack of effort at Umuahia and Ibadan, see *HR Deb*, 19 August 1952, 211. For accusations, see note 4 above, and also *HR Deb*, 18 March 1953, 532 f., and 19 March 1953, 540. Naturally, the charges were indignantly denied by the chief secretary. There is no sign from the figures for commissionings that there was such an attempt; if there was one, it was unsuccessful.

		Northern officers	Southern officers
Officers at December 1950		–	5
,,	,, 1951	–	6
,,	,, 1952	–	5
,,	,, 1953	2	7
,,	,, 1954	4	8
,,	,, 1955	5	10
,,	,, 1956	5	18

12. *HR Deb*, Written Answer, 16 March 1956; police establishment from *Federal Estimates* 1955–6. Since this establishment was

usually not filled, more than a quarter of the actual officers on duty would be Nigerians.

13. *HR Deb*, 21 March 1955, 423. *Daily Times*, 3 June 1957.

14. *Who's Who in Nigeria*, *Daily Times* publication, Lagos, September 1956. Major Ironsi, who was equerry to the Queen earlier in the year, is not included.

15. Pay in 1952, *HR Deb*, 19 August 1952, 204. Pay in 1956, *Daily Times*, 4 June 1957. See remarks on officers' pay in *1953 Conference Report*, 8.

16. Below are given the dates on which certain civil servants entered the senior service Scale A (the equivalent of a subaltern) and the date they were first appointed to a 'super-scale post' carrying a group 7 salary (£2292 in 1960, which was higher than the salary of a lieutenant-colonel in the Army at that time – £1880).

Eastern Region	Scale A	Group 7
B. N. Okagbue	1950	1959
P. E. Archibong	1951	1958
O. E. Ikpi	1954	1958
S. I. A. Akenzua	1952	1960
Northern Region		
Abdurrahman Okene	1954	1960
Yusufu Gobir	1956	1959
Bukar Shaib	1954	1960

17. Letters, e.g. *Daily Times* 13 September 1957. Number of applicants, see *HR Deb*, 20 February 1958, col. 107.

18. Figures taken from I. Nicholson's chapter on 'The Machinery of Government' in J. P. Mackintosh *et al.*, *Nigerian Government and Politics* (Allen & Unwin, 1966) 189.

19. *Defence White Paper 1957, Cmnd 124*, para. 68: 'The large reduction in the size of the forces will inevitably create a surplus of officers and NCOs.' This white paper also announced the ending of compulsory National Service, with the last intake in 1960. It is tempting to speculate that Nigerianization of the Army would have been more energetically pursued if Britain had ended National Service a few years earlier.

20. Pensions: *HR Deb*, 21 November 1958, cols. 2390–4. Cars: *HR Deb*, 12 August 1959, col. 1819. Prime Minister's remark: 20 February 1958, col. 107.

R

21. Easterners are categorized on the basis of tribal origin. If the classification were made on the basis of place of birth, both Nzeogwu and Ojukwu would count as Northerners, since they were both born in that region. Similarly it would be misleading to count the Ika-Ibo of the Mid-West with the Western Region, since they speak Ibo, and the officers from this group sided with Biafra at the time of the civil war. It seems that a calculation on this pattern had already been done in the Defence department, since, when the prime minister answered a question on the regional origin of Nigerian officers (*HR Deb*, Written Answer, 7, February 1959), his reply (that 22 officers of Eastern Region origin had been commissioned up to December 1958), can only be reconciled with the facts on the assumption that Ika-Ibo are being counted with the East.

  The ambiguity of the terms 'Ibo' and 'Easterner' was made full use of by propagandists on both the Federal and Biafran sides in the civil war.

22. Northern officers in the Police Force given in *HR Deb*, 18 April 1961, Written Answer.

  Region of Origin of Officers on C scale and Above in the Federal Public Service, at 1 March 1960:

Expatriates	1,724
West	1,429
East	1,092
Cameroons	57
North	29
Other African	67

  HR Deb, 20 April 1960

  (This group covers the 'senior service' and also the higher technical and executive grades.)

23. Calculations made from pp. 24 and 3 of *Matters Arising from the Final Report of the Parliamentary Committee on the Nigerianization of the Public Service* (Government Printer, Lagos, 1960) and also the establishment figures given in *Estimates of the Federal Government 1960–1*.

24. *Sunday Times*, 2 December 1956, quoting General Exham.

25. *Final Report*, 1959, 36.

26. Interview with General Gowon in *West Africa*, 15 July 1967. *Nigerian Citizen*, 27 April 1957.

27. See a letter in *Daily Telegraph*, 5 April 1967 from P. G. Harrington, who was formerly a captain in the Nigerian Army:

There always existed a visible rift between those who came up through the ranks in Nigeria and those who went to Sandhurst.

This has been mentioned to me a number of times by Nigerian officers. The same phenomenon is also apparently to be found in the Congolese Army (Crawford Young, *Politics in the Congo* (Princeton, 1965) 461).

28. There are some indications of this attitude in W. F. Gutteridge's book, *Military Institutions and Power in New States* (Pall Mall, 1964) especially 61, and 104.

There was a natural inclination on the part of British officers to go slow in the interests of thoroughness.

The matter-of-fact treatment of commissioned service as 'just another job' did not find favour with Britons brought up in an atmosphere where a certain militarist mystique is accepted.

CHAPTER IV

1. *Report of the 1953 Conference*, 4. The first meeting of the Advisory Council took place at Accra in January 1955. Mallam Abubakar represented Nigeria.

2. *Report of the Resumed Nigeria Constitutional Conference, September–October 1958, Cmnd 569*, para. 83.

3. *Parliamentary Debates, House of Commons*, Written Answer, 9 February 1962, 92. The announcement quoted in this answer made it clear that Defence co-operation would continue as before, in spite of the abrogation.

4. Details of the decisions are given in Haywood and Clarke, *op. cit.*, 482.

5. *HR Deb*, Written Answer, 20 November 1958, 98. This was a reversion to the system used before the Second World War.

6. *Final Report of the Parliamentary Committee on Nigerianization 1960* (Government Printer, Lagos) 35, gives the following figures for British NCOs and WOs:

April 1956	336
,, 1957	255
,, 1958	184
,, 1959	111
,, 1960	80

By March 1964 there were still 21 left, according to *HR Deb*, 14 March 1964, col. 198. Oral Answer.

7. One reason for the high rate of pay of seconded British officers was that before the Army passed under local control overseas allowances had been tax free, but now the full pay of seconded officers was liable to Nigerian income tax. The figures for the recruitment and run-out of contract officers are as follows:

Year	New Contracts	Left	Total remaining
1959	24	1	23
1960	18	4	37
1961	10	8	39
1962	2	6	35
1963	3	10	28
1964	–	19	9
1965	–	8	1

Table compiled from details of contract officers given in *Government Gazettes*.

8. For example: *HR Deb*, 19 August 1952, 209 (M. Bello Dandago); 18 March 1953, 525 (Mr Akinola); 16 March 1955, 337 (Mr Yellowe); 10 September 1957, col. 2095 (M. Hassan Yola); 3 March 1958, col. 711 (Mr Komolafe).

9. This and the following speech are in *Daily Service*, 30 April 1958 and 1 May 1958. Also see 14 May 1958. There is an account of the debate in Sklar, *Nigerian Political Parties* (Princeton, 1963) 280 f.

10. *HR Deb*, 14 March 1955, 164. Laughter was raised at a reference to Fani-Kayode's views, *HR Deb*, 17 January 1955, 93.

11. *HR Deb*, 12 August 1959, cols. 1824 and 1826; 14 April 1960, col. 1231.

12. *West African Pilot*, 4 July 1959. Ghana's projected increase in expenditure was not in fact achieved, according to the *Accountant-General's Statement* at the end of the financial year (Govt. Printer, Accra, 1961).

13. *HR Deb*, 14 April 1960, col. 1263.

14. The successive stages in Nigeria's change of policy can be traced in *HR Deb*, 16 February 1959, col. 535; 12 August 1959, col. 1826; and 14 April 1960, col. 1248.

15. See G. Bing, *Reap the Whirlwind* (MacGibbon & Kee, 1968) 257. One witness questioned by Mr Bing informed the enquiry: 'In 1946 in Burma a group of the opposition party dressed up in

military uniforms, stole an army truck and went into the cabinet room and massacred 14 of the entire cabinet.'

The Ghanaian major accused of complicity had served in Burma.

16. There are references in the press: *West African Pilot*, 23 March 1960 and 2 June 1960; *Nigerian Citizen*, 7 January 1959; *Daily Service*, 22 June 1960.

The most prescient comment was made by Ayo Ogunsheye, Director of the Extra-Mural Department of Ibadan University, *Daily Service*, 1 January 1959:

> When an African country (the Sudan) joined the ranks of the military dictatorships people could not help asking, 'Will it happen here?' One answer is that it cannot happen here because our Army is too small. That I do not find convincing. In relation to the area it had to cover, the Sudanese Army is proportionately smaller than the Nigerian. We can answer indirectly by asking, 'Why did the military intervene?' At the risk of over-simplification, because the civilians did not deliver the goods. The people expected good government and higher standards of living; instead they got inefficiency and corruption. Without suggesting that the Army can in fact do better than the politicians, the lesson is clear. If we do not want people to lose faith in parliamentary democracy we must make sure that it does not become a farce.

A similar point was made by M. Aminu Kano (NEPU) *HR Deb*, 14 April 1960, col. 1239.

17. Questions on the regional origins of officers: *HR Deb*, Written Answer, 7 February 1959. See also, the appeal of Abdullahi Musawa quoted in Ch. III, p. 53.

Other comments in parliament are *HR Deb*, 12 August 1959, col. 1812 and 18 January 1960, col. 201.

18. The NPC manifesto is in *Daily Times*, 4 December 1959.

The NCNC manifesto is in *Daily Times*, 7 and 9 October 1959.

One minor party also advocated an increase in military expenditure. This was the Dynamic Party of Dr Chike Obi, whose sole candidate was Dr Obi himself. He proposed the setting up of military training schools and an institute of guerrilla warfare (K. W. J. Post, *The Nigerian Federal Election of 1959* (Oxford, 1963) 313).

19. The Action Group manifesto is in *Daily Times* and *Daily Service*, 7 October 1959. The pledge of £500,000 was probably aimed

especially at the ex-servicemen in the Northern Region, particularly in the Middle Belt, where the Action Group was allied with the United Middle Belt Congress. Such voters would, of course, have been alienated by any open avowal of proposals to downgrade the Army.

Previously, when all the ex-servicemen in the Western House of Assembly were NCNC members from Ibadan or the Mid-West, the Action Group was less cordial towards them. The party newspaper, the *Daily Service*, reproved them on 11 May 1957: 'Ex-servicemen should not expect to be petted like spoiled children. They have to work for their living like anyone else.'

The AG policy paper on Internal Security is in *Daily Service*, 20 November 1959.

20. For details of the internal security precautions over the election period, see K. W. J. Post, *op. cit.*, 345-7. Also, *West African Pilot*, 14 November 1959; *Daily Times*, 20 November 1959; *Daily Service*, 1 December 1959, and *Daily Times*, 3 December 1959.

CHAPTER V

1. All details of the operations in the Cameroons are taken from *Royal Nigerian Army Magazine*, March 1961, especially pp. 20-3. Quotations from pp. 53 and 60.

2. e.g. Lt. Madiebo from the Recce Squadron, and Capt. Maimalari from Depot. Details of the moves of officers are given in *RNA Magazine* for March 1961 and May 1962.

3. Details of the dispositions of troops and the actions in this and subsequent paragraphs are taken from *RNA Magazine*, May 1962 and the long speech by the Minister of Defence in the debate on the Congo, *HR Deb*, 18 April 1961, cols. 1866-71.

4. *HR Deb*, 18 April 1961, col. 1871. The three officers who were moved from the battalion were expatriates, according to *West African Pilot*, 26 February 1962.

5. H. T. Alexander, *African Tightrope* (Pall Mall, 1965) 68. It is interesting that General Alexander suggests that a contributory factor to the Ghana Army mutiny was that Lt.-Col. Hansen (the Ghanaian C.O.) 'was perhaps sometimes not very moderate in applying discipline' (*op. cit.*, 68). This is the opposite fault to that imputed to Ironsi.

6. Allegations in *West African Pilot*, 6 February 1961. For alarmist reports, see, for example, *Daily Express* (Lagos) 22 February

1961. 'The massacre has begun. Today the Congolese Army staged the first offensive against the United Nations. . . .'

7. Ironsi's move to London was publicized as a promotion, but Ironsi himself was under no illusions about this, and felt very bitter that he had been let down by his officers (information from an officer of the battalion). On arrival in London Ironsi assumed the insignia of a brigadier for a few weeks, but he was not in fact promoted to this rank until March 1962. After eighteen months in the High Commission, he spent the year 1963 on a staff course at the Imperial Defence College, and then commanded the tail end of the UN Congo Force in 1964, with the local rank of major-general. On his return to Nigeria he reverted to brigadier, and took over 2 Brigade at Apapa, near Lagos.

8. *Nigerian Citizen*, 28 January 1961, quoting Ministry of Defence.

9. *HR Deb*, 18 April 1961, cols. 1862–5.

10. *NAM*, October 1963, 61. Other details of the Kasai operation will be found in Major R. Lawson's book, *Strange Soldiering* (Hodder, 1963) and in *RNA Magazine*, May 1962. The operation against Katanga in January 1963 is described in *West African Pilot*, 4 April 1963.

11. Calculations made from details given in *HR Deb*, 18 April 1961, cols. 1874–5.

   UN Allowance; all ranks, 65 Congolese francs daily (approx. 9s. 3d.).

   Nigerian Overseas Allowance; ranging from 5s. a day for a private to £1 a day for a colonel.

   Additional Family Allotment; 1s. 6d. to 2s. 9d. a day, according to rank.

   UN Leave Allowance; 375 Congolese francs a month.

12. There was also a detachment of the Nigerian Police in the Congo, which did not leave until January 1966.

   Immediately after the Nigerians left Sir Abubakar received a fresh request from the Congolese government for military assistance to deal with the rebellions in Kwilu and Orientale (*The Times*, 8 July 1964). The Nigerian Government promised to consider such military aid after the Federal elections (*West Africa*, 29 August 1964, 978), but this proved unnecessary as a result of Tshombe's mercenaries and the descent of the Belgian paratroops on Stanleyville.

13. See Harvey Glickman, *Some Observations on the Army and Political Unrest in Tanganyika* (Duquesne University, 1965).

14. *Observer*, 30 August 1964.

15. *West Africa*, 28 March 1964, 355.

16. *West African Pilot*, 14 September 1964.

17. There is a very full account of this incident in the chapter by Martin Dent in J. P. Mackintosh *et al.*, *Government and Politics in Nigeria* (Allen & Unwin, 1966) 461–507.

18. *West Africa*, 8 August 1964, 879. This was quickly denied by the police commissioner for the Northern Region, but later the premier of the North, Sir Ahmadu Bello, said that at least 11 police and 326 civilians had been killed by terrorists (*Debates of the Northern House of Assembly*, 27 February 1965, col. 115).

19. *NAM*, 1964, 71. By the end of the operation there were detachments from a number of different army units assisting in Tiv Division. Major Hassan Katsina (Inspector Recce) was one of the other senior officers involved.

20. *Observer*, 6 December 1964 and *West Africa*, 12 December 1964.

21. *Daily Express* (Lagos) 25 February 1965; *Nigerian Outlook*, 7 June 1965; *Nigerian Citizen*, 7 August 1965; *Federal Gazette*, 26 January 1966.

CHAPTER VI

1. The details in this paragraph are taken from *West African Pilot*, 9 March 1963; *HR Deb*, 10 January 1964, col. 3416; *Daily Express* (Lagos) 5 May 1965 and from many speakers in the obituary debate *HR Deb*, 4 May 1965. Allowance must be made for the traditional hyperbole on such occasions.

2. These figures are rounded to the nearest £50,000 and are taken from the annual *Reports of the Accountant General of the Federal Government* from 1956 to 1966. These relate to the sums actually expended, and are usually far below the estimates issued at the beginning of the financial year.

3. The authorized establishment of the Army was given in the *Financial Estimates of the Federal Government* from 1958 to 1962; thereafter the figure was treated as a military secret.

1958–59	7,599
1959–60	7,514
1960–61	7,480
1961–62	7,696
1962–63	7,816

In 1964, General Welby-Everard told a press conference that the Army would reach 10,500 by April 1965 (*Daily Times*, 2 May 1964).

4. Details of the stops and starts in recruit training at the Depot are given in *NAM*, 1963, 77 and *West African Pilot*, 16 April 1963 (speech by Alhaji Tako Galadima).

5. J. P. Mackintosh *et al.*, *Nigerian Government and Politics* (Allen & Unwin, 1966) 82. There is perhaps a rueful reference to Ribadu's previous demands by the Minister of Finance, Chief Festus Okotie-Eboh, in the obituary tribute:

> 'The entire Armed Forces will mourn a well-loved minister who was always ready to fight their battles unasked, and who nearly always fought them successfully.' (*HR Deb*, 4 May 1965, col. 1918.)

6. For comparison with Ghanaian Defence spending, it is more realistic to contrast the Ghanaian figures with the combined Nigerian Federal and Regional budgets since the costs of the Nigerian social services were largely paid by the Regions, though they are carried on the central budget in Ghana. Figures for the *actual* achieved recurrent expenditure over the period are as follows:

	Nigerian Army	Total Defence (Army, Navy, Air)	% of Fed. recurrent budget	% of Fed. and Regions recurrent budget
1958–59	£2,823,000	£2,978,000	8·5	3·1
1959–60	3,690,000	3,988,000	9·9	4·3
1960–61	3,979,000	4,427,000	9·6	4·3
1961–62	4,048,000	4,564,000	8·5	3·9
1962–63	4,082,000	4,707,000	7·8	3·6
1963–64	4,516,000	5,588,000	7·6	4·0
1964–65	5,168,000	6,591,000	8·8	4·0
1965–66	5,838,000	7,847,000	9·1	4·5

From *Accountant General's Annual Reports*. These figures are fairly close to the original estimates.

7. *West African Pilot*, 3 December 1966, quoting Col. Adebayo. Special intakes for Westerners in 1965, see advert in *Daily Express* (Lagos) 15 May.

8. *RNA Magazine*, 1962, 99.

9. Police figures from *HR Deb*, Oral Answer, 13 January 1966.

10. B. Dudley, 'Nigeria's Civil War', *Round Table* (January, 1968) 30, estimates the Ika-Ibo as 50 per cent of the Mid-West military.

11. *NAM*, 1963, 57.

12. *Daily Times*, 6 April 1963 – a UMBC press conference. *Daily Express* (Lagos) 30 March 1963 – Tarka speaks at the treason trial.

13. See speeches in *HR Deb*, 14 April 1960, cols. 1231–66. So also Dr Azikiwe, *Nigerian Outlook*, 18 November 1961. Such views were not entirely disinterested, as Ribadu later pointed out (quoted at p. 108).

14. 'The Armed Forces in Nigeria are not regimentalized, men from all over Nigeria being deliberately mixed in all units', *Notes on RWAFF* (1955, in War Office Library). I was told of the 1961 policy at the time.

15. *Daily Times*, 26 October 1963.

16. *HR Deb*, 2 April 1965, cols. 442 and 444.

17. *Nigerian Outlook*, 18 November 1961.

18. History of the unit is given in *RNA Magazine*, 1962, 100 ff. Its disbandment, *NAM*, 1964, 87 f.

19. *NAM*, 1963, 66. The writer adds: 'Other battalions have had a similar experience, though to a lesser degree.'

20. *West African Pilot*, 26 July 1961 and 26 February 1962. The reporter admitted that some other Nigerian officers did not share these views.

21. I was told by an officer of one case where a Southern officer punished a Northerner. The soldier who had been punished then complained to the minister that the penalty was the result of anti-Northern prejudice, and the minister then ordered the officer to revoke the punishment.

22. Tai Solarin, a columnist in the *Daily Times*, who had served in the RAF during the war, wrote:

> I still have the letter from one of the Nigerian soldiers in the Congo. They were ordered to appear within a specified time with full kit on the parade ground. Half an hour after the order should have been executed, there were hardly any soldiers on the parade ground. . . . I have myself seen a Nigerian army captain shout three times at a private soldier from whom he was expecting audience, which was never given (27 February 1964).

23. *Daily Times*, 4, 6, 8 and 14 February 1964 (Col. Imo). Bribery by recruits *HR Deb*, 14 April 1960, col. 1241.

24. *Daily Express* (Lagos) 31 October 1964. Previously in the Navy three British officers had been dismissed for smuggling and one court-martialled.

25. Both Dr Okpara's speeches are in *Nigerian Outlook*, 24 December 1964.

26. *West Africa*, 16 January 1965, 58.

CHAPTER VII

1. *Daily Times*, 15 August 1960, quoting a government release. The plan had been referred to by Sir Abubakar *HR Deb*, 12 August 1959, col. 1825.

2. Numbers on courses from *Daily Times*, 13 October 1960; *Nigerian Citizen*, 16 August 1961 and 4 March 1962. Pass rate calculated from the later commissioning notifications in the *Federal Government Gazette*.

3. The vacancy for one brigadier occurred unexpectedly when Brig. Goulson died in a car crash. Lt.-Col. Ademulegun was promoted to fill his post at 2 Brigade, Apapa; Ironsi remained as adviser to the High Commission in London after this promotion.

4. *West African Pilot*, 27 March 1962.

5. *Nigerian Citizen*, 24 March 1962, 9 January 1963 and 15 April 1963. *West African Pilot*, 14 January 1963 and 23 December 1963.

6. These categories cover most of the secondary school students known to me who considered an Army career at this time. Not all of them did eventually apply, and not all those were finally commissioned.

7. Advertisements in the *Federal Government Gazette*, 17 September 1959 and 8 May 1961, and in the local press shortly afterwards.

   From about 1963 onwards a school-leaver with these minimum qualifications found difficulty in getting employment as a clerk in Lagos, but not elsewhere in Nigeria, particularly in the North.

8. *NAM*, 1963, 79.

9. W. F. Gutteridge, 'Military Élites in Nigeria and Ghana', in *African Forum*, 1966, 38. The author was teaching at Sandhurst in 1960.

10. *HR Deb*, 18 April 1961, Written Answer, 79 sets out the official policy directive, as it was just before it was changed.

11. *Daily Times*, 13 October 1960, gives the official listing: North:

     Apolo, Bamigboye, Adamu, Abisoye, Obeya, Danjuma, Alabi. South: Kalu, Oluleye, Okon, Obioha, Ogbemudia, Ayo-Ariyo, Chiabi, Tataw. But in fact Alabi was from the Mid-West, educated in the North. He returned to the Mid-West after the July 1966 counter-coup, *West African Pilot*, 18 November 1966.

12. North: Shande, Abubakar, Yakubu, Usuman, Remawa. West: Bajowa, Armah (?). Mid-West: Afiegbe. Ibo: Okoye, Oji, Iwe, Iweanya, Nnamani, Idika, Anekwe, Egere, Nwobosi.

13. The original composition of the course can be calculated from *HR Deb*, 18 April 1961, Written Answer, which gives the total number of officer cadets in training in UK and Nigeria by region of origin; and the final success ratio from the commissions later noted in the *Government Gazette*.

14. See the party strengths as given in *A Guide to the Parliament of the Federation, revised to May 1961*, Government Printer, Lagos.

15. Cadet units were opened at government colleges at Keffi and Kaduna, and the provincial secondary schools at Kano, Sokoto, Bida and Zaria. In the South the only new ones were at Government College, Afikpo and Igbo Etiti Grammar School.

16. Before 1958 the Examination Council Report does not list boys and girls separately. These figures only refer to candidates taking the examination who were still at school. There was a similar disproportion between North and South in the numbers of private candidates taking the G.C.E. examination, e.g. 1960: Northern candidates, 1,171; rest of Nigeria, 16,665.

17. References to the number of candidates for the Army Entrance Examination for potential officers can be found in a number of places and are not fully comparable. The following figures give an indication:

       1953   9 applications
       1956   133 applications of which 67 sat the examination
     Dec. 1959   199 sat the examination
     July 1963   385 sat the examination.

     HR Deb, 12 March 1954, 218; *HR Deb*, 18 March 1957, col. 982; *Reports of the West African Examinations Council*, 1960 and 1964.

18. 13 February 1964.

19. Ibos: Dillibe (Enugu), Okafor (Owerri), Okeke (Onitsha), Onyekwe (Lagos), Isichie (Zaria). Mid-Westerners: Ogunro (Sapele), Tuoyo (Sapele). West: Onifade (Ilaro). Home towns are given in *Daily Times*, 12 January 1962 and 21 December 1963.

20. The following officers with combatant commissions certainly left the Army before 1966:

> To join Cameroons Army: Malonge, Chiabi, Tataw
> To join Air Force: Alao, Esuene, Ikwue, Odiwo
> Cashiered: Okafor, D.I.
> Dead: Ezeugbana, Ogbonnia, Sanda, ?Mbu.

21. This was the automatic reply to such allegations: 'If the member has any friends in the Army who feel they are not being promoted, there must be some reason for their being left behind' (Tako Galadima, *HR Deb*, 2 April 1965, col. 458).

22. The Army List at Independence (to be found in *Federal Government Gazette*, 6 October 1960) divided officers into those with regular commissions and those with short-service commissions. By 1966 all the latter (with the exception of Adigio and Brown) had been converted to regular commissions. Since this conversion made no difference to their seniority dates, this technicality has been ignored, and it is assumed that all officers at Independence were on one seniority list.

Often the officers who were superseded by Sandhurst trained officers had in fact been commissioned *after* them, but before 1960 they ranked *above* them since their commissions had been backdated to take account of their service in the ranks. For example, Lt. Imo was commissioned in 1955, but his commission was backdated to 1951 because of his other rank service; he thus had more than two years' seniority to Kur Muhammed at Independence, but was later superseded by him.

23. See Ch. III, note 27, p. 244.

24. To give an example of such grumbles: when Brig. Ademulegun became commander of 1 Brigade, Kaduna, the two majors on his taff were Ifeajuna (an Ibo) and a British officer; a year later both those posts were filled by Yorubas (Sotomi was brigade major and Adegoke was DAQMG). These appointments may be contrasted with the staff of Brig. Maimalari at 2 Brigade, Apapa, on the eve of the coup where the two majors were an Ibo – Ifeajuna and a Yoruba – Johnson. Maimalari was noted for his commitment to 'One Nigeria'; his appointment of Ifeajuna cost him his life.

25. Quoted from Janowitz, *The Military in the Political Development of New Nations* (Chicago, 1964) 58.

26. See Major Nzeogwu's first proclamation in Kaduna in January 1966, in which moral and political crimes (such as homo-

sexuality) are all alike made liable to the death penalty (quoted on p. 161). For Lt.-Col. Ogbemudia's regime in the Mid-West, see *West Africa*, 30 December 1967, 1685: 'Sixty young men and women were arrested in Benin following the Military Government's order banning loitering and public drinking between 9 a.m. and noon.'

27. *Africa and the World*, Vol. 3, No. 31, May 1967, 16.

28. See also his remarks 'I do not believe in Northernization' . . ., *Daily Times*, 15 and 18 March 1966.

CHAPTER VIII

1. I first heard of this attempted coup in 1961 from a senior British officer of 1 QONR and have since had it confirmed from another source.

2. There are detailed accounts of the crisis in the Action Group in J. P. Mackintosh(ed.), *Nigerian Government and Politics* (Allen & Unwin, 1966) 427–60, and in the chapter by R. L. Sklar, 'The Ordeal of Chief Awolowo', in G. M. Carter (ed.), *Politics in Africa – 7 cases* (Harcourt Brace & World, Inc., 1966) 119–65.

3. There is a full account of the trial by one of the defendants, L. K. Jakande, *The Trial of Obafemi Awolowo* (Secker & Warburg, 1966). One of the defendants, Chief Anthony Enahoro, was tried subsequently after he had been extradited from England. He has described his trial, at which much of the original evidence was repeated, in *Fugitive Offender* (Cassell, 1965).

   The evidence is highly confusing and contradictory. The prosecution claimed that there were two separate plots to overthrow the government by force – one by Dr Maja, one of the original defendants who turned Queen's evidence to testify for the prosecution, and the other organized by Chief Awolowo. (*West Africa*, 16 May 1964, 551.)

4. The evidence about Brig. Ademulegun is not given in the two books mentioned above, nor in the press reports, but it was widely known that he had been named during the trial, and this has been confirmed to me by a correspondent who covered the proceedings.

5. In 1968 the Military government in Sierra Leone was overthrown in a coup organized by two private soldiers (*West Africa*, 4 May 1968, 507) so it cannot be said that this is impossible, however unlikely such an event may have seemed at the time.

   Joseph Tarka was one of the defendants acquitted at the trial.

6. This possibility was talked of in Lagos at the time. It is not evidence, of course; but if such foreign help was not available, the plot becomes even more ludicrous.

7. Details of the moves of 2 QONR are taken from the full account in the *NAM*, 1963, 60.

8. The official result of the 1963 census (which was itself a recount after the first census result of 1962 had been rejected as inaccurate) was:

North			29,777,986
East	12,388,646	Total	
West and Mid-West	12,811,837	South	25,875,835
Lagos	675,352		

Seats in the Federal House were finally allocated:

North 167, South 145 (East 70, West 57, Mid-West 14, Lagos 4).

There is a full account of the census controversy and aftermath in J. P. Mackintosh, *op. cit.*, 545–609.

9. That such a bargain was struck at the conference is an inference only, but highly plausible. Richard Akinjide, an NNDP minister, even suggested that Dr Okpara had deliberately provoked the census controversy solely in order to be bought off with the establishment of the iron and steel industry in the East (letter to *West Africa*, 4 April 1964, 379).

10. In fact it is fairly clear that the census figures were deliberately inflated in both the South and the North. Stories of the deceptions used are legion, such as enumerators counting the same people at the front door of the house and then again at the back door, and mothers giving the Christian names of their children as if each name represented a separate child.

    Between the end of the census controversy and the Federal election a successful general strike took place in June. There were rumours of a possible military intervention (*West Africa*, 18 July 1964, 801), but nothing significant occurred.

11. There is a detailed analysis of the legal position in Mackintosh, *op. cit.*, 591 f.

12. *West African Pilot*, 2 and 4 January 1965. The UPGA view of the president's powers is given in Mackintosh, *op. cit.*, 586 f.

13. The heads of the services saw the prime minister on the morning of Friday, 1 January and the morning of Sunday, 3 January (*Daily Times*, 2 and 4 January 1965).

    There is a full account of the meeting between the president and the heads of the services in Mackintosh, *op. cit.*, 591 f., based, among other informants, on an interview with Major-General Welby-Everard (see p. 587). The meeting is also referred to briefly by W. Schwarz, *Nigeria* (Pall Mall, 1968) 173, but he places it before the election. Other versions are current of when the meeting took place and exactly what was said by the various participants, but it is generally accepted that Dr Azikiwe attempted to give orders to the heads of the services, by-passing Sir Abubakar, and that he was rebuffed.

The possibility that Dr Azikiwe might use his position in this way had been foreseen by Anthony Enahoro in 1960:

> As Head of State he will be Commander-in-Chief of our Armed Forces and his honoured position will enable him, if he wishes, to interfere more than any other man in the Federation, including the Prime Minister himself, with the Police, the Civil Service and other vital organs of the state.
>
> There is no need to argue about constitutional safeguards, which exist, I know them, but people who want to seize power do not bother about constitutional niceties. . . . We have seen in other countries, and Pakistan comes to mind, how easy it is for a Head of State who has pronounced political views and even ambitions to use the Armed Forces to climb to power and abolish the parliamentary system (*HR Deb*, 13 April 1960, col. 1146 f.).

14. For the region of origin of police commissioners, see *West African Pilot*, 11 April 1964, 'Top Posts for Northerners'. Odofin Bello was convicted on charges of corruption and abuse of office in 1966. The treasurer of the NNDP gave evidence that he had paid £5,000 to Bello before the election on the instructions of Chief Akintola (*West Africa*, 7 May 1966, 528 and 4 June 1966, 639). The verdict was reversed on appeal after the countercoup.

15. Ojukwu's battalion, 5 NA, should have moved its station to a new barracks at Kano before the December elections, but Ojukwu had delayed the move by making various objections. (Information from an officer of the battalion, given in 1964.)

16. The commanding officer of 2 NA, Lt.-Col. Njoku, was on sick leave and the battalion second-in-command was temporarily in command.

17. W. Schwarz, *Nigeria* (Pall Mall, 1968) 176.

18. After the confrontation was over Dr Azikiwe published his version of the events in 'State House Diary' (*Daily Times*, 13

January 1965). This exercise in self-justification was not welcomed by other UPGA leaders. Tarka told the annual conference
of the UMBC:

> The resultant publication of the State House Diary was and is
> in very bad taste and whoever did order the publication ought
> to be told so in plain language. . . . The main attempt to visit
> the sins of the constitutional crisis on the UPGA has simply
> misfired. The masses know too well who betrayed them. . . .
> It is not Okpara, Adegbenro, not Aminu Kano and just not I
> (*Nigerian Tribune*, 26 January 1965).

The conference to review the constitution, on which great stress
was laid by UPGA as a tangible benefit from the confrontation,
had not yet convened by the time of the military coup a year
later. There was disagreement about the composition of the
conference; the NPC proposals would have given a strong pro-
Northern majority (*West Africa*, 18 September 1965, 1054).

19. *West Africa*, 13 January 1968, 53.
20. There is an account of Lt.-Col. Banjo's conspiracy in 1967
    in Frederick Forsyth, *The Biafra Story* (Penguin, 1969) 118 ff.
    Major Ifeajuna was executed with him. According to Forsyth,
    Banjo attempted to involve Lt.-Col. Ejoor, the Federal governor
    of the Mid-West, but without success. Ejoor and Banjo had
    passed out of Sandhurst together in 1956.
21. All newspapers, 20 November 1965.
22. The cut in the price paid to producers by the Marketing Board had
    been inevitable for some time because of the world slump in
    cocoa prices, and had only been delayed till after the election.
    In spite of this, NNDP electoral propaganda had promised a
    rise in the cocoa price (see the advertisement in *Daily Express*
    (Lagos) 11 October 1965, item 5).
23. The significance of this editorial was noted by *Financial Times*,
    12 January 1966; *West African Pilot*, 14 January 1966 and
    Nigerian Outlook, 15 January 1966.
24. Sir Abubakar said in the interview quoted below:

> I was told the other day that a car was stopped in the region
> and its occupants were asked by the people who held them up
> to give them money. They answered, 'But we thought we had
> to shout, "Awo, Awo." ' The men replied, 'Should we eat
> Awo? Give us money.' But this is getting too serious. The
> thieves and thugs are taking part. And the AG and NNDP,

s

who have been organizing their hooligans are not now, I hear, paying them enough.

25. After Akintola's death, a reporter described an interview with him in December: 'It was clear to me that he would never voluntarily relinquish power, however much violence there was in the region; nor would he consider a coalition with his opponents, which was the only hope of peace' (*West Africa*, 22 January 1966, 93).

It is impossible to say how many died in the rioting in the Western Region. The official figure was 151 (*HR Deb*, 13 January 1966, col. 2867). On 3 January, the *Nigerian Tribune*, which had been keeping a tally of reported killings, gave a total of 567 deaths to that date. Other estimates gave a figure of 2,000 or more (*The Guardian*, 27 January 1966).

CHAPTER IX

1. *West African Pilot*, 8 November 1965. Number of dead, *ibid.*, 28 February 1966.
2. Obarogie Ohonbamu, *Nigeria, The Army and the People's Cause* (African Education Press, Ibadan, 1966) 25 and introduction. In the Federal election crisis Dr Ohonbamu had been one of the advocates of Dr Azikiwe's assumption of 'executive powers', *Nigerian Outlook*, 4 January 1965.
3. Lists of army commands in January 1966 are given in *January 15 – Before and After*, 29, *Nigeria, 1966*, 7, and *West Africa*, 28 January 1967, 125. Some discrepancies in the above lists have been corrected from information available in Lagos at the time. The list in the text is, I believe, accurate for the night of the coup.

Col. Kur Muhammed was substantive second-in-command of the Defence Academy at Kaduna. He was acting as chief of staff in Lagos in place of Col. Adebayo who was on a course in England, and his place at the Academy was temporarily held by Col. Shodeinde. Lt.-Col. Fajuyi had recently handed over command of 1 NA, Enugu to his second-in-command, Major Ogunewe, when he left to take command of Abeokuta garrison. His successor in command of 1 NA, Lt.-Col. Ejoor, was still in Lagos.
4. The most important pamphlets are listed in Section C of the Bibliography at the end of the book.
5. *The Guardian*, 26, 27 and 28 January 1966, articles by Patrick Keatley. Similarly, *January 15 – Before and After*, 13.

6. See his final interview, *West Africa*, 29 January 1966, 93.

7. *Constitution of the Federal Republic of Nigeria* (*Laws of Nigeria*, 1963, No. 20), Sec. 38, 'Procedure for the Removal of the President'.

   Sec. 87 (2) 'Whenever the President shall have occasion to appoint a Prime Minister, he shall appoint a member of the House of Representatives. . . .'

8. *January 15 – Before and After*, 14. This is also the interpretation of the meeting given in the independent *West Africa*, 22 January 1966, 105. All four participants in the meeting were murdered the same night, so it is impossible to know what was decided. (Richard Akinjide, who accompanied Akintola, may perhaps one day give a full account.) An alternative theory about the meeting is that given in W. Schwarz, *Nigeria*, 189 f., that it was held to consider reports of a conspiracy in the Army.

9. According to *The Guardian*, 28 January 1966, 'I have it on excellent authority that Ironsi was told to go on leave in October, but this was countermanded by Sir Abubakar.'

   The Eastern Inspector-General of Police, Edet, was sent on leave from 20 December to 5 March, and there was a rumour that he was being retired to make way for his deputy, Kam Selem, a Northerner. This was officially denied, *West African Pilot*, 7 January 1966. (Edet was recalled from leave after Ironsi took over.)

10. This follows the account in *West Africa*, 22 January 1966, 105 f.

11. *Daily Telegraph*, 17 January 1966 reported, 'According to the Nigerian Government, loyal troops have recaptured Kano.' Also information from Nigerian officers in the North at the time.

12. Major Okafor of Federal Guards normally had a Northern second-in-command, Capt. Garba. But this officer had just been sent with a party of Nigerian officers to assist in the supervision of the Indo-Pakistani truce in Kashmir, at the request of the United Nations – a fortunate coincidence for the conspirators.

   According to *Nigeria, 1966*, 7, Lt.-Col. Unegbe, the only Ibo officer murdered, was killed because he refused to hand over the keys of the Armoury. It seems rather strange that the conspirators should need access to arms and ammunition. There was a large store of weapons and ammunition available to Major Anuforo at Abeokuta, and Major Okafor also had quite enough under his own control at Federal Guards.

13. Major Nzeogwu told a reporter in Kaduna after he had surrendered to Ironsi:

We wanted to get rid of rotten and corrupt ministers, political parties, trades unions and the whole clumsy apparatus of the federal system. We wanted to gun down all the bigwigs in our way. This was the only way. We could not afford to let them live if this was to work. We got some but not all. General Ironsi was to have been shot. But we were not ruthless enough. As a result he and the other compromisers were able to supplant us (*Daily Telegraph*, 22 January 1966).

14. Njoku was awarded the Austrian medal for gallantry at the same time as Ironsi for the relief of the Austrian Medical Team, (*NAM*, 1963, 67). Igboba was also in Ironsi's battalion in the Congo (*Daily Times*, 11 March 1961).

   Major Igboba later boasted to me, 'This battalion saved the Federation in January.'

15. *Daily Telegraph*, 20 January 1966: 'Reports in Kaduna said that only a last minute telephone call from General Ironsi to Major Nzeogwu had prevented a march on the South by his troops.'

16. The *Nigerian Morning Post*, a newspaper owned by the Federal Government, had a headline on 17 January: 'Federal Troops in Full Control; Zanna for Prime Minister?' So also Schwarz, *op. cit.*, 197.

17. *West Africa*, 22 January 1966, 83; *Daily Telegraph*, 17 January 1966.

18. A visitor to Lagos was given this as an explanation of Sir Abubakar's death: 'Innocent Sir Abubakar may have been of corruption, but he had to be killed; were he in jail, a mere scribble on a piece of toilet paper smuggled by him to the British might have sent their commandos parachuting into Lagos' (*Africa Report*, March 1966, 10).

19. Dr T. O. Elias, who was present at the final cabinet meeting, gives this account in *Nigeria, the Development of its Laws and Constitution* (Stevens, 1967) 457.

20. *West Africa*, 29 January 1966, 127.

21. *January 15 – Before and After*, 89–91. *West Africa*, 29 January 1966, 127.

22. 'The thirty-two officers were men from the major tribes of Nigeria – Hausa, Ibo and Yoruba' (*Nigeria Crisis*, Vol. 1, 3).

23. Second-lieutenant Nwokocha has the same name and initials as a student who took the School Certificate at Plateau Provincial Secondary School, Kuru.

24. This assumes that G. S. Adeleke, N/245, who is named in

January 15 – Before and After, 89, as one of those imprisoned at Enugu, is an error for G. Adeleke, N/412.

Samuel Funsho Adeleke, the officer whose army number was N/245 was given an executive commission in 1962 after seventeen years in the ranks. He served with the Federal Army during the civil war and was buried with full military honours in 1968.

The other officer, G. Adeleke N/412 was given a regular commission in 1963 and disappears from the Federal Army after 1966. He is the only Yoruba officer (apart from the other named conspirators) who cannot be accounted for in the civil war.

25. It has been said that Ifeajuna comes from Onitsha, but according to an Ibo informant he is from the Mid-West.

26. Details of the companies and years of these officers can be found in the magazine of RMA Sandhurst, *The Wish Stream*, Vols. 12–15, 1958–1961. There is a parallel here with the officers from the classes of 1936–1939 from the Egyptian Military Academy, which supplied the nucleus of Col. Nasser's 'Free Officers Group' (see Vatikiotis, *The Egyptian Army in Politics*, (Indiana University Press, Bloomington, Ind., 1961) 54 f., for a full list).

27. Ironsi began his army career as a clerk in the ordnance stores. After commissioning in 1949 he was attached to a Stores Depot in England, and then worked in the Army Stores at Yaba, Lagos on his return to Nigeria. He was transferred to the infantry in 1951 after he had been acquitted at a court martial on a charge of theft.

28. Martin Dent's original report of this story in the *Observer*, 9 October 1966, was somewhat distorted in transmission. There is a fuller account in his article in *St Antony's Papers, No. 21*, (O.U.P., 1969).

29. *January 15 – Before and After*, 75, accuses Lt. Bello of being responsible for Ironsi's death.

30. *Government Statement on the Current Situation*, 2; *Nigeria, 1966*, 5.

31. *Daily Telegraph*, 17 January 1966.

32. *Daily Times*, 17 January 1966.

33. *Nigeria's Military Government, First Hundred Days*, entries for 8 March and 11 April 1966.

34. *West Africa*, 13 May 1967, 615.

35. Some of the more exaggerated Federal propaganda has claimed that all non-Ibo officers above the rank of major were killed on 15 January, or only escaped assassination by luck. In fact, apart from Gowon and Ironsi, the following Lt.-Cols. were in Nigeria at the time of the coup and remained alive: Ejoor (Urhobo),

Fajuyi (Yoruba), Banjo (Yoruba), Bassey (Efik), Kurobo (Ijaw), Effiong (Anang) and Peters (Yoruba – Army Medical Services).

36. There is a brave attempt to prove that the United States would really benefit from a Nigerian military coup because it would lead to greater centralization and efficiency, in *New Left Review*, July–August 1966, 54 ff.

37. There are no statistics available for the religious denominations of army officers; but if there were, it seems likely that this result of four Catholics out of five would count as a 'significant correlation' by the 'chi squared' test.

38. This view was affirmed by the World Muslim Congress in Karachi, *New Nigerian*, 1 May 1967. The Sardauna described as 'most encouraging' the conversion of 350,000 people to Islam during his sixteen-day tour of parts of Kano, Zaria, Bauchi, Plateau and Bornu provinces (*West Africa*, 30 October 1965, 1211).

39. *West Africa*, 26 February 1966, 237.

40. Ghanaian financial help for the thugs in the West was reported by the *New York Times*, 20 January 1966.

CHAPTER X

The journal *West Africa* gave a day by day summary of the events in the first three months of the Ironsi regime, and this was subsequently published as a pamphlet by the Lagos *Daily Times* press: *Nigeria's Military Government, the First Hundred Days*. Events not annotated here will be found in that publication, under the appropriate day, and also in the issue of *West Africa* a week later.

1. This is admitted by the Federal document, *Nigeria, 1966*, 8.

2. Account of the deaths of Adegoke and Odu is as given in *January 15 – Before and After*, 74.

3. Ejoor was sent by Ironsi from Lagos to Enugu over the weekend to take over 1 NA. On 17 January he announced that he was temporary military governor of the East (*Daily Times*, 18 January 1966).

4. This account was given by a friend of his shortly afterwards. According to the London press, he was taken out and executed after attempting to assassinate Ironsi. He was in fact imprisoned in the East, and later in 1967 commanded the Biafran invasion of the Mid-West.

5. Stories of mass killings, e.g. in *The Times*, 19 January 1966. Both the Federal document *Nigeria, 1966*, and the Eastern document

January 15 – Before and After, agree on the list of nine officers killed.

6. *West Africa*, 13 August 1966, 911.

7. I learnt of the existence of this order accidentally in April when attempting to draw ammunition for cadet range practices. Ammunition had been freely available before the coup.

8. The substantive majors passed over were Adekunle, Obasanjo, Chude-Sokei, Sotomi, Rotimi, Aniebo, Ayo-Ariyo and Obienu, as well as the majors in prison.

9. 'Reflections on the Nigerian Revolution', *South African Quarterly*, Vol. 65, No. 4 (1966) 421 ff. (The writer is anonymous but very well informed and gives a good picture of the early days of the Ironsi regime, especially the North.)

10. M. Janowitz, *The Military in the Political Development of New Nations* (Chicago, 1964) 1.

11. *New Nigerian*, 20 January 1966. Nzeogwu said, 'I made it clear a few days ago that it was not my job to rule. My job was to keep order.' (Quoted in *January 15 – Before and After*, 19.)

12. The special correspondent of the *Financial Times* reported 5 May 1966:

> Another encouraging sign is that the army officers seem to be well aware of their own limitations in the field of civil administration. General Ironsi sets the tone here – so far he has relied heavily on the senior civil servants, so much so that it is fair to say that it is the permanent secretaries who are really governing the country. . . . They meet frequently to put forward their policy 'recommendations' to their military masters. The result is that decisions are seemingly taken with more despatch than used to be the case.

13. Anwunah and Okwechime were commissioned from Sandhurst in 1956 and Nzefili in 1957. All three were promoted from major to lieutenant-colonel in May 1966. Nzefili had held a junior position in the railways before entering the Army in 1955. (*Daily Times*, 24 and 26 May 1966; *West Africa*, 30 July 1966, 868.)

14. *Daily Times*, 7 April 1966.

15. The instructions to the study groups made clear the sort of recommendations that would be most acceptable:

> (*a*) to identify those faults in the former constitution that militated against national unity and the emergence of a strong central government.

(b) to ascertain to what extent the powers of the former Regional Governments fostered Regionalism and weakened the central government. . . .

(Government Notice 863, *Gazette*, March, 1966.)

16. Isaac Boro was not executed. After the civil war began he was released from prison and commissioned in the Federal Army. He was killed in action in the Rivers area.

17. *The Times*, 26 April 1966. *Financial Times*, 5 May 1966 (headline) 'When will the Army begin to govern?' Similar well-meaning advice was given to Ironsi by *West Africa*, 2 April 1966, 370.

18. Translations in *Daily Times*, 27 April 1966, e.g. from *Gaskiya Ta Fi Kwabo* of 29 March:

The quiet way Northerners received the take-over since their leaders were killed does not mean that they were afraid. . . . Certain Northern military leaders were killed – those who had nothing to do with politics and committed no offence.

See also *West African Pilot*, 12 February 1966.

CHAPTER XI

1. For example: *West African Pilot*, 10 February 1966

The seed of tribalism watered in Nigeria in 1949 by Sir John Macpherson has grown to rend Nigeria into tribal entities. In his review of the Richards constitution Macpherson played up tribalism among the politicians and thus disarmed the nationalist camp. . . . The politicians of the First Republic preached tribalism in order to preserve their influence. . . . The New Regime is resolved to abolish, very ruthlessly if need be, the regionalism and unworkable constitution thrust upon us.

The historical accuracy of such an interpretation of recent history, is, of course, somewhat open to question.

2. See above. Ch. VIII, p. 139.

3. A prominent supporter of unification was Dr Aluko, a Yoruba, who was Professor of Economics at Ife University, and later at Nsukka. The FAO report is quoted in *West Africa*, 29 January 1966, 109.

4. *Report on the Grading of Posts in the Public Service of the Federation,*

Ministry of Information (Lagos, 1966). The quotations are from memoranda submitted to the chairman of the commission, Mr Ellwood, which are quoted in the report at p. 6.

5. *West African Pilot*, 12 February 1966. This speech at Lokoja by Mr Michael Asaju was quoted as an example of the 'trouble-making' that was still allowed to continue in the North.

6. According to the Northern account, 'Ironsi acted against good and sincere advice by some of his colleagues in the Supreme Council', *The Nigerian Situation, Facts and Background*, 7.

   According to the Eastern version, 'When the Council met, members found that, because of the general feeling of the meeting, they could not go very far' (*January 15 – Before and After*, 35).

   The views of Lt.-Col. Katsina have been quoted earlier in Ch. VII, p. 129.

7. *Daily Times*, 27 May 1966.

8. Ibo insolence is mentioned in *Nigeria, 1966*, 8 and in *The Nigerian Situation*, 5 f., and has been confirmed to me by several observers in the North. Of course, this display of bad manners does not excuse the murders which followed.

9. The official cost of living index for Kaduna, based on expenditure patterns of those earning less than £400:

	1966	1965 (for comparison)	
January	121·5	118·9	
February	121·3	117·5	
March	123·6	117·5	from *Northern States*
April	131·5	121·6	*Gazette*, 8 June 1967
May	133·4	125·9	
June	141·4	125·2	
July	138·7	126·2	

For Ibo dominance in trade in the North, cf. *Nigerian Citizen*, 10 February 1965; 'There was a virtual blackout of business life in Oturkpo, Benue province, when Ibo traders boycotted the main market, and Ibo traders refused to operate in the area.'

10. Both the Federal document, *Nigeria, 1966*, 8 f., and the Eastern document, *January 15 – Before and After*, 33 f., agree on the list of likely malcontents, except that the Eastern publication adds 'expatriates working in the North who feared displacement by Nigerians from other regions'.

11. A meeting in April 1966 of these two politicians with Maitama

Sule, the former NPC Minister of Mines, to concert tactics is reported by Martin Dent in his article in *St Antony's Papers*, No. 21, edited by K. Kirkwood (O.U.P., 1969).

12. *The Nigerian Situation, Facts and Background*, 7.

13. *New Nigerian*, 1 June 1966. Lt.-Col. Katsina announced, 'I have ordered troops to patrol the town of Kaduna *from now on*' (italics added).

14. The official casualty figures are in *West African Pilot*, 2 June 1966. Later Lt.-Col. Ojukwu claimed that 3,000 died in the May massacres (*West African Pilot*, 20 October 1966).

   David Loshak in the *Sunday Telegraph* gives the following totals by towns: Zaria 82, Katsina 75, Gombe 65, Gusau 65, Bauchi 55, Funtua 42, Yola 22, Jos 10, Kaduna 7, Kano 74 corpses at the hospital and at least 100 dead.

   Details of the riots given in the text are taken from the very restrained accounts in *West Africa* and from questioning of eyewitnesses.

15. *West African Pilot*, 9 June 1966. Other details in this paragraph will be found in the issues of *West Africa* for 11, 18 and 25 June 1966, and in the Nigerian daily press.

16. Major Nzeogwu gave his views on Ironsi's policies after he had been released from detention.

   Q. Was there anything you did not like in his administration?
   A. Yes, everything. First he chose the wrong advisers for the work that he half-heartedly set out to do. Most of them were mediocre and absolutely unintelligent. Secondly he was tribalistic in the appointment of governors. . . . We wanted to see a strong centre. We wanted to cut the country into small pieces, making the centre inevitably strong. We did not want to toy with power, which was what he did.
   Africa and the World, May 1967, 15.

17. Details in this paragraph from the Nigerian daily press, and in *West Africa* 2, 9, 16 and 23 July.

18. Samson O. O. Amali, *The Ibos and their Fellow Nigerians* (typescript, CMS Bookshop, Ibadan, 1967) 28, quotes a lament by an Idoma (Northern) soldier of 4 NA on the death of Lt.-Col. Largema. The translation runs:

   Our master who is our head here,
   They have tricked him along to a hotel in Lagos and killed him.

They have killed Brigadier Maimalari too.
They did not tell us, but we know what they have done.
They are soldiers! We are soldiers!

19. The Eastern document, *January 15 – Before and After*, 27 gives the information about Lt.-Col. Gowon's report.

20. This and the following complaint are taken from *The Nigerian Situation – Facts and Background* (Current Issues Society, Kaduna Gasiya Press, 1966) 7.

   The Military Forces Ordinance (No. 26 of 1960) Pt. VII, 'Pay Forfeitures and Deductions', Sections 149 and 150. In October 1964 when three naval officers were being court-martialled their counsel, H. O. Davies, complained to the court that the pay of his clients had been stopped before the verdict, contrary to regulations, and this was upheld. (*Daily Express* (Lagos) 23 October 1964.)

21. The Northerners promoted were Major Katsina to Lieutenant-Colonel; Major Akahan to A/Lieutenant-Colonel; A/Majors Shuwa Muhammed, Muhammed Murtala and Haruna to A/Lieutenant-Colonel. The Mid-Westerner was Major Morah (Pay Corps) to Lieutenant-Colonel. The Yoruba was Major Olutoye (Education Corps) to Lieutenant-Colonel. If any group of officers had any grievance over promotions, it was not the Northern officers, but the Yoruba. Five of the substantive majors who were passed over for promotion to A/Lieutenant-Colonel were Yoruba (Obasanjo, Sotomi, Adekunle, Ayo-Ariyo and Rotimi).

22. When Dr Nkrumah was faced with similar opposition in 1954, he created the Brong-Ahafo Region out of Ashanti, to splinter Dr Busia's National Liberation Movement. See D. Austin, *Politics in Ghana*, 292–7.

23. *Nigeria, 1966*, 8, claims that Northern recruits were deliberately rejected before the May riots. It is not clear that there was discrimination at this stage, but such rejections certainly took place in July.

24. Quotation is from *The Nigerian Situation – Facts and Background*, 8. The official Federal account, *Nigeria, 1966*, 9, also referred to the 'widely circulating rumours' of such a plot, but does not endorse their truth.

25. This was the interpretation first put on the news by the normally well-informed correspondent of the *New York Times* 30–31 July 1966 (International edition): 'The uprising reflects the mounting dissatisfaction of young Southerners in and out of the

Army. . . . The suspicion grew that Ironsi had sold out to the Moslem-dominated Northern Region.'

26. The speech by Commodore Wey in the *Verbatim Report of the Meeting at Aburi*, 22 f. gives a full account of the decision to ask Lt.-Col. Gowon to take over.

We were all in Police Headquarters. . . . Brigadier Ogundipe went out and when he came back and complained of 'when an ordinary sergeant can tell a brigadier "I do not take orders from you until my captain comes" '. Therefore it would have been very wrong, it would have been very unfair, to Ogundipe, or to any other person for that matter, to take command. And there is no point in accepting to be a commander of a unit you have no control over. . . .

If we did not have the opportunity of having Jack (Gowon) to accept, God knows, we would have been all finished, because all the people ran away and left us at the Police Headquarters. . . . Therefore if anybody accepted to lead them, well candidly, I doffed my hat for him.

Lt.-Col. Katsina described the situation in the North (at p. 24): 'I have seen a mutinied Army in Kano and if you see me trembling with fear, you will know what a mutiny is. . . . For two days I was there, where soldiers refused orders from a C.O., a Northerner, who had to run away.' (This quotation may refer to the events of September–October 1966.)

27. *West Africa*, 6 August 1966, 873 and 901.

28. List is in *January 15 – Before and After*, 67–73. It seems that this publication accidentally omits the names of the Ibo officers killed at Ibadan, so this is probably an underestimate.

29. I visited 2 NA barracks at Ikeja four days after Gowon took over. There was no 'secessionist flag' flying in front of battalion HQ then, as has been claimed by Eastern propagandists (*January 15 – Before and After*, 49).

30. See *West Africa*, 22 October 1966, 1222 and 5 November 1966, 1278. There are frequent references to the indiscipline in the Army during the latter months of 1966 in the weekly issues of *West Africa*. See also the article by Martin Dent, *op. cit.*, in note 11 above, p. 268.

31. Major Ekanem was travelling in a Land-Rover to Military Headquarters. He was stopped by soldiers guarding Carter Bridge and shot on the spot. As a result, exaggerated rumours of indiscriminate shooting quickly circulated, there was panic in the area and

mothers rushed to primary schools to take their children home (*Daily Times*, 2 August 1966). A typical remark at the time was, 'The old politicians may have been corrupt, but at least they did not go around shooting people.'

32. J. J. Johnson (ed.), *The Role of the Military in Underdeveloped Countries* (Princeton, N.J., 1962) 247 and 301.

33. The Military Government in Ghana set up an advisory body of civilians, including politicians, in June 1966. Presumably they took warning from the Nigerian riots.

34. Eduardo Santos, quoted in J. J. Johnson, *op. cit.*, 153.

35. *Verbatim Report of the Meeting at Aburi*, especially General Ankrah's opening speech, 7 f.

36. *Nigeria Crisis*, Vol. 4., *The Ad Hoc Conference on the Nigerian Constitution*, 1–11, 'Views of the Northern Delegation'.

37. Of course, any British governor who had acted in such a way as to provoke a crisis requiring troops from outside would not have been kept in his post very long by the British colonial secretary in London. But such external checks on gubernatorial autocracy were not obvious to Nigerians.

38. See, 'The Uganda Army, Nexus of Power' in *Africa Report*, December 1966, 37–9. Even these precautions do not preclude a coup. Obote was ousted by his own army commander in January 1971.

POSTSCRIPT

1. The seniority dates for promotion to substantive rank of these two are:

	Gowon	Ojukwu
2/Lt.	19 Oct. 1955	22 Sept. 1955
Lt.	9 Sept. 1957	22 Sept. 1957
Capt.	19 Oct. 1961	22 Sept. 1961
Major	9 Mar. 1963	7 Mar. 1963
Lt.-Col.	1 April 1964	1 April 1964

Ejoor, the military governor of the Mid-West and also a member of the Supreme Military Council, was also substantive lieutenant-colonel with effect from 1 April 1964.

2. Two examples of this leverage on Eastern policies may be given: Dr Eme Awa, *Federal Government in Nigeria*, (Univ. of California, 1964) 65:

> Some Ibo businessmen in the North say that at some time between 1957 and 1959 Northern leaders threatened to confiscate their property or to use subtle manoeuvres to destroy their business enterprises if the NCNC continued to agitate for the creation of a Middle Belt State and social reforms in the North. A delegation of Ibo businessmen saw the NCNC and urged them to desist. . . .

Also the remarks of Dr Okpara to an interviewer in *West Africa*, 16 January 1965, 58 (after the Federal election crisis):

> Okpara is giving no thought to secession. He asked me, 'What of our Easterners, perhaps 3,000,000 who work elsewhere in the Federation?'

3. *Nigerian Crisis*, Vol, 3, *Pogrom*; F. Forsyth, *The Biafra Story*, 75.
4. *Time Magazine*, 7 October 1966, quoted in Forsyth, *op. cit.*, 76, and in *Pogrom*. This account has been confirmed to me by an eyewitness.
5. In fact there was no trouble reported in the minority areas of the East at the time of Biafra's secession, and only fifteen officers from that area, including six with combatant commissions, chose to remain on the Federal side. (List in *January 15 – Before and After*, 82–8.) The most notable were Lt.-Col. Kurobo (Ijaw), later Nigerian ambassador in Moscow; Lt.-Col. Ekpo (Efik), later Chief of Staff, Supreme Military Headquarters; and Major Ally (from Obudu in Ogoja province), later Chief of Staff of III Div. Lt.-Col. Bassey (Efik), retired from the Army before the outbreak of war. During the Ironsi regime he had been acting brigadier in the North, and had a lucky escape during the counter-coup of July, having just gone off for a few weeks leave. He was later employed by the Federal Government as consul and then ambassador in Fernando Po.
6. *West Africa*, 10 June 1967, 772 f.
7. The figure of 120,000 is that given in the Scott report in *Sunday Telegraph*, 11 January 1970.

Joseph Tarka, the former UMBC leader who was brought into General Gowon's government as a civilian commissioner at the outbreak of the war, claimed that 80 per cent of the soldiers came from the Middle Belt (*West Africa*, 27 January 1968, 113).

8. *West Africa*, 17 June 1967, 803–5.

9. The full roll call of the officers listed in the table in Ch. III, p. 51, is as follows:

> Died before 1966: Ogbonnia (car crash), Ezeugbana (in Congo).
> Murdered in 1966: Ironsi, Ademulegun, Maimalari, Kur Muhammed, Shodeinde, Largema, Fajuyi, Pam, Unegbe, Ekanem, Okonweze, Okafor, D. O., Okoro.
> Retired to Cameroons Army: Malonge, Kweti.
> Governors and Ambassadors: Ogundipe, Adebayo, Bassey, Gowon, Ejoor, Katsina, Kyari, Kurobo, Ojukwu.
> Federal Army: Ekpo, Obasanjo, Sotomi, Olutoye, Akahan.
> Mid-West Area Command: Nwawo, Okwechime, Nzefili, Trimnell, Nwajei, Igboba, Ochei, Keshi.
> Biafran Army: Imo, Njoku, Effiong, Banjo, Anwunah, Madiebo, Akagha, Ogunewe, Eze, Amadi, Adigio, Brown, Ivenso, Okafor, D. C., Nzeogwu, Aniebo, Chude-Sokei, Ude.

10. Njoku was later imprisoned by Ojukwu, *West Africa*, 28 February 1970, 245.

11. F. Forsyth, *op. cit.*, 123.

12. For Nzeogwu's views, see the quotations above in Ch. VII, p. 129, and Ch. XI, note 16, p. 268.

13. Court-martial reported in *West Africa*, 1 June 1968, 650. Other officers imprisoned, see speech by Brig. Katsina, *West Africa*, 19 July 1969, 850.

> Scott Report in *Sunday Telegraph*, 11 January 1970:

> To supply the sudden expansion of the Army, the Federal Military Government sent purchasing teams, early in the war, to most European countries to obtain arms and ammunition. These teams, many of them led by senior officers and civil servants, soon succumbed to the temptations of personal gain and often purchased obsolete stocks of ammunition from the black market, much of which was subsequently found to be useless.

> Permanent Secretary's complaint, *Daily Telegraph*, 23 October 1969.

Sources and Select Bibliography

A. *Personal Details of Nigerian Officers*

The careers of all Nigerian officers from 1948 to October 1960 can be traced in the *London Gazette*, since they were all commissioned into the British Army. From November 1958 onwards these details are repeated in the *Federal Government of Nigeria Official Gazette*, and after 1960 this is the only source. According to the *Nigerian Military Forces Act*, sec. 11 (3), all commissionings and promotions of officers had to be noted in the *Official Gazette*; in fact, some details of European officers are omitted, and also a few Nigerian promotions, but all details of commissionings are complete.

The list of Nigerian officers who were trained at Sandhurst is available in the Royal Military College magazine, *The Wish Stream*, published twice yearly, but this does not give details of the schools attended in Nigeria.

For many of the earlier Nigerian officers, tribe, home town and other biographical details are given in the Nigerian newspapers at the time of commissioning. In the late 1950s, as more officers were commissioned, only brief details are available for each group of cadets, often only the home town. Biographies of the most senior officers are to be found in *The New Africans*, edited by S. Taylor (Reuters News Agency and Hamlyn, 1967).

Where no other information is available, tribal/regional origin can often be inferred from an officer's surname. The ethnic origin of the officers commissioned before September 1960 is almost certain, since the *London Gazette* gives all the forenames of officers. This practice was not normally followed by the *Official Gazette* except for the full list of Nigerian officers at Independence, given in the *Gazette* of 6 October 1960.

B. *The Nigerian Army*

i. MAGAZINES

Journal of the Nigeria Regiment, 1949, 1950.
Nigerian Military Forces Magazine, July 1956, July 1957.

Royal Nigerian Army Magazine, March 1961, May 1962.
Nigerian Army Magazine, October 1963, October 1964.

ii. BOOKS AND PAMPHLETS

Colonial Office, *Report on the West African Forces Conference, Lagos, 20–24 April 1953*, Cmnd. 6577 (1954).

Crown Agents (for Government of Nigeria), *The Nigeria Handbook, 1953*.

Haywood, A. and Clarke, F. A. S., *The History of the Royal West African Frontier Force* (Gale & Polden, Aldershot, 1964).

Lawson, R., *Strange Soldiering* (Hodder & Stoughton, London, 1963).

Nigeria Public Relations Department,
  Our Regiment (Crownbird Series, No. 29) 1953.
  Our Military Forces, 1956.
  Spearheads of Victory, not dated, ? 1945.

Notes on the Royal West African Frontier Force and the Stations in Which it normally Serves, no author or date stated, ? 1955 (copy in War Office Library, London).

Smyth, Sir John, *Bolo Whistler* (Muller, London, 1967).

Royal Nigerian Military Forces Ordinance, No. 26 of 1960.

iii. ARTICLES

Bassett, Rev. R. H., 'The Chaplain with the West African Forces', *Journal of the Royal Army Chaplains Department* (1950) 21–6.

Clarke, Brigadier F. A. S., 'The Development of the West African Forces in the Second World War', *Army Quarterly* (October, 1947) 58–72.

Gifford, Sir George, 'The Royal West African Frontier Force and its Expansion for War', *Army Quarterly* (July, 1945) 190–6.

Gutteridge, W. F., 'Military Élites in Nigeria and Ghana', *African Forum* (1966) 31–41.

Kirk-Greene, A. H. M., 'A Preliminary Note on New Sources for Nigerian Military History', *Journal of the Historical Society of Nigeria*, Vol. III (1964) 129–47.

Metteden, Alhaji, 'Recruiting in the North', *Nigeria Magazine* (1962) 13–17.

Stacpoole, Capt. H. A. J., 'The Dissolution of the Royal West African Frontier Force', *Journal of the Royal United Service Institution* (August, 1960) 376–86.

Swynnerton, Brigadier C. R. A., 'The First West African Infantry Brigade in the Arakan, 1944–1945', *Army Quarterly* (October, 1946) 48–60.

T

Ukpabi, S. C., 'The Origins of the West African Frontier Force', *Journal of the Historical Society of Nigeria*, Vol. III, No. 3 (December, 1966) 485–501.

'The Nigeria Regiment Between the Wars' (author not stated) *Empire and Commonwealth*, Vol. XXXV (September, 1960) 23.

C. The Military Government of General Aguiyi-Ironsi

i. PAMPHLETS AND DOCUMENTS ISSUED BEFORE AUGUST 1966

Aguiyi-Ironsi, Major-General J. T. U., *Budget Speech*, 31 March 1966, Federal Information Service.

Broadcast to the Nation, 24 May 1966, Federal Information Service.

Nigeria's Military Government, First Hundred Days, January 15, 1966–April 24, 1966 (Daily Times Press, Lagos).

The Nigeria Yearbook, 1966 (Daily Times Press, Lagos).

Ohonbamu, Obarogie, *Nigeria: The Army and the People's Cause* (African Education Press, Ibadan, February, 1966).

ii. PAMPHLETS AND DOCUMENTS PUBLISHED AFTER SEPTEMBER 1966, BY THE FEDERAL GOVERNMENT OR SOURCES FAVOURABLE TO IT

Issued by the Federal Ministry of Information, Lagos:

Government Statement on the Current Nigerian Situation, October 1966.

Nigeria, 1966, January 1967.

Meeting of the Nigerian Military Leaders at Aburi, 4–5 January 1967, March 1967.

The Challenge of Unity, July 1967.

The Struggle for One Nigeria, October 1967.

Amali, Samson O. O., *Ibos and their Fellow Nigerians* (mimeo 1967 from C.M.S. Bookshop, Ibadan).

Armstrong, R. G., *The Issues at Stake in Nigeria, 1967* (Ibadan University Press, October, 1967).

Current Issues Society, Kaduna, *The Nigerian Situation, Facts and Background* (Gaskiya Corporation, Zaria, 1966).

Dent, M., chapter in *St Antony's Papers No 21, African Affairs, No 3* (O.U.P., 1969).

Dudley, B. J., 'Nigeria Sinks into Chaos', *Round Table* (January, 1967) 42–7.

'Eastern Nigeria Goes it Alone', *Round Table* (July, 1967) 319–24.

'Nigeria's Civil War', *Round Table* (January, 1968) 28–34.

Legum, Colin, 'New Hope for Nigeria', *Round Table* (April, 1968) 127–38.

O'Connell, James, 'The Scope of the Tragedy', *Africa Report* (February, 1968) 8–11.

Panter-Brick, S. K., 'The Right to Self-Determination and Its Application to Nigeria', *International Affairs* Vol. 44, No. 2 (April, 1968) 254–66.

iii. PAMPHLETS AND DOCUMENTS PUBLISHED AFTER SEPTEMBER 1966 BY THE EASTERN REGION GOVERNMENT (BIAFRA) AND BY SOURCES FAVOURABLE TO IT

Ministry of Information, Eastern Nigeria, 'Crisis' Series:

Vol. 1. *Crisis 1966*

Vol. 2. *The Problem of Nigerian Unity*

Vol. 3. *Pogrom*

Vol. 4. *The Ad Hoc Conference on the Nigerian Constitution*

Vol. 5. *The North and Constitutional Development in Nigeria*

Vol. 6. *The Meeting of the Supreme Military Council at Aburi*

Vol. 7. *January 15 – Before and After*

The Verbatim Report of the Proceedings of the Supreme Military Council Meeting, Aburi, Ghana.

Birch, Geoffrey and George, Dominic St., *Biafra, The Case for Independence* (Britain–Biafra Association, February, 1968).

Ejindu, D. D., 'Nigeria, Major Nzeogwu Speaks, exclusive interview', *Africa and the World* Vol. 3, No. 31 (May, 1967) 14–16.

Forsyth, Frederick, *The Biafra Story* (Penguin, Harmondsworth, 1969).

Post, K. W. J., 'Is there a Case for Biafra?', *International Affairs*, Vol. 44, No. 1 (January, 1968) 26–39.

D. Other African Armies and Discussions of the Military in Politics

i. BOOKS AND PAMPHLETS

Afrifa, Col. A. A., *The Ghana Coup, 24 February 1966* (Cass, London, 1966).

Alexander, General H. T., *African Tightrope* (Pall Mall, London, 1965).

Andrzejewski, S., *Military Organization and Society* (Routledge, London, 1954).

Andreski, S. (same author as above, name changed), *Parasitism and Subversion* (Weidenfeld & Nicolson, London, 1966).

Bell, M. J. V., *Army and Nation in Sub-Saharan Africa*, Adelphi Paper 21 (Institute of Strategic Studies, 1965).

Bing, Geoffrey, *Reap the Whirlwind* (MacGibbon & Kee, London, 1968).

Chorley, K., *Armies and the Art of Revolution* (Faber, London, 1943).

Daalder, H., *The Role of the Military in Emerging Countries* (Mouton & Co., 'S-Gravenhage, 1962).

Finer, S. E., *The Man on Horseback* (Pall Mall, London, 1962).

Glickman, H., *Some Observations on the Army and Political Unrest in Tanganyika* (Duquesne University Press, Pittsburgh, Pa., 1965).

Gutteridge, W. F., *Armed Forces in New States* (O.U.P., 1962).

     Military Institutions and Power in New States (Pall Mall, London, 1964).

     The African Military Balance, Adelphi Paper 12 (Institute of Strategic Studies, August, 1964).

     The Military in African Politics (Methuen, London, 1969).

Hoskyns, Catherine, *The Congo Since Independence* (O.U.P., Oxford, 1965).

Huntington, S., *The Soldier and the State* (Harvard University Press, Cambridge, Mass., 1957).

Janowitz, Morris, *The Military in the Political Development of New Nations* (University of Chicago Press, Chicago, Ill., 1964).

Johnson, John J., *The Military and Society in Latin America* (Stanford University Press, Stanford, Calif., 1964).

Johnson, John J. (ed.), *The Role of the Military in Underdeveloped Countries* (Princeton University Press, Princeton, N.J., 1962).

Lee, J. M., *African Armies and Civil Order* (Chatto & Windus for Institute of Strategic Studies, London, 1969).

Lefever, E. W., *Crisis in the Congo* (Brookings Institute and Faber, London, 1965).

Tinker, H., *Ballot Box and Bayonet* (O.U.P., 1964).

Young, Crawford, *Politics in the Congo* (Princeton University Press, Princeton, N.J., 1965).

ii. ARTICLES

Berge, Pierre L. Van Den, 'The Role of the Army in Contemporary Africa', *Africa Report* (March, 1965) 13–17.

Brice, Belmont, Jr., 'The Nature and Role of the Military in Sub-Saharan Africa', *African Forum* (1966) 57–67.

Feit, Edward, 'Military Coups and Political Development', *World Politics* (1968) 179–93.

Glickman, Harvey, 'The Military in African Politics: A Bibliographic Essay', *African Forum* (1966) 69–75.

Greene, Fred, 'Towards Understanding Military Coups', *Africa Report* (February, 1966) 12–14.

Gutteridge, W. F., 'The Political Role of African Armed Forces', *African Affairs*, Vol. 66, No. 263 (April, 1967) 93–103.

Hopkins, Keith, 'Civil–Military Relations in Developing Countries', *British Journal of Sociology* (1966) 165–82.

Howe, R. W., 'Togo: Four Years of Military Rule', *Africa Report* (May, 1967) 6–12.

Kraus, J., 'Ghana without Nkrumah, Army in Charge', *Africa Report* (April, 1966) 16–20.

Mazrui, A. and Rothchild, D. S., 'The Soldier and the State in East Africa', *Western Political Quarterly* (March, 1967) 94 ff.

Mehden, F. R. and Anderson, C. W., 'Political Action by the Military in the Developing Countries', *Social Research* Vol. 28 (1961) 459–78.

Murray, R., 'Militarism in Africa', *New Left Review* (July–August, 1966) 35–59.

Weeks, G., 'The Armies of Africa', *Africa Report* (January, 1964) 4–9.

Welch, C. E., 'Soldier and State in Africa', *Journal of Modern African Studies*, Vol. 5, No. 3, 305–22.

'The Uganda Army: Nexus of Power' (author not stated), *Africa Report* (December, 1966) 37–9.

E. Nigerian Government and Politics

i. OFFICIAL GOVERNMENT DOCUMENTS

Federal Nigeria Official Gazette.
Western, Eastern, Northern Regions, Official Gazettes.
Staff Lists, Federal, West, East and North.
House of Representatives Debates, Lagos.
Senate Debates, Lagos.
Estimates of the Federal Government (yearly).
Reports of the Accountant-General of the Federation (yearly).
Report of the Commission appointed to make recommendations about the Recruitment and Training of Nigerians for Senior Posts in the

Government Service of Nigeria (The Foot Commission) August 1948.

The Nigerianization of the Civil Service: A Review of Policy and Machinery by Sir Sydney Phillipson and Mr S. O. Adebo (April, 1953).

Interim Report of the Special Committee on Nigerianization, June 1958.

Final Report of the Parliamentary Committee on the Nigerianization of the Federal Public Service, July 1959.

Matters Arising from the Final Report of the Parliamentary Committee on the Nigerianization of the Federal Public Service, August 1960.

Report of the Commission appointed to enquire into the fears of Minorities and the means of allaying them (the Willink Commission) July 1958.

Draft Defence Agreement Between the Government of the United Kingdom and the Government of the Federation of Nigeria, December 1960.

General Report and Survey on the Nigeria Police Force (yearly). (Last report available is that for 1963.)

The Economic Programme of the Government of the Federation of Nigeria, 1955–1960, Sessional Paper No. 2 of 1956.

Federation of Nigeria National Development Plan, 1962–1968

National Development Plan, Progress Report 1964, March 1965.

Report of the Commission on the Review of Wages, Salary and Conditions of Service of Junior Employees of the Governments of the Federation and Private Establishments, 1963–1964 (The Morgan Commission) April 1964.

Report of the Grading Team on the Grading of Posts in the Public Services of the Federation of Nigeria (The Ellwood Commission) 1966.

Northern Region Who's Who (North Public Relations Office, 1952).

Who's Who in the Eastern House of Assembly, 1952.

Who's Who in the Western House of Assembly, 1952.

Mid-West Legislature, Who's Who, 1964 (Ministry of Information, Benin).

Who's Who in the Eastern Region Legislature (Ministry of Information, Enugu, 1963).

Who's Who in the Northern Regional Legislature, 1957 (Government Press, Kaduna).

Who's Who in the West Nigeria Legislature (Government Printer, Ibadan, 1959).

Who's Who in the Federal House of Representatives (Federal Information Service, Lagos, July, 1958).

Guide to the Parliament of the Federation, amended to 31 May 1961 (Federal Information Service, Lagos).

ii. BOOKS

Arikpo, Okoi, *The Development of Modern Nigeria* (Penguin, Harmondsworth, 1967).

Awolowo, Obafemi, *Path to Nigerian Freedom* (Faber, London, 1947).
Awo: The Autobiography of Obafemi Awolowo (C.U.P., 1961).
Thoughts on the Nigerian Constitution (O.U.P., 1966).

Bello, Sir Ahmadu, *My Life, Autobiography of Sir Ahmadu Bello, of Sokoto* (C.U.P., Cambridge, 1962).

Coleman, J. S., *Nigeria: Background to Nationalism* (Berkeley, N.Y., 1958).

Davies, H. O., *Nigeria, the Prospects for Democracy* (Weidenfeld & Nicolson, London, 1961).

Dudley, D. J., *Parties and Politics in Northern Nigeria* (Cass, London, 1968).

Elias, Dr T. O., *Nigeria: The Development of its Laws and Constitution* (Stevens, London, 1967).

Enahoro, Chief Anthony, *Fugitive Offender* (Cassell, London, 1965).

Jakande, L. K., *The Trial of Obafemi Awolowo* (Secker & Warburg, London, 1966).

Mackintosh, J. P. (ed.), *Nigerian Government and Politics* (Allen & Unwin, London, 1966).

Obi, Dr Chike, *Our Struggle* (Pacific Printers, Yaba, 1955).

Perham, M., *Lugard, the Years of Authority* (Collins, London, 1960).

Phillips, C. S., Jnr., *The Development of Nigerian Foreign Policy* (Northwestern University Press, Evanston, Ill., 1964).

Post, K. W. J., *The Nigerian Federal Elections of 1959* (O.U.P., 1963).

Schwarz, W., *Nigeria* (Pall Mall, London, 1968).

Sklar, R. L., *Nigerian Political Parties* (Princeton University Press, Princeton, N.J., 1963).
Chapter on 'The Ordeal of Chief Awolowo' in G. M. Carter (editor), *Politics in Africa, 7 cases* (Harcourt, Brace & World, Inc., N.Y., 1966).

Tilman, R. O. and Cole T. (eds.), *The Nigerian Political Scene* (Duke University Press, Durham, N.C., 1962).

White, Stanhope, *Dan Bana* (Cassell, London, 1966).
Who's Who in Nigeria (Daily Times Press, Lagos 1956).

iii. ARTICLES

Awa, E., 'The Federal Elections in Nigeria, 1959', *Ibadan*, No. 8 (March, 1960) 4 f.

Dudley, B. J., 'Federalism and the Balance of Political Power in Nigeria', *Journal of Commonwealth Political Studies* (1966) 16–29.

Galadanchi, Mallam Usuman, 'The Northern Teacher', *Nigeria Magazine* (December, 1966) 300–4.

Jones, Vivian, 'Pioneer of Northern Education', *Nigeria Magazine* (1962) 26–34.

'Reflections on the Nigerian Revolution', *South African Quarterly*, Vol. 65, No. 4 (1966) 420–30 (author anonymous).

F. Nigerian Newspapers and Periodicals
(political bias shown in brackets)

i. DAILY

Daily Times (independent) Lagos.

Sunday Times (independent) Lagos.

Eastern Outlook (NCNC) Enugu, published to 1960, then changed name to *Nigerian Outlook* (NCNC) Enugu from 1960.

West African Pilot (NCNC) Lagos.

Daily Service (AG) Lagos, published to 1960.

Daily Express (AG) Lagos, published from 1960. (In 1965 supported NNDP and closed November 1965.)

Nigerian Tribune (AG) Ibadan.

New Nigerian (NPC) Kaduna, published from 1966.

ii. WEEKLY

Gaskiya Ta Fi Kwabo (NPC) Zaria, twice weekly, in Hausa.

Nigerian Citizen (NPC) Zaria, twice weekly until 1965 ceased publication.

West Africa (independent) originally published and printed in London, now printed in both London and Lagos.

G. Recent Books on Nigeria and the Nigerian Civil War

First, Ruth, *The Barrel of a Gun; Political Power in Africa and the Coup d'état* (Allen Lane, the Penguin Press, 1970).

Niven, Sir Rex, *The War of Nigerian Unity* (Evans, London and Ibadan, 1971).

Panter-Brick, S. K. (ed.), *Nigerian Politics and Military Rule: Prelude to the Civil War* (University of London, Athlone Press, 1970).

Thayer, George, *The War Business* (Weidenfeld & Nicholson, London, 1970).

Waugh, Auberon, and Cronje, Suzanne, *Biafra: Britain's Shame* (Michael Joseph, 1969).

Nicolson, I. F., *The Administration of Nigeria 1900–1960* (O.U.P., 1970).

Index

(Officers mentioned only in the tables on pp. 51, 122, 123, and 168 are not listed here.)

Abdullahi Magajin Musawa, 53
Abubakar Tafawa Balewa, Sir Alhaji, 7, 18, 37, 41, 53, 60, 61, 64, 66, 82, 91, 93, 94, 115, 131, 136, 142, 143, 145, 148, 149–50, 152, 154, 158, 159, 162, 164–5, 171, 175, 178, 184–5, 222, 224, 239, 245, 249, 259, 262
Aburi Conference (1967), 221, 228
Abyssinia, see Ethiopia
Achebe, Chinua, 156
Action Group (AG), 5, 7–10, 54, 61, 63–4, 68–9, 96, 102, 131–7, 139–40, 145–6, 150–2, 180, 218, 248, 259
Adamawa Province, 26, 93, 98
Adebayo, Col., 51, 56, 109, 122, 123, 134, 182–3, 260, 273
Adegbenro, Alhaji D. S., 132, 151
Adegoke, Major, 123, 181, 255
Adekunle, Lt.-Col., 123, 232, 264
Adelabu, Alhaji A., 28
Adeleke, Lt. G., 168, 262
Ademoyega, Major, 92, 113, 167, 170
Ademulegun, Brig., 35, 36, 38–9, 42, 45, 46, 55, 83, 89, 109, 122, 134, 144, 148, 157, 160, 161–2, 253, 255, 256
Agriculture, Ministry of, 188, 196
Aguiyi-Ironsi, see Ironsi
Ahmadu, Sultan Attahiru, 12, 29, 69–70
Ahmadu Bello, Sir Alhaji, see Sardauna
Air Force, 63, 66, 94, 96, 103, 168
Akagha, Major, 51, 123, 183, 273
Akahan, Lt.-Col., 40, 51, 52, 123, 182–3, 212, 230, 269
Akintola, Chief S. L., 18, 31, 63, 86, 131–3, 136–7, 138, 140, 143, 144, 152–5, 160–2, 164, 169, 178, 180, 222, 224, 258, 260, 261
Alexander, General, 80, 109, 248
Algeria, 2, 28, 89, 90, 231
Ally, Major, 113, 272
Aluko, Dr S., 127, 266
Aminu Kano, 8, 202, 247

Anglo-Nigerian Defence Agreement, 8, 59–60
Anthony, Major Seth, 34
Anuforo, Major, 92, 123, 170, 173–4, 217, 233, 261
Anwunah, Lt.-Col., 51, 53, 123, 187, 210, 265, 273
Armoured Car Squadron, see Recce Squadron
Armée Nationale Congolaise, 81, 84, 85
Army Act (1960), 140, 164, 209
Army Council (British), 17, 18, 60
Arthur, Lt. (Ghanaian Army), 173
Artillery, 61, 95, 102
Ashanti War, 12–13
Attorney-General, Dr T. O. Elias, 142–3, 262
Audu, Dr, 185
Australia, 102, 110
Austrian ambulance unit, Bukavu, 75–7, 79
Awolowo, Chief Obafemi, 11, 61, 63, 68, 131–7, 139, 154, 218, 222, 229
Azikiwe, Dr Nnamdi, 4, 8, 11, 14, 33, 103, 140, 142–6, 150, 159, 164, 169, 172–3, 222, 256, 258

Bamileke tribe, 71–2
Banjo, Lt.-Col., 44, 51, 123, 147, 170, 182, 233, 259, 264
Barracks and accommodation, 23, 94–5, 127
Bassey, Brig., 27, 36, 38–9, 45, 51, 119, 122, 123, 157, 162, 183, 227, 264, 272
Batista, President of Cuba, 10–11
Belgium, 75, 79, 81, 130, 165
Bello, Sir Ahmadu, see Sardauna
Bello, Odofin, Police Commissioner, 144, 258
Bello, Lt., 171, 263
Benin, 126, 163
Benue Province, 26, 90
Biafra, 229–34
Biobaku, Dr, 149
Bissalla, Lt.-Col., 122, 173, 231, 232
Boigny, M. Houphouet, 6

Bokassa, Col., 156
Bornu Province, 26, 36, 38, 204, 231
Boro, Isaac, 192, 266
Boys' Company, 17, 22, 112
British Policy, 4–6, 17–18, 24, 28, 33–4, 59–61, 166, 195, 197, 224, 271
Brown, Akpan, 96–7
Browne, Brig., 41
Bukavu, 75, 77, 78–82, 85, 162
Burma campaign, 13, 37, 73, 99, 229; coup, 66, 246–7
Burmi, Battle of, 12, 29

Cadet units, 17, 48, 96, 113, 117, 254
Calabar, 12, 27, 52, 63, 119
Cameroon Republic, 71–4, 255, 273
Canada, 102, 110
Car Basic Allowance, 42, 48, 50, 62
Casablanca Bloc, 88, 132
Castro, Fidel, 10
Census, 1952, 7, 25; 1962/63, 8–9, 138–9, 146
Chaplains, Army, 18, 62, 114
Chari Maigumeri, RSM, 37
Chief Justice, 142
Chief Secretary, 20, 31
Chukuka, Major, 168, 170
Command Secretary, 17
Commissions, types of officer, 52, 113–15, 119, 126
Commonwealth Prime Ministers' Conference (1966), 152, 154, 163
Compulsory military service, 96
Congo, 28, 69, 74–88 passim, 101, 105, 112, 125, 128, 130, 148, 155–6, 162, 165, 212, 218, 245, 248–9
Constitutional conferences, 4–5; of 1957, 60; of 1958, 61; proposed in 1965, 259; of 1966, 223, 227
Contract officers, 62, 236–7, 246
Corruption, 3, 105–6, 177–8, 234
Cuba, 10

Dahomey, 155–6
Dakakori, Niger Province, 26
Dan Fodio, 40; see also jihad
Dar-es-Salaam, 88–9
Dayal, Mr (U.N. representative), 78
Decorations, 12, 14, 27, 37, 39, 77–8
Defence Academy, see Military Academy, Kaduna
Defence Agreement, Anglo-Nigerian (1960), 61, 113, 132
Defence Council, 60, 61
Defence, Ministry of, 60, 93, 108, 113, 116; see also Ribadu and Inuwa Wada
Development Plan, 95, 110

Dipcharima, Zanna Bukar, 164, 171, 262
Discipline, military, 25, 41, 78–81, 104–5, 181–2, 217–18, 228, 229, 234, 252, 270
Disu, Mr A. K., 7
Dynamic Party, 64, 247

East Africa campaign (1916–18), 13, 26, 37
Eaton Hall Officer Cadet School, 34, 36, 50, 121, 227, 233, 241
Economic Committee of the Cabinet, 96
Edet, L., Inspector-General of Police, 143, 261
Edo College, Benin, 128
Educational Service, Army, 35, 113
Effiong, Lt.-Col., 51, 123, 233, 264, 273
Egba rebellion (1916), 13, 30
Egypt, 82, 231, 263
Ejoor, Lt.-Col., 51, 53, 56, 123, 157, 163, 176, 181, 190–1, 259, 260, 263, 264, 273
Ekanem, Major, 51, 216, 218, 270
Elias, Dr T. O., see Attorney-General
Elections, Federal (1959), 7–8, 54, 60, 67–9, 131; Federal (1964), 92, 106, 139–46, 149, 155, 159; Northern (1961), 9, 131; Eastern (1961), 131; Mid-West (1964), 138; Western (1965), 150–5, 160
Electoral Commission, 141, 142, 151
Enahoro, Chief Anthony, 32, 238, 256, 258
Enang, Chief, 99
Eneh, Mr G. O. D., 21–2, 30, 66, 67
Estimates, Army, 17, 18, 21, 41, 62–5, 94–6, 250–1
Ethiopia, 13, 32, 37, 86, 89, 90, 102, 110
European Common Market, 192
Executive commissions, 52, 114–15, 126, 169, 236–7, 263
Ex-servicemen, 14–15, 21, 98, 229, 248
Eze, Lt.-Col., 30, 41, 51, 53, 123, 233, 273
Ezera, Prof. Kalu, 175
Ezeugbana, Lt., 51, 78

Fajuyi, Lt.-Col., 38–9, 51, 77–8, 105, 123, 134, 157, 176, 182, 191, 212, 213, 260, 264
Fani-Kayode, Chief R. A., 64, 137
Federal Guard, Lagos Island, 95, 119, 136, 144, 147, 162, 181, 183, 208, 261

Food and Agriculture Organization (FAO), 266
Foot Commission (1948), 33, 34, 36
Force Publique, Congo, 74, 130
Forster, Major-General, 109
French Army in West Africa, 2, 3, 6, 14, 59, 66, 72
French Cameroons, 28, 64, 71–2
Fritz-Werners, 103

Gabon, 165
Garba, Capt., 119, 261
Gaskiya Ta Fi Kwabo, 193, 208
de Gaulle, General, 66
General Certificate of Education (GCE), 35, 111, 254; *see also* School Certificate
General Strike (June 1964), 155, 257
German East Africa, 13
Germany, West, 103
Ghana, 2–4, 6, 11, 15, 28, 34, 59–60, 63, 65–6, 74, 80, 83, 96, 132–5, 158, 173, 176–7, 246–7, 248, 251, 264, 269, 271
Gizenga, Antoine, 75
Gizengist troops, 77–9, 82, 84
Glover, Lt. R. N., 12
Gold Coast, *see* Ghana
Goldie, Sir George, 12
Goulson, Brig., 83, 253
Governor, British, 15, 33, 188, 189, 224, 271
Governor-General's cadetships, 49
Gowon, Major-General, 40, 52, 56, 120, 146–7, 158, 160, 162, 182–4, 209–10, 213–16, 218, 221, 227–9, 234, 270, 271
Graduates, 42–5, 49, 113–14, 168, 170, 229
Granville Sharp Commission of Enquiry, 66
Guinea, 6, 59, 82
Gulani, CSM Jibrin, 77
Guyana (British Guinea), 10
Gusau, 203

Hama Kim, MM, RSM, 27
Haruna, Lt.-Col., 113, 122, 173, 185, 231–2, 269
Hassan Katsina, Lt.-Col., 40, 52, 129, 182, 185–6, 189, 198, 201, 206, 214, 219, 250, 267–70
High Commission, British, 165, 204, 216
Hitler, Adolf, 11
Howeidy, Mallam, 185

Ibadan, College of Technology, 113
Ibadan, Government College, 40, 48, 128, 242

Ibadan University, 48, 180
Ibrahim Tako Galadima, 93, 100
Ifeajuna, Major, 113, 147, 162, 170, 177, 181–2, 233, 255, 259, 263
Igboba, Lt.-Col., 157–8, 162–3, 183, 262
Ikejiani, Dr, 174
Ikoku, Dr S., 176–7
Imams (in Army), 114–15
Imo, Lt.-Col., 37, 105, 227, 255
Imperial Reserve, 28, 224
Indian Army, 3, 58–9, 83, 86, 102, 110, 157
Indo-China, French, 2, 28
Indonesia, 82
Inuwa Wada, Alhaji, 93–4, 164, 202, 225
Ironsi, Major-General Aguiyi-, 1, 11, 27, 35–7, 45, 74–5, 77–8, 80–1, 88, 92, 109, 122, 127, 144, 148–9, 156–8, 160, 162–8, 170–3, 181–4, 187–8, 190–3, 198–216, 220–26, 242–3, 249, 253, 261–7
Isho, 155
Ivenso, Lt.-Col., 51, 123, 233
Ivory Coast, 6, 15, 97

Jagan, Cheddi, 10
Jalo, Lt.-Col., 232
Jibrin Gulani, CSM, 77
jihad, Fulani, 6, 26, 40
Johnson, J. M., Minister of Labour, 15

Kaduna College, *see* Zaria, Government College
Kam Selem, Police Commissioner, 144, 261
Kambona, Oscar (Tanganyika), 89
Kamerun, German, 13, 37, 71
Kano Riots (1953), 27, 203
Katsina College, *see* Zaria, Government College
Katsina Provincial Secondary School, 48
Keffi, Government College, 48
King's College, Lagos, 14, 45, 48, 112, 113, 117, 128, 239
Kurobo, Lt.-Col., 53, 157, 162, 183, 264, 272

Labour ministries, 189
Lagos City Council, 191
Lagos Technical College, 48
Lagos University, 149–50, 174
Lamizana, Col., 156
Largema, Lt.-Col., 105, 144, 157, 160, 162, 183, 204, 268
Lawson, Major, 84
Local government, 189

Longe, Chief, 30
Loshak, D., 204, 205
Lugard, Lord, 12, 13, 26, 186
Lumumba, Patrice, 74, 75, 79, 81, 82
Lundula, Gen., 78

Macpherson, Sir John, 33, 36, 266
Madiebo, Lt.-Col., 51, 53, 123, 210, 233, 248
Maigumeri, RSM Chari, 37
Maimalari, Brig., 36, 51, 102, 109, 122, 123, 136, 148, 157, 160, 162, 204, 248, 255, 269
Majekodunmi, Dr, 93
Malayan Army, 78, 85
Manifestos, election, 67–8, 139–40, 195
Mariere, Chief, 64
Matthews, Lt., 77
Mbadiwe, Dr, 148–9
Mbu, Matthew, 93
Medical Service, Army, 18, 49, 114, 119, 230–1, 236, 264
Mid-West Democratic Front (MDF), 138
Military Academy, Kaduna, 95, 110, 115, 124, 157, 161, 175, 230
Military School, Zaria, 112
Mirza, Iskander, 11
Mobutu, General, 75, 82, 83, 108, 155
Moma Fortlamy, Sgt., 32
Mons O. C. S., 34, 50, 52, 109, 111–13, 121, 168, 169, 232
Morgan, Lt.-Col., 81
Morah, Lt.-Col., 269
Moumié, Felix, 72
Muhammed, Col. Kur, 45, 51, 121, 123, 157, 160, 162–3, 183, 204, 255, 260
Muhammed Murtala, Lt.-Col., 49, 173, 185, 231–2, 269
Muhammed, Lt.-Col. Shuwa, 49, 173, 183, 185, 231, 269
Muhammadu Ribadu, see Ribadu
Mulele, Pierre, 85
Muslim religion, 26, 94, 152, 176, 186, 198; see also jihad
Myohaung, Battle of, 13

National Liberation Movement (NLM) Ghana, 4
National Plan, 94, 199
National service officers (British), 19, 47, 243
Navy, Nigerian, 63, 93, 94–5, 96, 106, 120, 143, 149, 171, 251
National Council of Nigeria and Cameroons (NCNC), 7–10, 54, 64, 67, 91, 93, 99, 106, 116, 131–3,

137–46, 148–52, 169, 185, 194–5, 205, 248
NCOs and WOs, British, 20–22, 62, 74, 101, 245
Nicholson, General, 34
Njoku, Dr Eni, 18, 149, 174
Njoku, Lt.-Col. Hilary, 18, 51, 77, 105, 122, 123, 158, 162, 183, 227, 233, 258, 262, 273
Nkrumah, Dr Kwame, 4, 6, 60, 63, 66, 109, 132, 135, 176–7
Niger Coast Constabulary, 12, 29
Niger (French), 6, 26, 65
Niger Province, 26, 93
Nigerian Military Training College, Kaduna (NMTC), 61, 108–10, 112, 115–17
Nigeria Regiment (up to 1956), 12–14, 18, 26
Nigerian National Democratic Party (NNDP), 138, 140–1, 144–5, 150–5, 161, 164, 169, 180, 185, 258, 259
Nigerianization, of NCOs, 21–2, 62, 245; of officers, 3, 33–58, 108–29 passim.
Northern Elements Progressive Union (NEPU), 6–8, 69, 201
Northern Nigeria Regiment, 12
Northern People's Congress, 5–11, 54, 67, 90–4, 106–7, 116, 119, 130–2, 136–46, 149, 152–3, 156–160, 164–5, 169, 175, 195, 201–2, 207–8, 218, 222–5
Nsukka University, 127, 172, 229
Nwajei, Lt.-Col., 51, 53, 123, 273
Nwawo, Lt.-Col., 37, 38, 51, 84, 123, 166, 233, 273
Nwokedi, Francis, 174, 187, 189, 219
Nzefili, Lt.-Col., 51, 53, 123, 163, 181, 182, 217, 265, 273
Nzeogwu, Major, 11, 51, 121, 123, 127, 129, 158, 161–9, 172, 176–7, 181, 185, 187, 200, 201, 209, 215, 222, 233–4, 244, 149, 255, 261, 265, 268, 273

Obande, Jacob, Minister of State for the Army, 93, 109
Obasanjo, Lt.-Col., 51, 123, 230, 231, 232, 265, 273
Obi, Dr Chike, 247
Obote, Dr (Uganda), 224, 271
Officer cadet schools, see under Teshie, Eaton Hall, Mons and Nigerian Military Training College
Officers, British, 2, 3, 18–20, 43, 50, 55–8, 62, 70, 79–81, 101, 104, 127, 224, 236–7, 239–40, 246

Ogbemudia, Lt.-Col., 126, 254, 256
Ogoja, Cpt. Emeka, 32
Ogoja Province, 27, 93, 272
Ogundipe, Brig., 27, 38, 51, 85, 109, 122, 123, 134, 148, 213–15, 227, 270, 273
Ogunewe, Lt.-Col., 51, 123, 157, 163, 183, 212, 260, 273
Ohonbamu, Dr Obarogie, 156, 260
Oil Rivers Protectorate, Irregulars, 12
Oji, Capt., 168, 233
Ojukwu, Mr Louis (later Sir Odumegwu), 31, 173
Ojukwu, Lt.-Col., 31, 49, 51, 92, 113, 123, 144, 147, 157, 162, 172, 182, 184, 190–1, 200, 208, 213–16, 221, 227–9, 233, 244, 258, 268, 271
Ojukwu, 2/Lt., 168, 209
Okafor, Lt.-Col. D. C., 51, 210, 273
Okafor, Major D. O., 51, 105, 119, 144, 147, 157, 168–70, 210, 217, 233, 261, 273
Okigbo, Dr, 187
Okon, Cpt. Bassey, 32
Okonkwo, Major, 230
Okonweze, Lt.-Col., 51, 123, 183, 273
Okotie-Eboh, Chief Festus, 94, 149, 162, 164, 251
Okoro, Lt.-Col., 51, 123, 183, 273
Okoye, Capt., 49
Okpara, Dr, 106, 139, 272
Okwechime, Lt.-Col., 51, 53, 122, 123, 187, 210, 265, 273
Olutoye, Lt.-Col., 51, 113, 123, 230, 269, 273
Olympio, President, 3
Omo-Bare, T., Police Commissioner, 144
Ondo Province, 27, 37
Onwuatuegwu, Major, 51, 91, 122, 123, 168, 170, 173, 233, 273
Ordnance Depot Mutiny (1952), 25
Ordnance Factory, 95, 103
Organization of African Unity (OAU), 89
Orizu, Dr, 164–5, 171–2

Pakistan, 58, 66, 102, 104, 110, 158
Pam, Lt.-Col., 22, 38–9, 51, 89, 91, 105, 120, 122–3, 144, 157, 162, 273
Pay, British officers', 43, 53–4, 62, 246; British NCOs', 21, 62; Nigerian officers', 42–3, 45–6, 48, 50, 53–4, 57, 62, 111–12, 127, 173; Nigerian ORs', 21, 22–3, 62, 87, 101–2, 130, 211, 249; in civil service, 45, 102, 112, 127, 243

Pay Corps, 114, 237
Pensions, Army, 50
'Peter Pan' (columnist Daily Times), 32, 192
Police, 18, 23, 25, 28, 40, 46, 54, 60, 62, 63, 68, 96, 98, 105–6, 128, 132, 136, 143–6, 149, 155, 178, 190, 218, 234; in Congo, 249
Price, Lt.-Col., 74, 77
Promotions, Army, 36, 44–6, 57, 58, 104, 109, 112, 120–4, 173–4, 185, 209–11, 214, 231–3; in civil service, 44–6, 112, 196–7, 243
Protestant missions, 26, 240
Public service commission, 47, 199–200, 211
Public Works Department, 23
Physical Training School, Army, 52

Quartermaster commissions, 114, 126, 217; see also Executive commissions
Queen Elizabeth, visit to Nigeria, 1, 30, 45, 243
Queen's Birthday Parade, 29
Queen's Own Nigeria Regiment (QONR, 1956–63), 1, 69; first battalion, 72–4, 81, 84–7, 97, 105, 130, 135, (1NA) 157, 163, 183, 212; second battalion, 72, 82, 85–7, 101, 105, 134–6, (2NA) 144, 155, 157–8, 162–3, 183, 213, 215, 270; third battalion, 72, 84, 87, 135, (3NA) 89, 91, 105, 157, 163, 183; fourth battalion, 72, 74–5, 77, 83–4, 87, 105, 135, (4NA) 155, 157, 163, 172, 182–3, 212, 238; fifth battalion, 72, 74–5, 78, 82, 85, 87, 135, (5NA) 91–2, 157, 163, 183
Queen's School, Ede, 128

Railways, 91, 174, 187, 265
Rassemblement Démocratique African (RDA), French West Africa, 6
Recce Squadron, 61, 69, 73, 74, 85, 87, 91–2, 95, 162, 163, 166, 170
Recruits, region of origin, ORs, 24–7, 97–100, 229; officer cadets, 37–40, 51–4, 114–19
Regimental Depot, Zaria, 15, 27, 40, 99, 157, 162, 163, 183, 203, 212, 233
Ribadu, Alhaji Muhammadu, Minister of Defence, 23, 33, 80, 93–6, 100, 102, 108–9, 113, 116, 120, 148, 164, 187, 210, 251
Rivers Province, 27, 39, 52
Roman Catholics, 26, 176, 264

Rosiji, Chief, 64
Rotimi, Major, 113, 123, 265, 269
Royal Niger Company Constabulary, 12
Royal West African Frontier Force (RWAFF), 12, 19, 24, 70, 103
Russians, 159–60

Sakiet (bombing), 63
Salami, Sgt. Akanbi, 32
Sandhurst, Royal Military Academy, 34–43, 46, 50, 52, 55, 57, 109, 111, 115, 118, 121, 148, 170, 210, 227, 231, 232, 233, 259, 263
Sandys, Duncan, British Minister of Defence, 47
Sardauna of Sokoto, Alhaji Sir Ahmadu Bello, 8, 29, 94, 144, 152–4, 158–61, 167, 176, 184–6, 197, 200, 202, 214, 222, 250, 264
Sawaba Party, Niger, 65
Schools, Army, 21, 62, 240
School Certificate Examination, 34, 35, 42, 45, 49, 111–12, 117
Schwarz, Walter, 205
Scott Report, 272–3
Selassie, Emperor Haile, 13, 32
Selem, Kam, Commissioner of Police, 144, 261
Sey, Lt., 36, 242
Shadrack, Lt., 52
Shande, Lt., 119
Shangev, Pte. Mailafia, 32
Shodeinde, Lt.-Col., 36, 51, 56, 109, 122, 123, 134, 161–2, 260
Shrivenham, Royal Military College of Science, 44
Sierra Leone, 6, 256
Signals, Army, 35, 55, 231
Soglo, Gen. (Dahomey), 155
Sokoto, 69, 203–4, 208, 212
Sokoto, Sultan of, 70, 206, 220
Solarin, Tai, 252
Sotomi, Major, 51, 123, 230, 265, 273
South Africa, 64
Southern Cameroons, 25, 52, 65, 71–4, 98, 118, 119, 144, 255, 273
Sudan, 3, 66, 247
Suez crisis (1956), 28
Sule Katagum, Alhaji, 185
Sule Kolo, Alhaji, 93

Tako Galadima, Ibrahim, 93, 100
Tanganyika, 13, 88–90, 218
Tapa, 135–6
Tarka, Joseph, 133, 135, 202, 252, 256, 259, 272
Technical arms, 22, 24–5, 35, 43, 53, 55, 69, 114, 229

Teshie Officer Cadet School, Ghana, 35, 52, 60, 113, 115, 241
Tivs and Tiv Division, 26, 32, 90–2, 99, 106, 140, 160, 178, 180, 202, 218, 221–2
Togo, 2, 3
Touré, M. Sekou, 6
Tshombe, M., 75, 85, 249

Uganda, 224–5, 271
Ugboma, Lt., 36, 242
Ughelli, Government College, 53, 128
Umar Lawan, Lt., 36, 38–9, 52, 242, 252
Umuahia, Government College, 39, 40, 48–9, 53, 242
Unegbe, Lt.-Col., 51, 56, 122, 123, 157, 162, 210, 261
Union des Populations Camerounaises, 71–2
Uniform of Nigerian Army, 103, 127
United Middle Belt Congress (UMBC), 67, 90–2, 202, 248
United Nations, and Cameroun, 71, 73; operation in Congo, 69, 74–88, 128, 148, 218
United Progressive Grand Alliance (UPGA), 139–42, 145–6, 149, 155–6, 172, 177, 202
United States of America, 102, 110, 175, 264
Upper Volta, 156
Uwakwe, Capt., 233

Von Lettow, 13

War Office, London, 15, 17–21, 23, 43, 46–7, 49, 60
Ward, Brig., 74
Weapons, 2, 65–6, 102–3, 127
Welby-Everard, Major-General, 104, 109, 143–5, 148, 219, 258
Wellington, Lt. Otu Amoo Kwa, 36, 242
West Africa Command, 15, 19, 59
West African Army Advisory Council, 18, 59–60, 245
West African Frontier Force (WAFF), 12, 33, 37
West African Forces Conference, 18, 28, 59
West African Military Academy, proposed, 34
West African Service Corps, 24
Wey, Commodore, 143, 149, 227, 270
Whistler, General, 36
Williams, Chief Rotimi, 63

290

Women's War (*yakin mata*), 13
Wushishi, Lt., 119

X Squad, Nigeria Police, 105

Yace, M. (Ivory Coast), 14
Yenagoa, 192

Yerima Balla, 98

Zanzibar, 10, 88
Zaria, Government College, 37, 40, 48–9, 53, 242
Zaria, College of Technology, 48, 113